D1522388

PUBLICATIONS OF
THE MANCHESTER CENTRE FOR ANGLO-SAXON STUDIES

Volume 12

# Leaders of the Anglo-Saxon Church
## From Bede to Stigand

PUBLICATIONS OF
THE MANCHESTER CENTRE FOR ANGLO-SAXON STUDIES

ISSN 1478–6710

Editorial Board

Donald Scragg

Richard Bailey
Timothy Graham
Nicholas J. Higham
Gale R. Owen-Crocker
Alexander Rumble
Leslie Webster

Published Titles

1. *Textual and Material Culture in Anglo-Saxon England: Thomas Northcote Toller and the Toller Memorial Lectures*, ed. Donald Scragg
2. *Apocryphal Texts and Traditions in Anglo-Saxon England*, ed. Kathryn Powell and Donald Scragg
3. *King Harold II and the Bayeux Tapestry*, ed. Gale R. Owen-Crocker
4. *The Place of the Cross in Anglo-Saxon England*, ed. Catherine E. Karkov, Sarah Larratt Keefer and Karen Louise Jolly
5. *Writing and Texts in Anglo-Saxon England*, ed. Alexander R. Rumble
6. *Anglo-Saxon Royal Diplomas: A Palaeography*, Susan D. Thompson
7. *Britons in Anglo-Saxon England*, ed. Nicholas J. Higham
8. *Edgar, King of the English 959–975: New Interpretations*, ed. Donald Scragg
9. *The Landscape Archaeology of Anglo-Saxon England*, ed. Nicholas J. Higham and Martin J. Ryan
10. *Place-names, Language and the Anglo-Saxon Landscape*, ed. Nicholas J. Higham and Martin J. Ryan
11. *A Conspectus of Scribal Hands Writing English, 960–1100*, Donald Scragg

BL, Additional 49598, fol. 118v: Benedictional of St Æthelwold: a bishop
(?Æthelwold) pronouncing a blessing.
© British Library Board. All Rights Reserved

# Leaders of the Anglo-Saxon Church
# From Bede to Stigand

edited by
ALEXANDER R. RUMBLE

THE BOYDELL PRESS

© Contributors 2012

*All rights reserved.* Except as permitted under current legislation
no part of this work may be photocopied, stored in a retrieval system,
published, performed in public, adapted, broadcast,
transmitted, recorded or reproduced in any form or by any means,
without the prior permission of the copyright owner

First published 2012
The Boydell Press, Woodbridge


ISBN 978-1-84383-700-8




The Boydell Press is an imprint of Boydell & Brewer Ltd
PO Box 9, Woodbridge, Suffolk IP12 3DF, UK
and of Boydell & Brewer Inc,
668 Mt Hope Avenue, Rochester, NY 14620, USA
website: www.boydellandbrewer.com


A CIP catalogue record for this book is available
from the British Library


The publisher has no responsibility for the continued existence
or accuracy of URLs for external or third-party internet websites referred
to in this book, and does not guarantee that any content on such websites is,
or will remain, accurate or appropriate.

Papers used by Boydell & Brewer Ltd are natural, recyclable products
made from wood grown in sustainable forests




Printed and bound in the United States of America

# Contents

# Illustrations

Photographs are reproduced by special permission of The British Library Board (Frontispiece, 6.2–3), the Master and Fellows of Corpus Christi College, Cambridge (6.1), The Trustees of Lambeth Palace Library (6.4), the city of Bayeux (6.5) and David Wright (6.6).

*Frontispiece*. BL, Additional 49598, fol. 118v: Benedictional of St Æthelwold: a bishop (?Æthelwold) pronouncing a blessing

*Figures*

*Table*

# Preface

The collection of papers published in this volume seeks to illustrate the important and various roles played by individual leading ecclesiastics in England, both within the church and in the wider political sphere, from the late seventh to the mid eleventh century. Individual chapters discuss not only the undeniable authority of Bede and Bishop Æthelwold but also the influence of less-familiar figures such as Bishop Wulfsige of Sherborne, Archbishop Ecgberht of York and St Leoba. The book draws new conclusions from both textual and material evidence which will demonstrate the influence (by both deed and reputation) of powerful personalities not only on the developing institutions of the English church but also on the secular politics of their time.

As is demonstrated in my introduction, theories of ecclesiastical leadership were expounded in contemporary texts on the role of bishops and heads of monastic houses. But how far did image or ideal reflect reality? Writers of biography have to weigh up the balance between an individual's character, acumen and talents and the norms of institutional training, expectations and duties of those in authority in the church. Which were outstanding, rather than merely doing the same as others of their status? How much room was there for individuals to use their office to promote new ideas?

It is clear that both episcopal and abbatial authority were of fundamental importance to the development of the Christian church in Anglo-Saxon England. Church leaders such as bishops and abbots were invested with a variety of types of power and influence. Their actions, decisions, and writings could change not only their own institutions, but also the national church, while their interaction with the king and his court affected the lives of many within wider contemporary society. It should not be forgotten, however, that occasionally a monk such as Bede, who was neither bishop nor abbot, could produce works of such lasting significance that they have moulded the views and attitudes of future generations of both religious and secular readers and worshippers, even unto the present day. The memory and reputation of other individuals discussed in the book, although considerable in their own lifetime and within their own church, have not endured in the same way. It is hoped that the present collection will serve as a reminder of their activities and provide some indications, where still possible, of their aims, image and character. The present volume is dedicated to the memory of the late Dr David Hill, Anglo-Saxonist and cartographer, who was an inspiration to many, colleagues and students alike.

Alexander R. Rumble
Manchester, 2011

# Contributors

Debby Banham, University of Cambridge

Nicholas J. Higham, University of Manchester

Joyce Hill, University of Leeds

Allan Scott McKinley, University of Birmingham

Gale R. Owen-Crocker, University of Manchester

Cassandra Rhodes, London

Alexander R. Rumble, University of Manchester

Martin J. Ryan, University of Manchester

Dominik Wassenhoven, University of Bayreuth

# Abbreviations

| | |
|---|---|
| *ASC* | The Anglo-Saxon Chronicle |
| AS Charters | Anglo-Saxon Charters (British Academy and Royal Historical Society series) |
| *ASE* | *Anglo-Saxon England* |
| BCS | Walter de Gray Birch, *Cartularium Saxonicum*, 3 vols. (London 1885–93) |
| BL | London, British Library |
| BN | Paris, Bibliothèque Nationale |
| Bod | Oxford, Bodleian Library |
| CCCC | Cambridge, Corpus Christi College |
| *CCSL* | *Corpus Christianorum, series latina* (Turnhout, 1953–) |
| Colgrave and Mynors | *Bede's Ecclesiastical History of the English People*, ed. Bertram Colgrave and R. A. B. Mynors (Oxford, 1969) |
| *Councils & Synods*, ed. Whitelock | *Councils & Synods with Other Documents Relating to the English Church*, ed. D. Whitelock, M. Brett and C. N. L. Brooke, I, i, *871–1066* [volume edited by D. Whitelock] |
| CSASE | Cambridge Studies in Anglo-Saxon England |
| *CSEL* | *Corpus scriptorum ecclesiasticorum latinorum* (Vienna, 1886–) |
| *DB+county abbreviation* | County volumes in the Phillimore *Domesday Book* series, general editor John Morris, 38 vols. (Chichester, 1975–92) |
| Douglas and Greenaway, *EHD* | *English Historical Documents*, II, *1042–1189*, ed. David C. Douglas and George W. Greenaway, 2nd edn (London and New York, 1981) |
| EETS | Early English Text Society os = Original Series ss = Supplementary Series |
| *EHR* | *The English Historical Review* |
| EPNS | English Place-Name Society |
| GDB | Great Domesday Book: The National Archives E.31/2 |
| *HBC* | *Handbook of British Chronology*, ed. E. B. Fryde, D. E. Greenway, S. Porter and I. Roy, Royal Historical Society Guides and Handbooks 2, 3rd edn (London, 1986) |
| HBS | Henry Bradshaw Society (London, 1891–) |
| *HE* | Bede, *Historia Ecclesiastica* |
| *HRH* | David Knowles, C. N. L. Brooke and Vera C. M. London, *Heads of Religious Houses, England and Wales*, I, |

|  | *940–1216,* 2nd edn with new material by C. N. L. Brooke (Cambridge, 2001) |
| JW | *The Chronicle of John of Worcester*: II, *The Annals from 450–1066,* ed. R. R. Darlington and P. McGurk, trans. Jennifer Bray and P. McGurk (Oxford, 1995); III, *The Annals from 1067 to 1140 with the Gloucester Interpolations and the Continuation to 1141,* ed. and trans. P. McGurk (Oxford, 1998) |
| KCD | Johannes M. Kemble, *Codex Diplomaticus Ævi Saxonici,* 6 vols. (London, 1839–48) |
| Ker, *Catalogue* | N. R. Ker, *Catalogue of Manuscripts Containing Anglo-Saxon* (Oxford, 1957) |
| LDB | Little Domesday Book: The National Archives E.31/1 |
| MGH | Monumenta Germaniae Historica |
| ODNB | *Oxford Dictionary of National Biography* (Oxford, 2004; online ed. 2006 (http://www.oxforddnb.com) |
| OE | Old English |
| OG | Old Germanic |
| ON | Old Norse |
| PASE | *Prosopography of Anglo-Saxon England* (http://www.pase.ac.uk/index.html) |
| PL | *Patrologia latina,* ed. J. P. Migne, 221 vols. (Paris, 1844–64) |
| Robertson, *AS Charters* | *Anglo-Saxon Charters,* ed. and trans. A. J. Robertson (Cambridge, 1939) |
| RS | Rolls Series |
| RSB | St Benedict of Nursia, *Regula* |
| Rumble, *Property and Piety* | Alexander R. Rumble, *Property and Piety in Early Medieval Winchester: Documents Relating to the Topography of the Anglo-Saxon and Norman City and its Minsters,* Winchester Studies 4, *The Anglo-Saxon Minsters of Winchester,* part iii (Oxford, 2002) |
| S (Sawyer) | P. H. Sawyer, *Anglo-Saxon Charters: An Annotated List and Bibliography,* Royal Historical Society Guides and Handbooks 8 (London, 1968), with additions and revisions by Susan Kelly and Rebecca Rushforth at http://www.esawyer.org.uk; quoted by number |
| VÆ | Wulfstan of Winchester, *Vita Sancti Æthelwoldi* |
| Whitelock, *EHD* | *English Historical Documents,* I, *c. 500–1042,* ed. Dorothy Whitelock, 2nd edn (London and New York, 1979) |

# Introduction
## Church Leadership and the Anglo-Saxons

ALEXANDER R. RUMBLE

FROM the time of the late sixth-century mission led by Augustine, who had been sent by the bishop of Rome to convert the pagan Anglo-Saxons to Christianity, the church in England was intended to follow a territorial pattern, like that already established on the Continent and previously in Roman Britain, based on the diocese and administered by bishops.[1] Groups of such dioceses would be subject to a metropolitan and within each diocese there could be ecclesiastical centres (*monasteria*, 'minsters' mostly led by abbots or abbesses) of lesser status than the bishop's cathedral and whose clergy would be under his higher authority. The structure was hierarchical, its justification stemming from powers invested in St Peter, the first bishop of Rome, by Christ himself.[2]

Although the administrative system that eventually emerged in England was not identical with the Continental one, the two archdioceses of Canterbury and York having an unequal number of satellites,[3] the expected episcopal and abbatial nature of leadership within the church was common to the whole country, even when the latter was still divided into a number of secular kingdoms. The Anglo-Saxon pattern was also different from that of the Romano-British and Irish churches. Cathedrals were not always in major urban centres as in late Roman Britain, though many were, and there was a clear distinction made between the offices of bishop and abbot such as was not always present in the early Irish church

---

[1] Cf. Barbara Yorke, *The Conversion of Britain: Religion, Politics and Society in Britain c. 600–800* (Harlow, 2006), pp. 149–52.

[2] Matt. XVI.18: 'And I say to thee: That thou art Peter; and upon this rock I will build my church, and the gates of hell shall not prevail against it'. Modern English biblical quotations are from the Douay-Rheims version, revised by Bishop Richard Challoner (1749–52).

[3] For a very short period there existed three archdioceses in England but that of Lichfield, created by King Offa of Mercia and consisting of seven dioceses in central and eastern England, did not survive after his death. See further J. W. Lamb, *The Archbishopric of Lichfield (787–803)* (London, 1964).

and its foundations in northern and western Britain. The importance of the diocesan bishop was further underlined by the canons of the Council of Hertford in 670/2.[4]

Primary definitions of the powers and responsibilities of episcopal and abbatial leadership came from biblical, patristic and conciliar texts. They were further expounded and reinforced by Anglo-Saxon writers through letters, homilies and treatises. How far a particular bishop, abbot or abbess succeeded in fulfilling his or her role within the church depended, however, both on the character of the individual and on the political climate of the age in which they lived. They were more likely to achieve success if working in conjunction with their peers in synod or when supported by royal or comital power.

Exceptionally, a scholar such as Bede[5] or Byrhtferth,[6] although neither bishop nor abbot, produced such writings as to influence not only his contemporaries but also future generations. These individuals, too, can be seen as leaders of the church but in a less public and more intellectual mode.

*Guidelines for the episcopal role*

The etymology of the term 'bishop', ultimately from Greek ἐπίσκοπος 'overseer', by way of Latin *episcopus* and OE *biscop*, reflects both its original and its continued significance within the church.[7] In the early

4   Catherine Cubitt, *Anglo-Saxon Church Councils c. 650–c. 850* (London and New York, 1995), pp. 8–11, 249–50. Bede, *HE*, IV. 5; Colgrave and Mynors, pp. 348–53. The second canon required: 'That no bishop intrude into the diocese of another bishop, but that he should be content with the government of the people committed to his charge'. The fifth canon required: 'That no clergy shall leave their own bishop nor wander about at will […]'. For a limitation on episcopal power in the third canon, see below, p. 19.
5   For a survey of Bede's works, see George Hardin Brown, *A Companion to Bede* (Woodbridge, 2009). For the political influence of his writings, see below, chapters 1 (Higham) and 2 (Ryan).
6   See *Byrhtferth's Enchiridion*, ed. Peter S. Baker and Michael Lapidge, EETS ss 15 (Oxford, 1995), with an account of his life and writings at pp. xxv–xxxiv.
7   The OE form was used by Ælfric to describe the one (Aaron) chosen by God for high religious office, that of hereditary high-priest of the Israelites, according to Numbers XVII–XVIII.1–20, see *Ælfric's Catholic Homilies: The Second Series, Text*, ed. Malcolm Godden, EETS ss 5 (Oxford, 1979), no. I, p. 4 (line 51). The Vulgate text, however, spoke of the office as a *sacerdotium* to be held by a *sacerdos*, see *Biblia sacra iuxta vulgatam versionem*, ed. Robert Weber, 5th edn by Roger Gryson (Stuttgart, 2007), pp. 205–6. The precedent of Aaron as God's appointee had also been used by Alcuin in a letter to Archbishop Eanbald II of York in 796: Stephen Allott, *Alcuin of York c. A.D. 732 to 804: His Life and Letters* (York, 1974, reprinted 1987), letter 6, p. 8. Elsewhere Aaron was referred to four times in the prayers used at the

Christian church the Greek term seems to have been applied to the leader of a local community of believers, responsible for maintaining the faith disseminated by the apostles of Christ.[8] The late first-/early second-century Pastoral Epistles of Paul, composed in his name but after his death,[9] include two sets of injunctions governing the behaviour of bishops. The first is in the First Letter to Timothy, bishop of Ephesus (III.1–7):[10]

1. A faithful saying: if a man desire the office of a bishop, he desireth good work.
2. It behoveth therefore a bishop [Vulgate 'oportet ergo episcopum'][11] to be blameless, the husband of one wife,[12] sober, prudent, of good behaviour, chaste, given to hospitality, a teacher.
3. Not given to wine, no striker, but modest, not quarrelsome, not covetous, but
4. One that ruleth well his own house, having his children in subjection with all chastity.
5. But if a man know not how to rule his own house, how shall he take care of the church of God?
6. Not a neophyte: lest being puffed up with pride, he fall into the judgment of the devil.
7. Moreover he must have a good testimony of them who are without. lest he fall into reproach and the snare of the devil.

The text goes on to distinguish bishops from the lesser role of deacon (1 Tim. III. 8–10, 12–13).[13]

The writer of the Letter to Titus (I.5–9) described the desired character of bishops in somewhat similar vein although not clearly distinguishing them from ordinary priests:[14]

ordination of a bishop, see Dorothy Bethurum, *The Homilies of Wulfstan* (Oxford, 1957), p. 353, note on lines 21–5 of homily XVII.

[8] Clare Drury, 'The Pastoral Epistles', in *The Oxford Bible Commentary*, ed. John Barton and John Muddiman (Oxford, 2001), ch. 73, pp. 1220–33, at pp. 1224–5. Ultimately, the role of bishop descended from that of the apostles, charged to be witnesses to the teaching of Christ in Acts I.8: 'But you shall receive the power of the Holy Ghost coming upon you, and you shall be witnesses unto me in Jerusalem, and in Judea, and Samaria, and even to the uttermost part of the earth'; and in Luke XXIV. 46–8: 'And he said to them: Thus it is written, and thus it behoved Christ to suffer, and to rise again from the dead, the third day. And that penance and remission of sins should be preached in his name, unto all nations, beginning at Jerusalem. And you are witnesses of these things'. For Wulfstan's use of the subsequent verses in Luke, see below, p. 10, n. 43.

[9] On their authorship, see Drury, 'Pastoral Epistles', pp. 1220–1. Paul died *c.* AD 65.

[10] For commentary, see Drury, 'Pastoral Epistles', pp. 1224–5.

[11] *Biblia sacra*, ed. Weber and Gryson, p. 1833.

[12] This stipulation was later modified by the expectation of celibacy for bishops by AD 400, see Henry Chadwick, *The Early Church* (Harmondsworth, 1967), p. 175.

[13] For commentary, see Drury, 'Pastoral Epistles', p. 1225.

[14] For commentary on this epistle, see Drury, 'Pastoral Epistles', pp. 1230–3. For a brief

5. For this cause I left thee in Crete, that thou shouldest set in order the things that are wanting, and shouldest ordain priests in every city, as I also appointed thee:
6. If any be without crime, the husband of one wife,[15] having faithful children, not accused of riot, or unruly.
7. For a bishop must be without crime, as the steward of God: not proud, not subject to anger, not given to wine, no striker, not greedy of filthy lucre.
8. But given to hospitality, gentle, sober, just, holy, continent.
9. Embracing that faithful word which is according to doctrine, that he may be able to exhort in sound doctrine, and to convince the gainsayers.

At least from the time of Irenaeus (bishop of Lyons in 180), these letters were treated as part of the canonical Pauline epistolary corpus and were thus disseminated throughout Christendom within the New Testament.[16] All three Pastoral Letters were quoted in the *Regula Sancti Benedicti*.[17] Pope Gregory the Great referred to the First Letter to Timothy in *responsio* 1 of the *Libellus Responsionum*, in relation to a bishop's conduct in church, and quoted the Letter to Titus in *responsio* 8 (concerning admission to church or holy communion of those with various categories of perceived bodily uncleanliness).[18] In the early eleventh century, parts of both the First and Second Letters to Timothy were translated by Ælfric in an expansion made to one of his homilies.[19] The injunctive phrasing of 1

---

account of bishops in the early church, see Stephen Neill, 'The Historic Episcopate', in *Bishops*, ed. [William G. H. Simon] the Bishop of Llandaff (London, 1961), pp. 41–50, especially pp. 43–8.

[15]  As above, p. 3, n. 12.

[16]  For the New Testament canon, see F. F. Bruce, *The Books and the Parchments* (5th edn, London, 1991), pp. 97–104.

[17]  For references, see *RB 1980: The Rule of St Benedict in Latin and English with Notes*, ed. Timothy Fry (Collegeville MN., 1981), p. 590.

[18]  The *Libellus Responsionum*, Gregory's answers to questions put to him by his missionary Augustine, as reported by Bede, makes up most of *HE*, I.27; Colgrave and Mynors, pp. 78–103. Bede used both letters to Timothy in his own narrative in *HE* (at I.15; II.19; III.17; and IV.1: Colgrave and Mynors, pp.93–4, 201–2, 265–6, 343–4). Note also the use of 2 Tim. in the letter of Pope Boniface V quoted by Bede at II.3 (Colgrave and Mynors, pp. 172–3). Titus I.7–9 and I Tim. III.3 were quoted in the Anonymous *Vita Sancti Cuthberti* (IV.1) in relation to the saint's conduct as bishop of Lindisfarne, see *Two Lives of Saint Cuthbert: A Life by an Anonymous Monk of Lindisfarne and Bede's Prose Life*, ed. and trans. Bertram Colgrave (Cambridge, 1940, pbk edn 1985), pp. 110–11.

[19]  *Ælfric's Catholic Homilies: The First Series, Text*, ed. Peter Clemoes, EETS ss 17 (Oxford, 1997), no. XVII (*Dominica secunda post Pasca*), pp. 313–16 with the considerably expanded text at pp. 535–42. Lines 146–8 are from 1 Tim. VI.10 and lines 157–84 are partly from 2 Tim. III.1–5, see Malcolm Godden, *Ælfric's Catholic Homilies: Introduction, Commentary and Glossary*, EETS ss 18 (Oxford, 2001), 143–4. See also, below, p. 9, and n. 38.

Tim III.2 may also have influenced the wording of texts by Wulfstan on the duties of bishops.[20]

From the late sixth century an aid to bishops as to their general conduct was available in the form of Gregory the Great's *Regula Pastoralis*, a handbook for those churchmen placed in authority over others, the general importance of which was deemed so great that its Latin text was later translated into the vernacular by King Alfred.[21] Certain of Gregory's answers in the *Libellus Responsionum*, widely disseminated as part of Bede's *Historia Ecclesiastica*, were also of particular and lasting significance to the Anglo-Saxon episcopacy. They included the statement (*responsio* 1) that non-monastic bishops and their household should take only a fourth part of the income of the diocese 'for purposes of hospitality and entertainment' with the rest being divided between the clergy, the poor and church repair, but that bishops who, like Augustine, were monks should possess all things in common with their fellow monks. *Responsio* 6 concerned the consecration of bishops in England in the presence of at least three or four existing bishops, while *responsio* 7 advised in connection with future relations between bishops of Britain and Gaul.[22]

Bede, in his *Epistola ad Ecgberhtum episcopum* of 734, recommended to Archbishop Ecgberht of York that he should meditate on the scriptures and read the Letters to Timothy and Titus and Gregory's *Regula Pastoralis* or his homilies

> [...] that your speech may always be seasoned with the salt of wisdom, more elevated than common diction, and may shine forth more worthy of the divine hearing.[23]

Bede's letter is one of a number of advisory missives, addressed by individual Anglo-Saxon churchmen to particular archbishops of Canterbury or York, which have survived. Some of their content is specifically focused on the role of the metropolitan as a senior bishop.[24] For example,

---

[20] Particularly in the text *Incipit de synodo*, see below, pp. 12–13.

[21] *PL* 77, 13–128; *King Alfred's West Saxon Version of Gregory's Pastoral Care*, ed. Henry Sweet, EETS os 45, 50 (London, 1871–2). For Alcuin's recommendation of it to his pupil Archbishop Eanbald II of York in 796 as 'a model of life and teaching' and 'a mirror of a bishop's life', see Allott, *Alcuin of York*, no. 7 (at p. 11).

[22] *HE*, I.27; Colgrave and Mynors, pp. 78–81, 86–9.

[23] *Venerabilis Baedae Opera Historica*, ed. C. Plummer, 2 vols. (Oxford, 1896), I.405–23, at p. 406; Whitelock, *EHD*, no. 170, pp. 799–810, at p. 800.

[24] Within their own diocese, the archbishops carried out the same duties as ordinary bishops, but in relation to their archiepiscopal province they had the right to consecrate their suffragans, over whom they had precedence, and a duty to coordinate their work. In England, the bitter contention between Canterbury and York as to which metropolitan had the legal right of national primacy was a post-Conquest dispute, but one which engendered a number of supposedly pre-Conquest papal documents. See

a letter from Boniface (archbishop of Cologne since 745)[25] to Archbishop Cuthberht of Canterbury in 747 spoke of their common duty as follows:

> The work of our ministry is in one and the same cause, and an equal oversight of churches and people is entrusted to us, whether in teaching or in restraining or in admonition or in protecting all classes of the clergy or the laity.[...] Our responsibility toward churches and peoples is greater than that of other bishops on account of the pallium entrusted to us and accepted by us, while they have the care of their own dioceses only.[26]

Other parts of the same letter, however, are applicable to all of episcopal rank:

> [...] a dread necessity impels us to present ourselves as an example to the faithful [...] the teacher is to live so justly that his deeds shall not contradict his words [...] He is set over the Church of God to this end, that he not only may set an example of right living to others, but, through his dutiful preaching, may bring every man's sins before his eyes and show him what punishment awaits the hard of heart and what reward the obedient.[27]

Likewise, Alcuin in 793, three years before becoming abbot of St Martin's at Tours, wrote to the newly-appointed Archbishop Æthelheard of Canterbury:

> You have received the pastoral rod and the staff of brotherly comfort, one to rule, the other to console, that the deserving may have comfort and the rebellious may feel your correction.[...]
> Remember that the bishop is the envoy of the Lord God and the holy law must be sought from his lips, as we read in the prophet Malachi.[28] He is a watchman, put in the highest place; so he is called 'bishop', meaning 'overseer', for he must look ahead for the whole army of Christ and give wise advice on what to avoid and what to do. Bishops are the lights of the holy church of God, the leaders of the flock of

---

Frank Barlow, *The English Church 1000–1066*, 2nd edn (London, 1979), pp. 232–8; R. W. Southern, 'The Canterbury Forgeries', *EHR* 73 (1958), pp. 193–207.

[25] *The Letters of Saint Boniface*, trans. Ephraim Emerton, with new introduction and bibliography by Thomas F. X. Noble (New York, 2000), no. 47, pp. 85–9.

[26] *Letters of Saint Boniface*, trans. Emerton, no. 62, pp. 114–19, at p. 114. For the *pallium*, see Wilhelm Levison, *England and the Continent in the Eighth Century*, Ford Lectures 1943 (Oxford, 1946, reprinted 1998), pp. 18–22; and Lamb, *Archbishopric of Lichfield*, Appendix, pp. 54–61.

[27] *Letters of Saint Boniface*, trans. Emerton, p.117.

[28] Referring to Mal. IV.5: 'Behold I will send you Elias the prophet, before the coming of the great and dreadful day of the Lord.'

Christ. They must boldly raise the standard of the holy cross in the front line and stand without fear before every attack of the enemy....[29]

The same writer, in 796 in a letter to his ex-pupil Eanbald, who had just been elevated to the rank of archbishop of York, exhorted him as follows:

Let not your tongue cease preaching, nor your feet visiting the flock entrusted to you, nor your hands working for the giving of alms and the building up of God's holy church in every place. Be a model of every man's salvation, an example of the religious way of life, a comfort to the unhappy, an encouragement to the hesitant. Let firmness of discipline, confidence in truth and every promise of good be seen in you. Do not be excited by worldly pomp, or softened by rich food and vanity of dress, or deceived by flattery, or upset by the opposition of critics, or broken by sorrow, or carried away by joy. [...]

Do everything decently and in good order. Fix a time for reading and hours for prayer. Mass should have its proper time. A wise use of the day is wisdom with God. Enjoy eating in moderation and fasting in purity. Wash your face in penitence and anoint your head with love that all may be acceptable to God, who has chosen you as his priest. For every high priest, who is taken from among men, is placed on men's behalf before God [ .] God's priest must be the preacher of his word and will to the people and intercede for them as a mediator between God and men.[...]

Do not think yourself a lord of the world but a steward. Do not let the number of your relations make you greedy, as if you ought to collect an inheritance for them – the opportunity will be there, if the tinder of greed, the root of all evil, is set alight.[...]

Let your companions be of respectable conduct, not known by the extravagance of their dress, but by their moral standing.[...] Let them not gallop bawling over the fields after the fox, but ride with you singing psalms in harmony.[...]

Your grace should provide teachers for the boys. There should be classes for reading, singing and writing separate from the clergy, and separate teachers for each class, so that the boys are not idle and do not run about playing silly games and forming frivolous habits.[30]

Such letters were in the first instance private and were intended to give personal support and advice to their recipient but, through having become included in posthumous collections of missives associated with notable churchmen such as Boniface and Alcuin, have been given wider circulation

---

[29] Allott, *Alcuin of York*, letter 48, pp. 61–3, at pp. 61 and 62.
[30] Allott, *Alcuin of York*, letter 6, pp. 6–10, at pp. 7, 8 and 9. See also below (Hill), pp. 150–1.

over more than twelve hundred years.[31] Any beneficial effect of the advice they contained on the thought and conduct of the recipient would have been first displayed to his fellow bishops at the provincial church councils which had become a more regular feature of ecclesiastical administration in England from the time of Theodore of Tarsus, archbishop of Canterbury in the later seventh century.[32] Thus, the canons of the Council of *Clofesho* in 747, attended by south-Humbrian bishops, are thought to have been influenced by Boniface's letter to Archbishop Cuthberht in that year.[33] Seven of these canons related to episcopal responsibilities and authority.[34] Later, the Council of Chelsea in 816 made an important reaffirmation of the rights of bishops over religious life within their particular dioceses.[35] Such meetings of episcopal colleagues were essential for church unity but also as the means by which archiepiscopal authority could be exercised. They continued a regulatory institution exemplified by important councils of the early Christian church (for example at Nicaea in 325 and Chalcedon in 451),[36] and mirrored those held in Francia.[37]

In the later Anglo-Saxon period, two of Ælfric's homilies bore on the role of bishop and the high status accorded to those so designated. In his First Series homily for *Dominica secunda post Pasca* he described bishops ('ælc biscop 7 ælc lareow') with reference to the biblical motif of 'the Good Shepherd' (from Ezechiel XXXIV, also applied to Christ in John X. 11 and 14). Bishops are required to guard 'godes folc' ('God's

---

[31] For two later Anglo-Saxon letters giving advice to a bishop and an archbishop, see Barlow, *English Church*, p. 64.

[32] For Theodore's influence, see Cubitt, *Church Councils*, pp. 8–13.

[33] Cubitt, *Church Councils*, pp. 102–10. The canons are edited in *Councils and Ecclesiastical Documents Relating to Great Britain and Ireland*, ed. Arthur West Haddan and William Stubbs, 3 vols. (Oxford, 1869–78), III. 362–76; for discussion, see Cubitt, *Church Councils*, pp. 100–52, and *eadem*, 'Pastoral Care and Conciliar Canons: The Provisions of the 747 Council of *Clofesho*', in *Pastoral Care before the Parish*, ed. John Blair and Richard Sharpe (Leicester, 1992), pp. 193–211, at pp. 195–8. For the location of *Clofesho*, see Cubitt, *Church Councils*, pp. 304–6; also, Simon Keynes, 'The Councils of *Clofesho*', Brixworth Lecture 1993 = University of Leicester Vaughan Paper 38 (Leicester, 1994), particularly 13–17, 49–50.

[34] Canons 1–7; *Councils and Ecclesiastical Documents*, ed. Haddan and Stubbs, III.363–5.

[35] Canons 4, 7 and 8: *Councils and Ecclesiastical Documents*, ed. Haddan and Stubbs, III.580–3. See Cubitt, *Church Councils*, pp. 191–203, 285; and Nicholas Brooks, *The Early History of the Church of Canterbury: Christ Church from 597 to 1066* (Leicester, 1984), pp. 175–6.

[36] Chadwick, *Early Church*, pp. 130–2, 203–5.

[37] See Rosamond McKitterick, *The Frankish Church and the Carolingian Reforms, 789–895*, Royal Historical Society Studies in History (London, 1977), pp. 11–17, 23–4.

people') from the depredations of the wolf (i.e. the Devil).[38] In his Second Series homily *De natale Domini* he used the vernacular term *biscop* in specific references to Christ, firstly representing the Latin of his source 'Christum verum sacerdotem' as 'se ðe is soð biscop' ('he who is the true bishop') and later avowing Christ to be 'soðlice ealra biscopa biscop. and ealra cyninga cyning' ('truly bishop of all bishops and king of all kings').[39]

However, Ælfric's Latin letter to Archbishop Wulfstan of York, datable 1002×1005, indicates that he did not always find the expected high standards of behaviour among the bishops he encountered. In it he complained:

Sed valde dolendum est, quia his diebus tanta neglegentia est in episcopis, qui deberent esse columpne aecclesiae, ut non adtendant divinam scripturam, nec docent discipulos qui sibi succedant in episcopatum, sicut legimus de sanctis viris, qui multos perfectos discipulos successores sibi reliquerunt, sed honores seculares et cupiditates vel avaritiam sectantes, plus quam laici mala exempla subditis prebentes. Non audent de iustitia loqui, quia iustitiam nec faciunt nec diligunt. Vacant potationibus honorifice in aula, non lectionibus cum clero aut monachis, et nolunt scire quid sit opus episcopi. Certe nos timemus valde ut eorum neglegentia fides deficiat in ista insula, et nimium miror quomodo ausi sunt vendere sanctam crisma; emunt oleum vili pretio et consecratum magno vendunt pretio, cum Dominus dicat. 'Gratis accepistis, gratis date'. Ergo omnes benedictiones et inpositiones manuum dare gratis deberent sicut apostoli fecerent, qui non habuerunt villas nec agros. Sed avaritia hoc non sinit.[40]

---

[38] *Ælfric's Catholic Homilies: The First Series*, ed. Clemoes, no. XVII, pp. 313–16, 535–42, at p. 314 (lines 23–4). On the use of the Letters of Timothy in this homily, see above, p. 4, n. 19. Although much of this homily was drawn from the earlier one by Gregory the Great and the expansion of it by Haymo of Auxerre, Ælfric's introduction of the 'bishop and teacher' was original, see Godden, *Ælfric's Catholic Homilies: Introduction*, p. 138. Bede also used 'the Good Shepherd' motif in his *Epistola ad Ecgberhtum*, see Whitelock, *EHD*, no. 170, p. 807. For its use in monastic texts, both in relation to the abbot and to King Edgar, see below, p. 15 and p. 16, n. 76. For its employment by Archbishop Wulfstan, see below, pp. 11 and 17.

[39] *Ælfric's Catholic Homilies: The Second Series*, ed. Godden, no. I, p. 4 (line 58) and p. 7 (lines 166–7). Ælfric's source for the first instance was Pseudo-Augustine, *Sermones* (now attributed to Ildefonsus of Seville), see Godden, *Ælfric's Catholic Homilies: Introduction*, pp. 347–8.

[40] *Councils & Synods*, ed. Whitelock, no. 45, pp. 242–55, at pp. 253–4. 'But it is greatly to be deplored that there is such a great lack of care these days in the bishops, who ought to be pillars of the church [cf. Gal. II.9], that they do not apply themselves to divine scripture, nor teach pupils who might succeed them in the episcopate, as we read of the holy men who left many perfect pupils as their successors, but, pursuing secular honours and desires and avarice, they more than laymen are furnishing bad examples to subordinates. They do not dare to speak about justice, because they neither do nor love justice. They give time with honour to drinking-bouts in the hall [but] not

Ælfric also accused the same bishops of being incompetent in their liturgical duties, saying too many collects at Mass or altering their wording as
well as changing or expanding other parts of the canonical rite.[41]

Ælfric's comments were made fairly soon after Wulfstan became archbishop and may perhaps have helped to persuade the latter to compose
various (undated) texts which spelled out the duties of bishops in some
detail. Thus, Wulfstan included in his treatise now known as the *Institutes
of Polity* several sections about the role of bishops within the nation, as
follows:[42]

> (5) *Concerning the Nation's Councillors*[43]
> [...] And bishops are heralds[44] and teachers of God's law, and they must
> preach justice and forbid injustice; and he who scorns to listen to them,
> let him settle that with God himself. And if bishops neglect to punish
> sins or forbid injustice, nor make known God's law, but mumble with
> their jaws where they ought to cry out,[45] woe to them for that silence!
> [...] Alas, grievous is the burden which God's herald must bear if he
> will not earnestly forbid injustice.[...]

to readings with clergy or monks, and they do not wish to know what a bishop's work
is. Certainly we are very afraid that the faith in this island will disappear because of
their lack of care, and I am exceedingly amazed at how they have dared to sell the
holy chrism; they buy oil at a cheap price and sell it consecrated at a great price,
although the Lord says [Matt. X.8] "freely have you received, freely give". Therefore
they ought to give freely all benedictions and layings on of hands as the apostles did
who had neither country-houses nor domains. But avarice does not permit this.' [my
translation].

41  *Councils & Synods*, ed. Whitelock, p. 254.
42  For a critical edition from the three extant manuscripts, see Karl Jost, *Die 'Institutes of
    Polity, Civil and Ecclesiastical': Ein Werk Erzbischof Wulfstans von York*, Schweizer
    anglistische Arbeiten 47 (Bern, 1959). The translation given here is from *Anglo-Saxon
    Prose*, trans. and ed. Michael Swanton (London, 1993, reprinted 1996), pp. 187–201.
    Swanton follows Jost's numbering of the sections but, where there is a difference, adds
    in brackets the numeration from the earlier edition by Benjamin Thorpe, *Ancient Laws
    and Institutes of England*, Record Commission, 2 vols. (London, 1840), II. 304–40.
43  Wulfstan later reused much of section 5, and part of section 6, in his homily for the
    consecration of a bishop, perhaps delivered in 1014 or 1020, see Bethurum, *Homilies
    of Wulfstan*, no. XVII, pp. 242–5, 351–3. Wulfstan began by quoting the Vulgate
    text of Luke XXIV.49–51, which records Christ's devolution to the apostles of the
    preaching of his message; cf. above p. 3, n. 8.
44  Translating OE *bydelas*, see BL, Cotton Nero A. i, part 2, fol. 109 (s. xi in.). The
    first part of this sentence was reused by Wulfstan in the lawcode I Cnut (datable
    1020×1022); see *Councils & Synods*, ed. Whitelock, no. 64, pp. 468–506, at p. 485
    (ch. 26).
45  The same fault was referred to by Wulfstan in his admonitory text to bishops: *Councils
    & Synods*, ed. Whitelock, no. 55, pp. 413–17, at p. 414. Also in *Sermo Lupi ad Anglos*,
    ed. Dorothy Whitelock (Exeter, 1976, reprinted 1980), p. 66, line 192.

(6) *Likewise, concerning Bishops*[46]

Bishops must attend to books and prayers, and over and again call on Christ by day and night and diligently intercede for all Christian people. And they must learn and teach correctly, and diligently enquire about the deeds of the people. And they must preach and carefully give an example of the spiritual duty of a Christian nation. And they must not willingly consent to any injustice, but diligently support every righteousness. They must bear in mind the fear of God and not be all too slothful for fear of the world. But let him who will, always take care diligently to preach God's law and forbid unrighteousness. For the shepherd will be found weak for the flock, who will not defend the flock which he must keep, at least with a cry, if he can do nothing else, if any despoiler of the people begin to ravage.[47] There is no despoiler so evil as the Devil himself. He is forever concerned with one thing – how he can most ravage men's souls. So those shepherds who have to shield the people against the despoiler of the nation must be very watchful and earnestly crying out. Those are bishops and priests who must protect and defend the spiritual flock with wise teaching, so that the ravening werewolf do not too greatly rend nor devour too many of the spiritual flock. And he who scorns to listen to them, let him settle that with God himself.[…]

7(8) *Likewise*[48]

The daily work of a bishop is rightly: his prayers first and then his book-work, reading or writing, teaching or learning, and his Church hours at the correct time, always together with those things which pertain to it, and washing the feet of the poor and his distribution of alms and the direction of works where it be necessary. Good manual crafts befit him also, and that those in his household cultivate crafts, so that at any rate no one too idle dwell there. And it also befits him well that in a meeting he over and again disseminate divine teaching to the people with whom he then is.

8(9) *Likewise*[49]

Wisdom and prudence always befit bishops, and that those that attend them have honourable ways, and that they practise some special craft also. Nothing useless ever befits bishops: not folly nor stupidity, nor too much drinking, nor childishness in speech, nor idle buffoonery of

---

[46] Some of this section was repeated in *Institutes of Polity*, section 11(19) concerning priests, see *Anglo-Saxon Prose*, trans. and ed. Swanton, pp. 193–6, especially p. 194.

[47] For the biblical motif of 'the Good Shepherd', also employed elsewhere by Wulfstan (who himself used the Latin pen-name *Lupus* 'wolf') in *Institutes of Polity*, section 13 on abbots (see below, p. 17) and section 11(19) on priests, and in I Cnut, ch. 26.1–4 (see above, n. 44), see further, above, pp. 8–9, and n. 38.

[48] This section was apparently drafted later than the others quoted here, see *Sermo Lupi ad Anglos*, ed. Whitelock, p. 26.

[49] *Anglo-Saxon Prose*, trans. and ed. Swanton, pp. 190–2.

any kind, not at home nor on a journey, nor in any place. But wisdom
and prudence are appropriate to their rank, and gravity befits those that
attend them.

Other vernacular texts concerning bishops, composed by Wulfstan but
distinct in origin from the *Institutes of Polity*, have survived in the same
manuscripts as the latter and have sometimes been confused with it.[50]
One is the text which Felix Liebermann named *Episcopus*.[51] This was
specifically focused on the role of bishops, possibly being prepared for
promulgation at a synod. It emphasized the supervisory and adjudicatory
duties of a bishop.

1.  Every direction ['ælc rihting'] belongs to a bishop, both in reli-
    gious and in secular things.
2.  He must first direct ['gewissian'] the men in orders ['gehadode
    men'], so that each of them may know what it rightly befits him to
    do and also what they ought to declare to laymen.
3.  He must ever be intent on reconciliation and on peace, as eagerly
    as he can.
4.  He must eagerly settle disputes and make peace, along with those
    secular judges who love right.
6.  He must not consent to any injustice, neither wrong measure nor
    false weight; but it is fitting that every law, whether law of a
    borough or law of a country district ['landriht'], should go by his
    advice and his witness [...].
9.  [...] bishops must always dictate judgements along with secular
    judges, so that, if it is in their power, they do not consent that any
    wrong springs up there.[52]

Another Wulfstanian composition (now known by its rubric *Incipit de
synodo*) consists of a set of injunctions to bishops which was apparently
to be promulgated at a provincial synod.[53] Besides sections which call for
unanimity and mutual support between bishops,[54] there are more injunctions relating to episcopal mien and behaviour:

7.  It befits bishops ['Bisceopum gebyreð']["]55 that there ever be good
    teaching in their households, and, wherever they may be, let them

[50] E.g. by Benjamin Thorpe in *Ancient Laws and Institutes of England* (London, 1840,
    reprinted 2004).
[51] *Die Gesetze der Angelsachsen*, ed. F. Liebermann, 3 vols. (Halle, 1903–16), I.477–9.
    Re-edited, with translation, in *Councils & Synods*, ed. Whitelock, no. 56, pp. 417–22.
[52] *Councils & Synods*, ed. Whitelock, pp. 418–20.
[53] *Councils & Synods*, ed. Whitelock, no. 54, pp. 406–13.
[54] Sections 3–5, 10–12.
[55] This is the opening formula of each section of this text. It may be deliberately echoing
    the wording of 1 Tim. III.2, see above, p. 3.

always be intent on wisdom and consider every folly unworthy of them.

8. It befits bishops that they be not too fond of sport, nor care too much for dogs or hawks, or worldly display or vain pride.

9. It befits bishops that they be not too avaricious either at ordination or at consecration or at penance, and do not in any way acquire anything wrongly.[56]

13. It befits bishops that they both order their own way of life rightly and admonish men of every order ['ælces hades men'] to what is right.[57]

In yet another admonitory text which is untitled but circulated with the others already mentioned,[58] Wulfstan began with the statement that

1. Bishops must always preach God's law and forbid wrong [...][59]

and included several statements of bad conduct apparently being pursued by some of his fellow bishops,[60] some of them closely comparable with those listed in the letter to him from Ælfric,[61] while exhorting them to reform their behaviour as well as to give alms and hospitality:

7. [...] it always befits us very rightly that we eagerly gladden God's poor with money and with food, as far as we can do so.

8. And also it is fitting for us that we give friendly hospitality to our friends, as is seemly.[62]

A further, non-Wulfstanian, early eleventh-century text relating to bishops survives in manuscripts from Sherborne and the New Minster, Winchester.[63] This is concerned with mutual prayers and spiritual support between bishops and, in the Sherborne version, between bishops, abbots and abbesses.[64]

It will have been noted that several common themes recur in the material quoted above. The central position within the church in England of bishops, gathered under an archbishop, is without contention. There is above all else an emphasis in the texts on correct preaching and teaching

---

[56] Cf. Ælfric's allegations in his Latin letter to Wulfstan about bishops charging for baptism and confirmation, see above, p. 9 and n. 40.

[57] *Councils & Synods*, ed. Whitelock, pp. 410–12.

[58] *Councils & Synods*, ed. Whitelock, no. 55, pp. 413–17.

[59] *Councils & Synods*, ed. Whitelock, p. 413.

[60] Sections 2–7, 9–13.

[61] See above, pp. 9–10.

[62] *Councils & Synods*, ed. Whitelock, pp. 415–16.

[63] *Councils & Synods*, ed. Whitelock, no. 53, pp. 402–6: surviving in Paris, BN, lat. 943, fol. 163v; and BL, Cotton Titus D. xxvii, fols. 17v–18.

[64] Sections 8–10.

by bishops in order to maintain the church's authority over Christian belief within each diocese. Bishops were called upon not only to maintain justice but also to mediate dissension. They were expected to sustain the poor, while giving a good example of behaviour to all by avoiding greed, bad company and showiness. They were required to work together, and with their abbatial colleagues, in both promoting and exemplifying the message of the apostolic church. Although the expectations laid upon bishops ought to have been familiar to those appointed to the episcopacy, the writings of Ælfric and Wulfstan in particular suggest that some appointees at least did need a constant reminder of their proper behaviour and duties. The criticisms they made of bishops who drank, hunted, engaged in an inappropriate pursuit of wealth and neglected their liturgical knowledge were perhaps aimed, however, at those who were from a secular background in the church rather than at those who had been schooled in the monastic virtues of humility and obedience.[65]

## Guidelines for the abbatial role

While the function of the bishop was exercised as part of the rigid structure of a church hierarchy with its apex in the bishop of Rome and its base in the parish priest, the role of abbots and abbesses was intended to be confined to the nurturing of their own specific monastic community. In early monasticism this role was that of a charismatic desert figure who imparted spiritual teaching and support to a small number of individual disciples.[66] The Aramaic term used in fourth-century Egypt to describe such a figure was *abba* 'father', whence Greek and Latin *abbas* (becoming OE *abbod* 'abbot'; with Latin *abbatissa*, OE *abbodisse* for the feminine equivalent 'abbess'). By the sixth century, the word denoted the head of a fixed monastic community, responsible, in the manner of a parent, for the spiritual welfare and discipline of its members.[67] This was the usage of the word in the rule of St Benedict (*RSB*), which here borrowed heavily from the earlier *Regula Magistri*.[68] The abbot was portrayed in the role of a father, but also as a servant of Christ who was the Supreme Shepherd and owner of the souls of the flock of believers dwelling within the monastery. The abbot was expected to teach by both word and example,

---

65  On monks and non-monks in the late Anglo-Saxon episcopate, see Margaret Deanesly, *Sidelights on the Anglo-Saxon Church* (London, 1962), pp. 104–9; also Barlow, *English Church*, pp. 62–95 and table at p. 63.

66  See C[laude] P[eifer], 'The Abbot', in *RB 1980*, ed. Fry, pp. 322–78, especially pp. 332–43.

67  On the parental nature of abbacy, see further, below, ch. 3 (Rhodes).

68  P[eifer], 'The Abbot', pp. 323, 346–53.

treating each monk as a separate personality and gearing his teaching accordingly.[69] The principal guidelines for the abbatial role were set out in chapter 2 of *RSB* as follows:

2.1.  To be worthy of the task of governing a monastery, the abbot must always remember what his title signifies and act as a superior should.

2.2.  He is believed to hold the place of Christ in the monastery [...]

2.4.  Therefore the abbot must never teach or decree or command anything that would deviate from the Lord's instructions.

2.11.  Furthermore, anyone who receives the name of abbot is to lead his disciples by a twofold teaching:

2.12.  he must point out to them all that is good and holy more by example than by words, proposing the commandments of the Lord to receptive disciples with words, but demonstrating God's instructions to the stubborn and the dull by a living example.

2.30.  The abbot must always remember what he is and remember what he is called, aware that more will be expected of a man to whom more has been entrusted.

2.31.  He must know what a difficult and demanding burden he has undertaken: directing souls and serving a variety of temperaments, coaxing, reproving and encouraging them as appropriate.

2.32.  He must so accommodate and adapt himself to each one's character and intelligence that he will not only keep the flock entrusted to his care from dwindling, but will rejoice in the increase of a good flock.

2.33.  Above all, he must not show too great concern for the fleeting and temporal things of this world, neglecting or treating lightly the welfare of those entrusted to him.

2.34.  Rather, he should keep in mind that he has undertaken the care of souls for whom he must give an account.

2.38.  Whatever the number of brothers he has in his care, let him realize that on judgment day he will surely have to submit a reckoning to the Lord for all their souls – and indeed for his own as well.

2.39.  In this way, while always fearful of the future examination of the shepherd about the sheep entrusted to him and careful about the state of others' accounts, he becomes concerned also about his own,

2.40.  and while helping others to amend by his warnings, he achieves the amendment of his own faults.[70]

---

[69] P[eifer], 'The Abbot', pp. 366–7. Cf. *RSB*, ch. 2.11–12, 23–5; *RB 1980*, ed. Fry, pp. 172–5, 177.

[70] *RB 1980*, ed. Fry, pp. 171, 173, 177, 179.

The personal qualities required of anyone chosen as abbot were not, however, listed until chapter 64:

> 64.2.   Goodness of life and wisdom must be the criteria for choosing the one to be made abbot […]
>
> 64.9.   He ought […] to be learned in divine law […]. He must be chaste, temperate and merciful.
>
> 64.16. Excitable, anxious, extreme, obstinate, jealous or oversuspicious he must not be. Such a man is never at rest.
>
> 64.17. Instead, he must show forethought and consideration in his orders, and whether the task he assigns concerns God or the world, he should be discerning and moderate [.][71]

With the gradual adoption of the *RSB* as the guide for regular life in the monastic houses founded in Anglo-Saxon England,[72] and particularly with the reinforcement of Benedictinism in the mid-tenth-century kingdom,[73] these criteria became the norm against which abbatial behaviour was to be judged. The *RSB* also directed that the election of an unsuitable person as abbot should be prevented by the local bishop and other abbots and Christians of the area.[74] In the New Minster Refoundation Charter, King Edgar took it upon himself, and put the obligation on his successors, both to defend the monks and to support the abbot in enforcing the provisions of the *RSB*.[75] Edgar's role as supporter and protector of the monks was also reported in the *Regularis Concordia* and in the OE text known as 'King Edgar's Establishment of Monasteries'.[76] All three of these texts were almost certainly composed by Bishop Æthelwold of Winchester.[77] In

---

[71] *RB 1980*, ed. Fry, pp. 281, 283.

[72] C[laude] P[eifer], 'Introduction', in *RB 1980*, ed. Fry, pp. 118–19. For the mixed character of the rules followed in early Anglo-Saxon monastic houses, see Sarah Foot, *Monastic Life in Anglo-Saxon England c. 600–900* (Cambridge, 2006), pp. 50–8. For influences on, and modifications of the *RSB* made in Gaul and Francia which influenced its usage in England, see Eric John, '"Secularium Prioratus" and the Rule of St Benedict', *Revue Bénédictine* 75 (1965), 212–39.

[73] See *Tenth-Century Studies: Essays in Commemoration of the Millennium of the Council of Winchester and* Regularis Concordia, ed. David Parsons (London and Chichester, 1975). For a revised chronology, see Julia Barrow, 'The Chronology of the Benedictine "Reform"', in *Edgar, King of the English 959–975*, ed. Donald Scragg (Woodbridge, 2008), pp. 211–23.

[74] Ch. 63.3–6, *RB 1980*, ed. Fry, pp. 280–1.

[75] S 745; Rumble, *Property and Piety*, no. IV, ch. xiv (p. 88), where the kings are to play the part of the 'Good Shepherd' (cf. above, p. 9, n. 38). Note also that the abbot is specifically stated in the same document (ch. xxi; p. 91) to be liable to punishment in accordance with the *RSB*.

[76] *Regularis Concordia Anglicae nationis monachorum sanctimonialiumque*, ed. and trans. Thomas Symons (London and Edinburgh, 1953), proem. 2 (pp. 1–2); *Councils & Synods*, ed. Whitelock, no. 33, pp. 142–54, at pp. 149–51. Edgar appears as 'Good Shepherd' in *Regularis Concordia,* proem. 3 (p. 2; cf above, p. 9, n. 38).

[77] Dorothy Whitelock, 'The Authorship of the Account of King Edgar's Establishment

the latter two, the task of overseeing the welfare of the nuns in England was deputed by Edgar to his consort, Ælfthryth.[78] In 'Establishment' the abbesses were instructed 'to be deeply loyal and to serve the precepts of the holy rule with all their hearts'.[79] They were expected to be of exemplary character and behaviour similar to that of the abbots, being equally bound by the *RSB*, and it is noteworthy that the text in one of the surviving manuscripts of Æthelwold's OE translation of it has been linguistically adapted for feminine use.[80]

Presumably because the criteria had already been firmly established and confirmed, Archbishop Wulfstan did not seem to have felt the need to elaborate much on the abbatial role in his *Institutes of Polity*, merely writing:

*13 Concerning Abbots*
It is right that abbots and especially abbesses constantly dwell fast in the monasteries and always diligently take care of their flocks and ever set them a good example and preach properly, and never care too greatly or all too frequently about the cares of the world in vain pride, but concern themselves most often with sacred needs. So it befits abbots and men in monastic orders.[81]

There is, however, criticism of some unidentified monastic superiors in *Polity*, section *14 Concerning Monks*. These superiors, Wulfstan stated, were not preventing some of the monks for whom they were responsible from wandering outside the monasteries and indulging in lustful and vain behaviour.[82] This is an interesting counterweight to the triumphant

of Monasteries', in *Philological Essays: Studies in Old and Middle English Language and Literature in Honour of Herbert Dean Meritt* (The Hague, 1970), pp. 125–36, at p. 131; Michael Lapidge, 'Æthelwold as Scholar and Teacher', in *Bishop Æthelwold: His Career and Influence*, ed. Barbara Yorke (Woodbridge, 1988, pbk edn 1997), pp. 89–117, at pp. 95–103. For references to textual parallels between the New Minster charter and the other two texts, see Rumble, *Property and Piety*, p. 66, nn. 10–11.

78 *Regularis Concordia*, ed. and trans. Symons, proem. 3 (p. 2); *Councils & Synods*, ed. Whitelock, no. 33, at p. 150.

79 'þæt hi inholde sin and þæs halgan regoles ge[b]odum eallum mode þeowigen': *Councils & Synods*, ed. Whitelock, no. 33, at p. 153.

80 BL, Cotton Claudius D. iii (s. xiii); see Mechthild Gretsch, 'Æthelwold's Translation of the *Regula Sancti Benedicti* and its Latin Exemplar', *ASE* 3 (1974), 125–51. On this manuscript, probably written at Wintney, Hants, see Francisco José Álvarez López, 'A Comparative Analysis of the Palaeography of the Manuscripts Containing the Æthelwoldian Translation of *Regula Sancti Benedicti* Written in England', Ph.D thesis (University of Manchester, 2009), pp. 177–202.

81 *Anglo-Saxon Prose*, trans. and ed. Swanton, pp. 197–8.

82 '[...] it is truly an evil that some are too proud and all too vain, and too given to wandering, and too profitless, and all too empty of every good deed, and too wicked in secret lustfulness: inwardly worthless and outwardly indignant. And some who should, if they would, be champions of God within their monasteries are apostates. That is,

description of the monastic reform found in the previous generation in the texts composed by Æthelwold, although it needs to be seen both in the context of an ancient opposition between wandering and static monasticism[83] and in relation to Wulfstan's apocalyptic style.[84] A further criticism of contemporary monastic behaviour was, however, made by Wulfstan in the lawcode VIII Æthelred (issued in 1014), which stated (ch. 31.1):

> And henceforth we desire that abbots and monks live more in accordance with the rule than they have been in the habit of doing up till now.[85]

Both these criticisms by Wulfstan support the modern view that the Benedictine reform in England had lost its initial force by the early eleventh century.[86]

## *Bishops and abbots in the English church*

The presence of both bishops and monastic superiors in the ecclesiastical hierarchy of the Anglo-Saxon church reflected a universal dichotomy within Christianity between the obligation to preach the faith to the public and the desire to contemplate it in seclusion. The former obligation was laid primarily upon the bishops and their subordinate priests, while the opportunity for contemplation and prayer within a monastic community

---

those wretches who have cast off orders and dwell in sin among worldly affairs. All too widely everything is going badly. So much is it worsening widely among men, that those in orders who through fear of God were at one time the most profitable and most laborious in divine ministry and in scholarship, are now everywhere well nigh the most useless, and never labour much at any needful matter on behalf of God nor on behalf of the world, but do all for pleasure and for ease, and love gluttony and vain joy, stroll about and wander and play the fool all day, chatter and sport and do nothing of any use. That is a detestable life that they live thus; it is the worse that the superiors do not amend it moreover; nor some of them conduct themselves as they should [...]': *Anglo-Saxon Prose*, trans. and ed. Swanton, p. 198.

83  *RSB*, ch. 1.10–11 categorised these 'gyrovagues' as the worst kind of monk; see *RB 1980*, ed. Fry, pp. 170–1, 319. Canon 4 of the Council of Hertford (670/2) had directed '[t]hat monks shall not wander from place to place, that is, from monastery to monastery, unless they have letters dimissory from their own abbot [...]': Bede, *HE*, IV.5; Colgrave and Mynors, pp. 350–1. Note the lawcode V and VI Æthelred (composed by Wulfstan and promulgated at Enham, Hants, in 1008), ch. 6, which placed 'that monk who has no monastery' under the control of the bishop: *Councils & Synods*, ed. Whitelock, no. 49, pp. 338–73, at p. 348.

84  For discussions of Wulfstan's style, see Bethurum, *Homilies of Wulfstan*, pp. 87–98; and A. P. McD. Orchard, 'Crying Wolf: Oral Style and the *Sermones Lupi*', *ASE* 21 (1992), 239–64.

85  *Councils & Synods*, ed. Whitelock, no. 52, pp. 386–402, at p. 398.

86  Cf. Barlow, *English Church*, pp. 65, 104, 311–12.

was regulated by those of abbatial rank. Although early on there seems to have been some lack of distinction between the relative influence of bishop and abbot in those northern and western districts of England whose churches had been founded by Irish missionaries,[87] for most of the Anglo-Saxon period there was a clear difference between the religious powers of the two officials. Thus certain rites were always reserved to the local bishop as the senior priest in a diocese: those of confirmation, the ordination of priests and abbots, the consecration of churches and of the chrism.[88] Abbots on the other hand, at least early in the period, did not themselves need to be priests if there were access to one within the monastic community or nearby.[89]

The relative authority of bishop and abbot in England was a subject which was clarified only gradually by the decrees of church councils.[90] Although canon 3 of the Council of Hertford (670/2) stated 'that no bishop shall in any way interfere with any monasteries dedicated to God nor take away forcibly any part of their property',[91] this did not affect the right, given by the *RSB*,[92] of the local bishop to be involved in the election of abbots (and abbesses) in his diocese. This right was strengthened by the Council of Chelsea (816), whose fourth canon gave to the bishop the power of appointing abbots following 'consent and consultation' with the respective monastic community ('familia').[93] Canon 8 of the same council gave new powers to the bishop to act against the use or appropriation of

---

[87] P[eifer], 'Introduction', in *RB 1980*, ed. Fry, pp. 114–15. For the possibility of an individual being both bishop and abbot in 7th century Ireland, see Thomas Charles-Edwards, 'The Pastoral Role of the Church in the Early Irish Laws', in *Pastoral Care before the Parish*, ed. Blair and Sharpe, pp. 63–80, at p. 67. On Irish influences at Lindisfarne, see Clare Stancliffe, 'Cuthbert and the Polarity between Pastor and Solitary', in *St Cuthbert, his Cult and his Community to AD 1200*, ed. Gerald Bonner, David Rollason and Clare Stancliffe (Woodbridge, 1989, reprinted 1998), pp. 21–44, at pp. 39–42. For references to some Irish missionaries elsewhere in England, see *Charters of Malmesbury Abbey*, ed. S. E. Kelly, AS Charters 11 (Oxford, 2005), 4.

[88] Barlow, *English Church*, p. 243; Alan Thacker, 'Monks, Preaching and Pastoral Care in Early Anglo-Saxon England', in *Pastoral Care before the Parish*, ed. Blair and Sharpe, pp. 137–70, at p. 137. Abbesses could be ordained by deacons, see Thacker, *ibid.*, p. 138. For the bishop's role in the ordination of priests, see *Councils & Synods*, ed. Whitelock, no. 57, pp. 422–7 (early 11th century).

[89] P[eifer], 'The Abbot', p. 377; Thacker, 'Monks, Preaching and Pastoral Care', p. 146. Abbesses of course would always need access to a priest in close proximity to their communities.

[90] In this they continued a theme begun by canon 4 of the Council of Chalcedon (451) which placed monks under the authority of their diocesan bishop, see Brooks, *Early Church*, p. 176. The English church seems also sometimes to have been influenced by decisions made at church councils in Francia, see Cubitt, *Church Councils*, pp. 102–4, 201–2, 244.

[91] Bede, *HE*, IV.5; Colgrave and Mynors, pp. 350–1.

[92] Chs. 64.3–6 and 65.3: *RB 1980*, ed. Fry, pp. 280–1, 284–5.

[93] Brooks, *Early Church*, pp. 175–6; Cubitt, *Church Councils*, p. 194.

monastic property by secular individuals,[94] a problem detailed by Bede in 734.[95]

Despite these rulings, a number of complicating factors and developments confront us when seeking to define further the relationship between bishops and their abbatial colleagues before 1066.

First, as has been often stated in recent years, there is nearly always some doubt about the exact significance of the word *monasterium* when used in any particular Anglo-Saxon text or document.[96] It might refer to various sorts of religious community: a proprietary monastery still controlled by its founder's family; a monastic house following a strict rule, but often also fulfilling some sort of more general pastoral function within its lands or neighbourhood;[97] or a parochial mother-church in an area, with a number of subsidiary centres of worship.[98] Some of these *monasteria* would be under the direct control of the local bishop, others would not.

Second, some uneven transfer of behaviour or attitude might well have arisen when an abbot became promoted to bishop during the course of his career. Sometimes, as the Christian faith spread and where a new episcopal see was made from an existing *monasterium*, as envisaged by Bede in *Epistola ad Ecgberhtum*, then the abbot, if suitably qualified, might be transmuted into a bishop through election by his community.[99] At other times throughout the period, abbots were advanced to the office

---

94  Brooks, *Early Church*, p. 176; Cubitt, *Church Councils*, pp. 194–5. See also John, "'Secularium Prioratus'". Canon 5 of the Council of *Clofesho* (747) had decreed that bishops should visit secular *monasteria*, see Cubitt, 'Pastoral Care and Conciliar Canons', pp. 195–6.

95  Bede, *Epistola ad Ecgberhtum*, in *Venerabilis Baedae Opera Historica*, ed. Plummer, I.405–23; Whitelock, *EHD*, no. 170, pp. 804–6.

96  See Sarah Foot, 'Anglo-Saxon Minsters: A Review of Terminology', in *Pastoral Care before the Parish*, ed. Blair and Sharpe, pp. 212–25; and Thacker, 'Monks, Preaching and Pastoral Care', pp. 139–52. John Blair, *The Church in Anglo-Saxon Society* (Oxford, 2005), pp. 3–5, favours use of the term 'minster' to cover all of the possible significances of *monasterium*.

97  Thacker, 'Monks, Preaching and Pastoral Care', pp. 153–64.

98  For examples, see P. H. Hase, 'The Mother Churches of Hampshire', in *Minsters and Parish Churches: The Local Church in Transition 950–1200*, ed. John Blair (Oxford, 1988), pp. 45–66; and Steven Bassett, 'Church and Diocese in the West Midlands: The Transition from British to Anglo-Saxon Control', in *Pastoral Care before the Parish*, ed. Blair and Sharpe, pp. 13–40, especially Fig. 1.5.

99  'Therefore I would consider it expedient that after a great council has been held a site among the monasteries should be procured, both by pontifical consent and also royal edict, where an episcopal see may be made. And in case the abbot or monks should try to oppose or resist this decree, permission is to be given them to choose for themselves from their number someone who may be ordained bishop and take episcopal charge of as many of the adjacent places as belong to the same diocese, along with that monastery; or if perchance no one can be found in that monastery who should be ordained bishop, yet it is to depend on their investigation according to the statutes

of bishop in existing sees. Thus, Abbot Hræthun of Abingdon appears to have become bishop of Leicester in 814×816, while Abbot Coenwulf of Peterborough became bishop of Winchester in 1006.[100] Conflicts of interest, or some administrative or logistical problems, might arise when such bishops retained their abbeys after their promotion. Examples of such retentions are Abbot Aldhelm of Malmesbury who kept the abbacy after becoming bishop of Sherborne in c.705,[101] and Abbot Æthelgar of the New Minster, Winchester, who kept that position after becoming bishop of Selsey in 980.[102]

Third, there were the potentially confusing effects of the introduction by the proponents of the Benedictine reform in the reign of Edgar of the new and uniquely English institution of the monastic cathedral in which the bishop was *in loco abbatis*.[103] In order to avoid potential or actual conflicts of power within a monk-bishop's own cathedral church the bishop was never, however, officially called abbot and a deputy, equivalent to the later prior,[104] was allowed to take over the day to day supervision of the monastic community. Provision was made in the *Regularis Concordia* for the election of bishops in such monastic sees, adapting the wording of chapter 64.1 of the *RSB*[105] and adding the involvement of the king:

Prefato equidem synodali conciliabulo hoc adtendendum magnopere cuncti decreverunt, ut abbatum ac abbatissarum electio cum regis consensu et consilio sanctę regule ageretur documento. Episcoporum quoque electio uti abbatum, ubicumque in sede episcopali monachi regulares conversantur, si Domini largiente gratia tanti profectus inibi monachus repperiri potuerit, eodem modo agatur; nec alio quolibet modo dum eiusdem sunt conversationis a quoquam presumatur. Si autem, imperitia impediente vel peccatis promerentibus, talis qui tanti gradus honore dignus sit in eadem congregatione repperiri non potuerit,

---

of the canons, who is to be ordained bishop of their diocese [...]': Whitelock, *EHD*, no. 170, p. 804.

[100] *Charters of Abingdon Abbey*, ed. S. E. Kelly, AS Charters 7–8 (Oxford, 2000), ccxii; *Charters of Peterborough Abbey*, ed. S. E. Kelly, AS Charters 14 (Oxford, 2009), 115.

[101] *Charters of Malmesbury*, ed. Kelly, pp. 107–8.

[102] Æthelgar kept the abbacy until 988, when he became archbishop of Canterbury. However, when in 983 he acquired meadow-land outside Winchester, later owned by the New Minster and to become the site of Hyde Abbey, he was styled solely as bishop of Selsey: see S 845; Rumble, *Property and Piety*, no. IX (pp. 149–55), and p. 95, n. 149.

[103] Barlow, *English Church*, pp. 102–4. On their uniqueness, see Patrick Wormald, 'Æthelwold and his Continental Counterparts: Contact, Comparison, Contrast', in *Bishop Æthelwold*, ed. Yorke, pp. 13–42, at pp. 37–41.

[104] Sometimes called 'dean' before 1066, see Margaret Deanesly, *Sidelights on the Anglo-Saxon Church* (London, 1962), pp. 162–8.

[105] *RB 1980*, ed. Fry, pp. 280–1.

ex alio noto monachorum monasterio, concordi regis et fratrum quibus dedicari debet consilio eligatur. Qui ordinatus videlicet episcopus in omnibus eundem morem regularem cum monachis suis quem abbas tenet regularis, diligenti cura et magnopere excellenti iugiter sine intermissione custodiat; nec episcopatus occasione regulę precepta tumidus vel obliviosus temere intermittat, sed quantum [excellit honore tantum] cum grege sibi subiecto sancto excellat et opere.[106]

Winchester and Sherborne, the sites of the two most ancient West Saxon dioceses, were reconstituted as monastic sees in 964 and 998 respectively.[107] The exact dates, but not the eventual fact, of the reconstitution of Canterbury and Worcester are still the subject of debate.[108] Three of these sees were held by the leaders of the monastic faction in the reign of Edgar, all of whom had previously been abbots elsewhere (Dunstan

---

[106] *Regularis Concordia*, proem. 9: text from *Councils & Synods*, ed. Whitelock, no. 32 (pp. 133–41), at pp. 139–40. The following translation is from *Regularis Concordia*, ed. and trans. Symons (p. 6): 'It was further decided by the whole assembly at this Synodal Council that another very important matter should receive attention; namely, that the election of abbots and abbesses should be carried out with the consent and advice of the King and according to the teaching of the Holy Rule. Thus wherever monks live the monastic life in a bishop's see, the election of the bishop shall be carried out in the same way as that of an abbot if, by the Lord's grace, a monk of sufficient worth be found in that see; nor shall anyone presume to act in any way contrary to this so long as such a manner of life is led in that place. But if, owing to their ignorance or sinfulness, there shall not be found in that community one worthy of so high a dignity, let a monk be chosen from another monastery that is well-known, with the consent of the King and the counsel of the brethren to whom he is to be presented. As for him who is chosen to be bishop, he shall live with his monks, unceasingly and with exceeding diligence and care keeping to the monastic life in everything, as would the abbot of a monastery. Nor shall he, by reason of his episcopal office, proudly or forgetfully dare to neglect the ordinances of the Rule but, as he excels in honour, so let him, together with the flock subject to him, excel also in holy deeds.'

[107] For Winchester (the Old Minster), see S 817–18; Rumble, *Property and Piety*, nos. V, ii (pp. 109–12) and V, xiv (pp. 98–135), '964×975' (late 10th/early 11th century). The latter section, in a passage (p. 133) adapted from *Regularis Concordia*, proem. 9, specifically excluded a 'canon' from being bishop there. For Sherborne, see David Farmer, 'The Monastic Reform of the Tenth Century and Sherborne', in *St Wulfsige and Sherborne: Essays to Celebrate the Millennium of the Benedictine Abbey 998–1998*, ed. Katherine Barker, David A. Hinton and Alan Hunt (Oxford, 2005), pp. 24–9; with S 895: ed. and trans. Simon Keynes, 'King Æthelred's Charter for Sherborne Abbey, 998', in *St Wulfsige*, ed. Barker *et al.*, pp. 10–13 and below, ch. 8 (Hill).

[108] For Canterbury, see Brooks, *Early History*, pp. 255–60. For Worcester: P. H. Sawyer, 'Charters of the Reform Movement: The Worcester Archive', in *Tenth-Century Studies*, ed. Parsons, pp. 84–102; Julia Barrow, 'The Community of Worcester, 961–c. 1100', in *St Oswald of Worcester's Life and Influence*, ed. Nicholas Brooks and Catherine Cubitt (London and New York, 1996), pp. 84–99; and Eric John, 'The Church of Worcester and St Oswald', in *Belief and Culture in the Middle Ages: Studies Presented to Henry Mayr-Harting*, ed. Richard Gameson and Henrietta Leyser (Oxford, 2001), pp. 142–57.

at Glastonbury; Æthelwold at Abingdon; and Oswald at Ramsey, which he continued to hold when he became bishop of Worcester).[109] The institution of the monastic cathedral did not spread further before 1066, however, though three of the four named above,[110] and the few others instituted after the Norman Conquest,[111] lasted until the Dissolution. Problems arose when (contrary to the *Regularis Concordia*) a non-monk was given such a monastic see. Perhaps the most infamous example of this was Stigand, who held both Winchester and Canterbury in plurality and lived a blatantly secular life.[112]

Finally, possession of a papal privilege of exemption would have allowed an abbot to bypass the power of both bishop and king, although the evidence for this in England before 1066 is exiguous and has been challenged.[113]

## *Other heads of communities*

Besides bishops and abbots, we should also note that other superiors, called variously deans, priors or 'elders', were usually in charge of the larger secular 'colleges' of priests or canons which existed in various places before 1066.[114] Some at least of these may have followed non-Benedictine rules of behaviour. However, although there exists a bilingual (Latin and OE) version of the rule of Chrodegang of Metz (*c.* 755), it is

---

[109]  Three commemorative volumes have been produced on these individuals: *St Dunstan: His Life, Times and Cult*, ed. Nigel Ramsay, Margaret Sparks and Tim Tatton-Brown (Woodbridge, 1992); *St Æthelwold*, ed. Yorke; and *St Oswald*, ed. Brooks and Cubitt.

[110]  The bishopric of Sherborne was united with that of Ramsbury under Bishop Hereman (1058–78), upon whose death the see was moved to Salisbury and became secular: *HBC*, pp. 220, 222, 270.

[111]  Later conversions to monastic cathedrals were Durham and Rochester (1083), Norwich (by September 1101), Ely (1109), and Carlisle (1133). See *John Le Neve: Fasti Ecclesiae Anglicanae 1066–1300, II, Monastic Cathedrals (Northern and Southern Provinces)*, compiled by Diana E. Greenway (London, 1971), 32, 78, 58, 47, and 21, respectively. Also, the monastery at Bath became a cathedral priory in 1090 and that at Coventry in 1102: *HRH*, pp. 27, 40.

[112]  See below, chapter 9 (Rumble).

[113]  On such papal privileges, see Levison, *England and the Continent*, pp. 24–33; cf. Brooks, *Early Church*, pp. 177–9, 184–6, and Cubitt, *Church Councils*, pp. 197–9. Note that Eric John ("'Secularium Prioratus'", p. 222 and n. 1) challenged Levison's position on particular papal documents, while Susan Kelly has suggested a re-dating of some forgeries, see *Charters of St Augustine's Abbey, Canterbury and Minster-in-Thanet*, ed. S. E. Kelly, AS Charters 4 (Oxford, 1995), lxiv–lxv.

[114]  For such 'colleges', see David Knowles and R. Neville Hadcock, *Medieval Religious Houses: England & Wales* (revised edn, London, 1971), pp. 411–46. Also Blair, *Church in Anglo-Saxon Society, passim*.

not certain that this rule was followed in England until after the Norman Conquest.[115]

Archbishops, bishops, abbots, abbesses and deans (etc.) represented various levels of spiritual leadership within the Anglo-Saxon church. Members of the episcopate and some abbots also occur in the historical record in a number of other roles, attending on and advising the king, judging or pleading in lawsuits, holding or disposing of estates, mediating disputes, acting as ambassadors, organizing national or local defence, commissioning or creating buildings and works of art, and being members of powerful kinship groups, to name but a few.[116] Whatever the activity in which they were engaged, however, they were expected to act in accordance with the dignity of their position in the church and the specific rank to which they had been elected. As the studies in the present volume illustrate, many leaders of the Anglo-Saxon church did succeed both in nurturing their specific religious communities and in consolidating Christian influence on law and government.

---

[115] *The Old English Version of the Enlarged Rule of Chrodegang*, ed. Brigitte Langefeld (Bern, 2003); *eadem*, '*Regula canonicorum* or *Regula monasterialis uitae*? The Rule of Chrodegang and Archbishop Wulfred's Reforms at Canterbury', *ASE* 25 (1996), 21–36. Cf. Blair, *Church in Anglo-Saxon Society*, pp. 345, 361–2.

[116] See PASE, *passim*. For a study which demonstrates the many activities of Anglo-Saxon bishops, see Mary Frances Giandrea, *Episcopal Culture in Late Anglo-Saxon England* (Woodbridge, 2007). For the dioceses, see Barlow, *English Church*, pp. 162–82, and map of principal churches at p. 161. For the abbeys, see Knowles and Hadcock, *Medieval Religious Houses*, *passim*. For the names of later Anglo-Saxon heads of religious houses, see *HRH*.

# 1

# Bede and the Early English Church

NICHOLAS J. HIGHAM

IN 731, Bede completed his *Historia Ecclesiastica nostrae insulae ac gentis in libri v* – his 'Ecclesiastical History of our island and people in five books', a work which he entitled internally the *Historia Ecclesiastica gentis Anglorum* (in the opening line of the Preface and in the headings of the contents lists which open each book).[1] The core of the title is, however, the same in each case, the *Historia Ecclesiastica.* Unsurprisingly, Bede made frequent use of the word 'ecclesia' meaning 'church' across this work; it occurs 378 times.[2] This term has several different significances, however, which we need to distinguish before we can really discuss Bede's conception of, and attitude towards, the early English church.

'Ecclesia' is frequently used in the *Historia Ecclesiastica* to refer to the universal Christian church, occurring in such phrases as 'catholica et apostolica ecclesia' ('the catholic and apostolic church'), 'ecclesia sua' ('his church', i.e. 'Christ's church'), 'ecclesia catholica' ('the catholic church') and 'omnis ecclesia' ('the whole church'), all taken from V. 21, which features Abbot Ceolfrith's letter to King Nechtan. This document was, of course, urging unity on the Picts as regards the calculation of Easter, so made frequent use of the terminologies of universality and conformity, of which such phrases form a central part. This was a terminology with which Bede was very familiar, appearing as it does in the New Testament, most famously in Matt. XVI.18, in a passage which reappears in *HE* III. 25, but elsewhere also in the Epistles of St Paul.[3]

The word is also used to refer to the 'ecclesia Anglorum' ('the church of the English'), so to a particular fragment of the universal church, which

---

[1] Throughout, all references are to the edition and translation by Colgrave and Mynors, henceforth *HE*.

[2] Book I has sixty instances, II seventy-four, III seventy-nine, IV eighty-one and V seventy-seven. The Preface has seven. The most instances in a single chapter is thirty-three in I. 27. For the detailed distribution, see Putnam F. Jones, *A Concordance to the Historia Ecclesiastica of Bede* (Cambridge Mass., 1929), pp. 168–72.

[3] E.g. 1 Cor. XII.27; Rom. XII.5; and Eph. I.22–3.

occurs in all forms some sixteen times – and it is here that our interest will naturally gravitate at a later point of this chapter.

However, Bede also made occasional use of 'ecclesia' in reference to a fragment of this fragment: so, for example, he refers to the 'ecclesia Cantuariorum' ('the church of the men of Kent') in his Preface, when identifying the theatre in which Pope Gregory's disciples first operated in Britain, and the 'ecclesia Cantiae' ('the church of Kent') in II.20 as the final resting place of King Edwin's treasures, which had been taken south by Paulinus in the 630s and were still reputedly on display in the eighth century. This last phrase is ambiguous: it could mean 'the [senior] church in Kent', so the archdiocesan church at Canterbury, or it could mean the church as a collective noun for the Christians in Kent, in which case these treasures were perhaps distributed across several different sites. That Paulinus ultimately became bishop of Rochester may suggest that it is the latter which we should prefer, on the assumption that individual items may well have been at both diocesan sites, at least, but Bede was arguably using such terminology somewhat loosely and was dependant on the phraseology used by his informants in such instances. However, regional names are uncommon in combination with 'ecclesia' in the singular, being exclusive to 'Kent' and the 'men of Kent'; there are occasional plural references, such as to 'the churches of the Northumbrians',[4] but this should perhaps be considered alongside the group following, as conveying a somewhat different and less corporate meaning.

At the far end of this spectrum of meanings, 'ecclesia' frequently means an individual church, or a specific group of churches at a particular place,[5] such as 'ecclesia Lindisfarnensis' – the church of Lindisfarne. In some instances this is quite specifically the physical building: so, for example, Bede used the word 'ecclesia' of the church of St Alban outside *Verulamium* in I.7, which was 'of wonderful workmanship' ('mirandi operis'). Otherwise it was also used of the community of priests associated with a particular religious centre, and the wider congregation. That was, indeed, the earlier meaning of the term. So, for example, we have 'Lundoniensis ecclesia' ('the church of London') used to locate 'the religious priest Nothhelm' in the Preface, which may quite specifically mean the diocesan church of St Paul's but may equally well signify the whole diocesan clergy and Christian community there and the various churches

---

4   *HE*, IV.2 (Colgrave and Mynors, pp. 334–5, the reference is to Ædsi 'cantandi magister Nordanhymbrorum ecclesiis' but translated there as '[singing master in] the Northumbrian churches').

5   Taking the point that most major church sites were in fact close-knit groups of churches; see Catherine Cubitt, 'Universal and Local Saints in Anglo-Saxon England', in *Local Saints and Local Churches in the Early Medieval West,* ed. Alan Thacker and Richard Sharpe (Oxford, 2002), pp. 423–53, at p. 444.

where they officiated. Specific insular churches named in this way are Lindisfarne,[6] Hexham,[7] York,[8] London,[9] Canterbury,[10] Rochester,[11] and Ripon,[12] all of which were, of course, diocesan churches, so Bede seems to have used such phrases exclusively in the context of a community of clergy at the centre of a diocese.

This plurality of meanings should not, of course, surprise us, since it mirrors that of our own word 'church'. In *The Concise Oxford Dictionary* we find the following meanings of 'church' as a noun: 'building for public Christian worship, especially according to established religion of country'; 'all Christians'; 'an organized Christian society of any time, country, or distinguishing principle'; 'organization, clergy and other officers, of a religious society or corporation', and 'clerical profession'.[13] We need to tread carefully, therefore, when attempting to explore just what Bede meant by the phrase 'ecclesia Anglorum', the extent to which he was committed to a particular vision of an English church, and just how that fitted into his view of English history.

On one level, it seems fairly clear that Bede thought of the entirety of English Christianity in the present as a single whole; he portrayed his countrymen as obedient to Rome via an archdiocese centred at Canterbury. He described that archdiocese in the present in his penultimate chapter (V.23), noting the death of Archbishop Berhtwold on 13 January 731, and the succession of Tatwine in June (which is the latest event to which he referred in this work). He then listed the occupants of the various dioceses, beginning in Kent and moving outwards to Essex, East Anglia, the West Saxons, the Mercians and their satellites, and finally the Northumbrians. By so doing Bede was establishing the key characters with authority over and responsibility for the English church *in toto* at the time of writing. This was clearly a single pyramidal structure, focused on Canterbury but encompassing all Anglo-Saxon England and Bede reported this factually, with a sense of a concentric geographical vision, and without apparent demur.

But this had not always been the case. In Bede's *Historia*, the English church was long divided between a Rome/Francia-orientated network

---

6  *HE*, Preface (pp. 6–7); III.12 (pp. 252–3); IV.12 (pp. 370–1), 27 (pp. 430–1: twice); V.1 (pp. 454–5).
7  *HE*, III. 2 (pp. 216–17: twice); IV.28(26) (pp. 438–9: twice); V.2 (pp. 456–7: twice).
8  *HE*, III. 28 (pp. 316–17); IV.23(21) (pp. 408–9); V.6 (pp. 468–9), 23 (pp. 558–9).
9  *HE*, Preface (pp. 4–5).
10 *HE*, II.7 (pp. 156–7), 18 (pp. 196–7); III.7 (pp. 236–7); IV.1 (pp. 328–9), 5 (pp. 348–9: in report of Council of Hertford).
11 *HE*, II. 8 (pp. 158–9), 20 (pp. 204–5); III.14 (pp. 254–5), 20 (pp. 278–9: twice).
12 *HE*, III.28 (pp. 316–17).
13 *The Concise Oxford Dictionary of Current English*, ed. H. W. Fowler and F. G. Fowler, 5th edn (Oxford, 1964), p. 213.

centred on Canterbury and an Anglo-Scottish church, centred at Lindisfarne in Northumbria; this structural disunity was a consequence of the
collapse of the Roman mission to the north and then the arrival of Scottish missionaries in the 630s. Although these incomers were putatively
much respected by their contemporaries in the Gregorian mission,[14] and
Bede was himself keen to sing their praises a century later,[15] differences
regarding the dating of Easter and the shape of the tonsure marked a
significant divide and they looked not to Rome but to Iona for spiritual
guidance and authority. The union of the English Church under Canterbury and Rome occurred in 664 at the so-called Synod of Whitby,[16] at
which the Scottish party was defeated and following which those who
were unwilling to compromise withdrew from England. Bede invested
heavily in his account of this meeting, devoting to it the fourth longest
chapter in the work (III.25), and incorporating several lengthy but apocryphal speeches on either side, building massively on the much shorter
(but arguably still apocryphal) treatment it had received in Stephen's *Vita
Wilfridi*.[17] The latter text could at least call upon memories of Wilfrid's
own account of the exchanges, albeit decades after the event, but there is
no evidence that Bede was able to draw upon eye-witness or even second-
hand accounts external to that earlier source, so his version is more to do
with what he thought should have been said than what actually occurred.
It is short of historicity, therefore, but it is worth emphasizing that Bede
presented this as a seminal event; the re-construction is laced with references to the greater authority of the universal church – as 'tota Christi
ecclesia' ('the whole church of Christ') and 'universalis ecclesia' ('the
universal church') – as well as to the unity of the English church, 'omnis
Anglorum ecclesia' ('the whole church of the English'). It is a highly
rhetorical piece, which is clearly designed to persuade his audience of the
veracity of the decision there arrived at; so the Northumbrians were right
to have shifted their spiritual allegiance from Iona to the universal and
Roman, and thus unite the church.[18] At the same time Bede was eager to
sustain the reputation of the Scottish clergy within the full pastoral tradi-

---

[14] Such was Bede's contention in *HE*, III.25 (pp. 296–7), in the prologue to discussion
of the Synod of Whitby, where he particularly singled out Aidan in this regard.
[15] In the *HE*, but not, a few years earlier, in his *Greater Chronicle*, which noticeably
passes over the Scottish mission in total silence: see Nicholas J. Higham, *(Re-)Reading
Bede: The* Ecclesiastical History *in Context* (London, 2006 ), pp. 118–46.
[16] Catherine Cubitt, *Anglo-Saxon Church Councils, c.650–850* (London, 1995), pp.
89–90, 150, 289, 316–17.
[17] *The Life of Bishop Wilfrid by Eddius Stephanus*, text, translation and notes by Bertram
Colgrave, (Cambridge, 1927), ch. x.
[18] For comment, see Robert W. Hanning, *The Vision of History in Early Britain* (New
York, 1966), pp. 82–3,who sees this as Bede equating the Romans with the New Law
and the Scots and Britons with the Old Law.

tion expounded by Pope Gregory,[19] despite their error on this particular issue.

Bede then went on to detail efforts to provide a successor for Archbishop Deusdedit, and the eventual arrival in 669 of Archbishop Theodore, Pope Vitalian's choice as a replacement after an English candidate, Wigheard, had died at Rome before his appointment could be confirmed.[20] Within this re-telling, this was the event which brought the union of the English church to fruition and of which Bede clearly approved. Theodore's arrival, thereafter, is one of the rhetorical highlights of his *Historia*, elaborated as a highpoint of English Christianity, and the most recent such to be recognized fulsomely in this work.[21] Bede opened book IV with it, and he clearly massaged his material to achieve that effect. His euphoria was unstinting, claiming that Theodore was 'gladly welcomed and listened to by all',[22] that he gave full instruction to the clergy, that he was the first archbishop 'whom the whole church of the English ('omnis Anglorum ecclesia') consented to obey', and that both he and Hadrian were so learned that they attracted a throng of students to whom they taught Scripture, the art of metre, astronomy, computation, Latin, Greek, and even sacred music. He added:

> Neque umquam prorsus, ex quo Brittaniam petierunt Angli, feliciora fuere tempora, dum et fortissimos Christianosque habentes reges cunctis barbaris nationibus essent terrori, et omnium uota ad nuper audita caelestis regni gaudia penderent, et quicumque lectionibus sacris cuperent erudiri, haberent in promtu magistros qui docerent.[23]

This was a veritable golden age, therefore, in which kings and bishops worked in harmony for the greater good of a Christian people.

---

[19] *HE*, III.26 (pp. 308–11). For comment, see Thomas M. Charles-Edwards, 'Bede, the Irish and the Britons', *Celtica* 15 (1983), 42–52, who foregrounds the Irish willingness to preach to the English as the reason Bede thought of them so highly. If this be thought excessive – since he did not take such a rosy view of the Franks, for example, despite their missionary efforts – then the reason for Bede's attitude may have more to do with contemporary politics: Higham, *[Re-]Reading Bede*, pp. 205–8.

[20] *HE*, III.29 (pp. 318–19).

[21] Earlier we have the reigns of Edwin (*HE*, II.9–20), and Oswald (*HE*, III.1–13), both of which are treated as rhetorical highpoints. The only possible candidate for a more recent one is the conversion of Iona to Roman practices by Egbert in 721: *HE*, V.22 (pp. 552–5), but that did not include any reference to the wider political community or the virtues of kings, as had featured in the earliest episodes.

[22] *HE*, IV.2 (pp. 332–3). This mirrors quite closely Bede's claims regarding the Scottish clergy in *HE*, III.26 (pp. 309–11), but virtually no others.

[23] 'Never had there been such happy times since the English first came to Britain; for having such brave Christian kings, they were a terror to all the barbarian nations, and the desires of all men were set on the joys of the heavenly kingdom of which they had only lately heard; while all who wished for instruction in sacred studies had teachers ready to hand': *HE*, IV.2 (pp. 334–5).

It was, of course, Theodore and Hadrian who were largely responsible for establishing the system of monastic learning in England on which Bede had based his whole life as a scholar (even though he is not known to have been their pupil himself) and it should be remembered that Benedict Biscop, the founder of Wearmouth/Jarrow, was closely involved in their project, as Theodore's guide on the journey, and temporarily as the abbot of SS Peter and Paul in Canterbury on his arrival. That the joint foundation of Wearmouth/Jarrow was similarly dedicated to SS Peter and Paul was surely no coincidence, so Bede's own monastic life to an extent explains his enthusiasm for Theodore.

The English church was, therefore, in the present a single archdiocese and Bede delighted in the membership of the universal church which it afforded his own countrymen. However, given that he copied Gregory's letter to Augustine (in 601) into the *Historia* (I.29), he was clearly well aware that the so-called 'apostle of the English' had originally suggested that, if conversion proceeded appropriately, the English church be organized as two separate archdioceses, each with twelve bishoprics. According to Gregory's plan, there should have been a single head only so long as Augustine was alive, after which the two archbishops should enjoy equal authority each within their own sphere of influence. Both should receive a *pallium* direct from Rome, with 'he who was first consecrated ... reckoned senior' ('ut ipse prior habeatur, qui prius fuerit ordinatus'), and they should share the leadership of the English church, 'taking counsel together and acting out of zeal for Christ' ('concordi actione quaeque sunt pro Christi zelo agenda disponant').[24] A *pallium* was indeed sent to Paulinus at York, so this plan was in the process of being implemented in the early 630s, but King Edwin was killed before it could take full effect and his bishop fled south. This aborted the attempt to raise York to archdiocesan status in the first generation of the Gregorian mission, and no subordinate dioceses had been established before this disaster struck. Indeed, it left York without even a bishop until the 660s.

Under this somewhat awkward system of dual management by a pair of archbishops, however, Gregory had clearly conceived of a single church for the English; he apparently originated the key phrase 'ecclesia Anglorum' which occurs in the same letter to Augustine to which reference has already been made:

Et quia noua Anglorum ecclesia ad omnipotentis Dei gratiam eodem Domino largiente et te laborante perducta est, usum tibi pallii [...] concedimus'.[25]

---

[24] *HE*, I.29 (pp. 106–7).
[25] 'And because the new church of the English has been brought into the grace of

It also occurs in three separate passages in the *Libellus Responsionum*, the very long set of Gregory's replies to Augustine's questions which Bede included almost verbatim as I.27, for example:

> [...] siue in Romana siue in Galliarum seu in qualibet ecclesia aliquid inuenisti, quod plus omnopotenti Deo possit placere, sollicite eligas, et in Anglorum ecclesia, quae adhuc ad fidem noua est, institutione praecipua, quae de multis ecclesiis colligere potuisti, infundas.[26]

This correspondence was probably the earliest source in which Bede came across the phrase 'ecclesia Anglorum', but it was also where he found another term of relevance to this discussion. Gregory's first answer suggests that when Augustine had originally written he had referred to himself not as bishop of the 'ecclesia Anglorum' but as 'episcopus Cantuariorum ecclesiae' – 'bishop of the church of the people of Kent'. Presumably, Augustine was only too well aware of how limited his remit actually was among the English in 601 and styled himself accordingly, but Gregory was more ambitious for his deputy; he had sent a mission to the English, not just the Kentishmen, so Augustine would be the leader of that larger mission, not just a local bishop, and he sent him the *pallium* and ordained him archbishop, with instructions regarding the development of a whole network of subordinate bishops. It is interesting to note that this same phrase 'ecclesia Cantuariorum' was used twice by Bede in his Preface, but it is not a style which he adopted otherwise; there is no reference, for example, to the 'church of the East Angles', 'the church of the Northumbrians' or 'the church of the *Gewisse*', so in this area Bede seems to have limited himself quite closely to phrases he had come across in pre-existing texts reaching him from Canterbury.

Given that Bede was himself born *c*.672/3, the unification of Anglo-Saxon Christendom at the Synod of Whitby in 664, under the presidency of the senior Northumbrian king of the day, and Theodore's enthrone-ment as the first undisputed archbishop of the whole English church in 669, were seminal events which conditioned the world in which he grew up, particularly once he had entered Wearmouth, *c*.678/9. Bede there-after spent his entire life as a monk of Wearmouth/Jarrow, within a wider English church which remained subject to the authority of a single arch-diocese at Canterbury, and more distantly to Rome. In his youth, this was a comparatively interventionist archdiocese; Theodore presided over the

---

Almighty God, through the bounty of the Lord and by your labours, we grant to you the use of the pallium [...]': *HE*, I.29 (pp. 104–5).

[26] '[...] if you have found any customs in the Roman or the Gaulish church or any other church which may be more pleasing to Almighty God, you should make a careful selection of them and sedulously teach the Church of the English, which is still new in the faith, what you have been able to gather from other churches': *HE*, I.27 (pp. 80–3).

church until his death in 690 (by which time Bede was in his late teens) and, since the late 670s, had been sub-dividing the greater sees, even in the teeth of the opposition of their incumbents, such, most famously, as Wilfrid I. Bede was a close associate of Acca, his own diocesan bishop at Hexham, at the time of writing, and seems to have been supportive of Theodore's policy of sub-dividing the larger dioceses which he had inherited, although his sympathy for Wilfrid I and respect for the papal support he had received made expressing such views somewhat problematic.[27] But he went out of his way to praise several of Wilfrid's successors to parts of the newly sub-divided see, and argued in favour of further sub-division in his *Epistola ad Ecgberhtum* in 734,[28] so his general position is reasonably clear: he favoured smaller dioceses within Northumbria and had no apparent difficulty with these having been initiated through a policy emanating from Canterbury.

Bede also included in his *Historia Ecclesiastica* notice of some at least of Theodore's synods, such as those at Hertford in 670, and Hatfield *c*.679,[29] copying out selected passages of the synodal books which he clearly had before him, which had presumably reached him from Canterbury. This may imply a degree of complacency on Bede's part regarding the pan-English authority of the archbishops of Canterbury, at least as long as Theodore was alive. Thereafter, however, he alluded to few synods, although it is not clear whether this was due to a lack of interest or a lack of documentation: Austerfield in particular was omitted, but there is passing reference to one by the river Nidd (V.19).

As his treatment of him in II.1 makes clear, Bede was a keen admirer of Gregory the Great and his inclusion of the latter's correspondence regarding the future structure of the English church surely conditioned Bede's own sympathies. Given that this information was contained in a letter which he had probably had to source from Rome, it seems unlikely that Gregory's plan for the English church was widely known in Britain before 731, when dissemination of the *Historia Ecclesiastica* began to publicise it. Yet York was raised to the status of an archdiocese four years after the *Historia* began to circulate and Bede's *Epistola ad Ecgberhtum* in 734 seems to take for granted the bishop of York's ability to sub-divide

---

[27] Bede's third longest chapter, *HE*, V.19 (pp. 516–31), was an obituary of Wilfrid offered in the most fulsome terms, at greater length than his comparable treatment of Gregory at the notice of his death in II.1 (pp. 122–35).

[28] Bede, *Epistola ad Ecgbertum episcopum*, in *Venerabilis Baedae Opera Historica*, ed. C. Plummer (Oxford, 1896), pp. 405–23. For a translation, see *Bede: The Ecclesiastical History of the English People*, ed. Judith McClure and Roger Collins (Oxford, 1994), pp. 341–57.

[29] *HE*, IV.5 (pp. 348–53), and 17(15) (pp. 384–8).

Northumbria's still overly large sees, and only an archbishop could do that.

The question arises, therefore, of just when York's claim on archdiocesan status became widely known. It has long been argued by Walter Goffart that Bede wrote in 731 in the full knowledge that plans were afoot for York to be elevated, and in support of one branch of the Northumbrian church in the contest to control the new archdiocese.[30] However, it has to be said that there is remarkably little evidence within this work that he had been particularly interested in York in recent years, at least once John of Hexham, his old friend and mentor, had died in 721. According to Bede (*HE*, V.6), John had recently resigned the see to retire to Beverley and had appointed his priest, Wilfrid II, to the see. In later chapters of the *Historia,* we have three highly retrospective references to Wilfrid's association with York (V.19), a fleeting mention of Acca's presence there in his youth (V.20), so again a highly retrospective remark, and a fleeting mention of the current incumbent of the see, Wilfrid II (V.23), alongside every other bishop in England. Bede's interest in Bishop John presumably stemmed from his earlier tenure of the see of Hexham, since it was in that capacity that he had known him at Jarrow, and had, of course, been ordained by him, and he was far more interested in Acca, at Hexham, than either Bosa or Wilfrid II at York. Bede did not avoid the subject of York in recent times, therefore, in the way that he avoided over-much discussion of recent kings, but he certainly made no allusion to the see's archdiocesan claims in a context later than the 630s. The Northumbrian bishoprics were accorded the distinction in the present (V.23), that they lay under the rule of Ceolwulf, whereas all the other bishoprics lay under the 'over-kingship' of Æthelbald of the Mercians, but on its own it is rather too much to read into that an anticipation of the Northumbrian archdiocese that was still several years away. That said, Bede surely knew what he was doing by publicising the earlier arrangement that had fallen into abeyance almost a century before.

Precisely what expectations were circulating from the 660s onwards regarding the status of York is now difficult to determine. Following the Synod of Whitby, the Northumbrian kings seem to have intended that there should be two bishops, one for the Bernicians, effectively maintaining the tradition of the Scottish Church in all but name, and one at York, where Paulinus's see was to be resurrected for the Deirans. In the north Oswiu successfully established a certain Tuda as bishop, whom Bede described as having been educated and consecrated bishop among

[30] Walter Goffart, *The Narrators of Barbarian History (AD 550 800): Jordanes, Gregory of Tours, Bede and Paul the Deacon* (Guildford, 1988), pp. 235–328.

the southern Irish, but he died soon after of the plague.[31] Alhfrith's choice for York was Wilfrid, the Romanist whom he had already appointed to head his new monastery at Ripon, who now journeyed south to Canterbury to seek consecration, but the death of Deusdedit made it necessary for him to go on to Gaul. Wilfrid then delayed his return from Gaul, probably because his patron, the sub-king Alhfrith, had rebelled against his father unsuccessfully and he and his circle had lost all influence, so Northumbria may well have looked far less welcoming to Wilfrid.[32] By this point, however, Oswiu seems to have realized that York had been the sole Roman diocese in the north and that reappointment separately to a Bernician see would not carry support from the Roman church, for the moment at least. Instead, in Wilfrid's continuing absence, he now promoted Chad to York. Chad was abbot of Lastingham and brother to Cedd, whom Oswiu had previously promoted as bishop of the East Saxons, so this was an appointment made from within the core of Oswiu's established clerical circle.

But the question remains, had any of the leading figures in this fast-changing reconfiguration of the Northumbrian church actually realized that York might again be raised to archdiocesan status? The obvious answer has to be 'Yes', since Paul the Deacon had been active in Paulinus's ministry in the early 630s, so can reasonably be expected to have known of his elevation, and he was present at Whitby in 664, so there was ample opportunity for the dissemination of this information to Wilfrid, at least. Even if he failed to pass on this information, it still seems likely that the knowledge was retained in Kent, at Rochester and/or Canterbury, so the presence of senior Northumbrians there involved in detailed discussions with the Kentish clerical establishment in 664 arguably provided another opportunity for this information to emerge. That said, there is no sign that any of Oswiu, successive popes of the period or Wilfrid did actually have this intention, or even this information. Oswiu seems to have interested himself in the appointment to Canterbury precisely because he was now recognizing the southern archdiocese as the senior authority throughout

---

[31] *HE*, III.26 (pp. 308–9) and 27 (pp. 312–13). The name Tuda is British, not Irish or Anglo-Saxon, so it seems likely that Tuda was a Northumbrian who, like many others, had gone to Ireland for his education, in which case this is another of the British-named Northumbrian community who achieved prominence in the church, to be placed alongside such figures as Chad and Cædmon. My thanks to Professor Richard Coates for confirmation of the origin of the name.

[32] The whole issue is highly obscure, but Bede's laconic comment (in *HE*, III.14; pp. 254–5) should probably be interpreted in this way. See David P. Kirby, *The Earliest English Kings* (London, 1991), pp. 102–4; Nicholas J. Higham, *The Convert Kings: Power and Religious Affiliation in Early Anglo-Saxon England* (Manchester, 1997), p. 260. Alhfrith certainly disappears from history at this point; his conflict with his father is likely to have been centred on the succession.

the English church, and he and his successors welcomed Theodore to the north and fully recognized his authority. If Bede's remarks at the beginning of *HE*, III.29 are broadly accurate, then Oswiu and Egbert, king of Kent, sent Wigheard

> antistitem ordinandum Romam [...] quatinus accepto ipse gradu archiepiscopatus catholicos per omnem Brittaniam ecclesiis Anglorum ordinare posset antistites.[33]

Neither is there is any hint in Pope Vitalian's letter to Oswiu, which Bede quoted later in the same chapter, that Canterbury was other than the sole archdiocese. Nor do any of the supposedly papal declarations copied into the *Vita Wilfridi* betray any realization at Rome that York was other than a large diocese. And Wilfrid does not seem to have been seeking archdiocesan status for himself as bishop of York, or was in any sense aware of its past elevation; Stephen normally termed Wilfrid either 'episcopus' or 'pontifex', which here read as synonyms, often adding 'sanctus' or 'beatissimus' when alluding to Wilfrid. There are only two passages where he implied any greater status than this for York: in ch. x, Colman was termed 'Eboracae civitatis episcopus metropolitanus' ('metropolitan bishop of the city of York'), and the same phrase was then applied to Wilfrid in ch. xvi. However, this seems to have been Stephen's way of distinguishing the peculiar status of Colman (who was not, of course, bishop of York at all) as the sole bishop of the various peoples ruled by Oswiu, to which role Wilfrid was in turn appointed. His meaning seems to have been that both were bishops over an extensive diocese including English, Scots, Britons and Picts, not that they had archdiocesan rights or powers. Use of 'archiepiscopus' in this text is reserved for Canterbury; Paulinus in his sole appearance in this text is termed 'episcopus'.[34] Where Wilfrid is represented as styling himself, it is as 'humilis et indignus episcopus' ('humble and unworthy bishop'), and York is 'episcopatus'; when he is represented as being described by Theodore it is as 'sanctissimus episcopus' ('most holy bishop').[35] The response of a synod at Rome to Wilfrid's appeal styled him 'Deo amabilis Wilfrithus episcopus' ('Bishop Wilfrid, beloved of God') and Pope John later reputedly addressed him as 'Beatus Wilfrithus, Deo amabilis episcopus' ('The blessed Wilfrid, a

---

[33] 'to Rome to be consecrated bishop so that, when he had received the rank of archbishop, he could himself consecrate catholic bishops for the English churches throughout the whole of Britain': *HE*, III.29 (pp. 318–19).

[34] *Vita Wilfridi*, ch. xvi. Stephen used the term on sixteen occasions, applying it to four different individuals, all but one of whom were at Canterbury, the other being in Francia.

[35] *Vita Wilfridi*, chs. xxx, li, xliii.

bishop beloved of God').[36] Stephen certainly used 'episcopus' of popes and archbishops, as well as bishops, but when doing so he normally distinguished them by the accompaniment of superlatives: Agatho was, for example, termed 'sanctissimus ac ter beatissimus episcopus sanctae ecclesiae catholicae urbis Romae' ('the most holy and thrice-blessed Bishop of the Holy Catholic Church in the city of Rome').[37] Wilfrid received no such treatment and it is fair to say that Stephen's language distinguishes quite effectively between archbishops, on the one hand, and bishops, among whom must be counted Wilfrid. So despite the obvious fact that archdiocesan status would have given Wilfrid a degree of immunity from Theodore's plans to divide his see, his apologist never made that claim on his behalf.

We must doubt, then, that the archdiocesan status of York was a factor in the re-organization of the northern English church following Whitby. This does not mean that the knowledge of Paulinus's elevation was entirely lost in 664, since Paul the Deacon presumably provides a sufficient link to be sure that the information was available were it needed; but it does suggest that there was no political will to pursue this option. Without support and with the passage of years, it was effectively moribund and may even have been entirely forgotten by the 720s. More compelling, therefore, than the view that Bede wrote in 731 in awareness of the coming struggle for York, and as a mouthpiece for one particular faction contesting that event, is the proposition that York's earlier status was all but lost by the time Bede was preparing to write and that he had only very recently come across, or been reminded, of the earlier situation. If that were the case, then the Northumbrian establishment only discovered that Gregory had intended that York should be an archdiocese, and that Paulinus had actually achieved that status, from the pages of the *Historia Ecclesiastica*. King Ceolwulf appointed his cousin, Ecgberht, to the see in 732, once Wilfrid II had retired to the contemplative life, and they were successful in petitioning for its elevation to archdiocesan status in 735, one presumes very largely on the basis that Gregory had demonstrably so intended. Bede's *Epistola ad Ecgberhtum* in the previous year anticipates their success and demonstrates that he was by then involved in that project, which he had arguably actually put in train in 731 simply by publicising Gregory's letter. That Ecgberht's brother, Eadberht, then took the crown in 737, on Ceolwulf's abdication and voluntary tonsuring, suggests that the whole matter of archdiocesan status was part of a complex political strategy, perhaps agreed in 731 when Ceolwulf was temporarily deprived of the kingship and involuntarily tonsured. Bede had sent his manuscript

---

[36] *Vita Wilfridi*, chs. xxxii, liii.
[37] *Vita Wilfridi*, ch. xxix.

to Ceolwulf pre-completion, in the summer of 731, and seems to have had comment back before final 'publication' later that year, which presumably provided the earliest opportunity to take advantage of the new information which it contained.

The Northumbrian establishment may well have been attracted by the prospect of removing their several bishops from the oversight of an archbishop whose election was increasingly influenced by the Mercian royal court – it must be remembered that the new incumbent in June 731 was indeed a Mercian – but it may also have been interested in the possibility that Northumbrian archbishops might take their turn, on grounds of seniority, as heads of the whole English church. Both Ecgberht and Nothhelm became archbishops in 735, but Nothhelm died only four years later, leaving Ecgberht as the senior churchman in England, right up until his death in 766. This may not have been a position which gave him much practical authority, but there is a case for supposing that Ecgberht intended his *Dialogus* for an audience encompassing the entire English church.[38] Under Gregory's plan, he certainly had the right so to do across the bulk of his long and distinguished tenure. Ecgberht was, therefore, the senior churchman in England for at least twenty-seven years, and perhaps for thirty-one. And he was a figure on the wider stage: he received his *pallium* from Rome, and was the first English prelate so to do outside of Canterbury since Paulinus; he received letters from Pope Paul I and from Boniface (the English missionary-bishop in Germany), the latter requesting works of Bede, and was surely very largely responsible for the creation of the famous school at York, of which Alcuin was the best known graduate. Alcuin acknowledged his debt to Ecgberht in his great poem *De patribus, regibus et sanctis Euboricensis ecclesiae* describing him in glowing terms and remarking on his royal ancestry, his generosity and charity, his excellence as a teacher, his patronage of churches and his skill in choosing suitable candidates for ordination.[39] Ecgberht's status as the senior English churchman, perhaps from 735 and certainly from 739, was arguably of considerable value to the Northumbrian regime headed by his brother King Eadberht from 737 to 758, which was the most stable and influential that Northumbria experienced throughout the century.[40]

---

[38] For Dr Martin Ryan's examination of this text, see below, chapter 2. I am grateful to him for access to his work prior to publication.

[39] *Alcuin: The Bishops, Kings and Saints of York*, ed. Peter Godman (Oxford, 1982), lines 1251–87.

[40] Alcuin remarks of Eadberht that he was 'extending the bounds of his own kingdom, subduing the enemy's forces in many a terrible defeat'; *Alcuin*, ed. Godman, lines 1275–6.

## *Bede and the 'ecclesia Anglorum'*

Let us return to Bede. One thing which stands out from the *Historia Ecclesiastica* is the comparative poverty of Bede's use of the phrase 'ecclesia Anglorum', or minor variants thereof. As established at the start of this chapter, these two words occur in combination in this work only sixteen times. In practice, however, three of these are in Gregory's *Libellus Responsionum* and another in his letter to Augustine in 601 (I.29), and yet another in a passage referring back to that same letter at a later point in the work (IV.27), so in passages which were effectively authored by others and here copied verbatim. Another four offer a plural, so have a rather different meaning – 'the churches of the English': such occur in the context of Wilfrid's introduction of Catholic practices to 'the churches of the English', for example, in IV.2; as an alternative way of Pope Vitalian's describing the English archdiocese in IV.1 – 'ecclesiis Anglorum archiepiscopum'; and as the theatre in which Adamnan had witnessed catholic practices, in V.15. These should perhaps be discounted, as bearing an alternative meaning closer to the use of 'ecclesia' to signify a specific church. If we discount Gregory's five instances as well, this leaves a mere seven occasions on which the phrase was used which might be independent.

Most of these, however, are also likely to have derived from written sources which Bede utilized. Let us take, for example, the passage in *HE*, IV. 2, already quoted, which begins

> Peruenit autem Theodorus ad ecclesiam suam secundo postquam consecratus est anno sub die sexta kalendarum Iuniarum, dominica, et fecit in ea annos xx et unum menses tres dies xxvi.[41]

Given the detail and the claims offered, it seems very likely that this was based on a textual or oral communication derived ultimately from Abbot Albinus at Canterbury, so the phrase 'omnis Anglorum ecclesia' 'the whole church of the English', which occurs only a few lines further on, may well also have been his. Theodore had found himself in the 670s as an outsider having to build virtually from scratch a pan-English archdiocese, and it seems very likely that the rhetoric supportive of that process continued to the present at Canterbury, so was capable of influencing passages in Bede's work which relied heavily on input from Albinus and Nothhelm. Albinus was, of course, one of Theodore's star pupils at his new school,[42]

---

[41] 'Theodore came to his church on Sunday, 27 May, in the second year after his consecration, and there he spent twenty-one years, three months, and twenty-six days': *HE*, IV.2 (pp. 332–3).

[42] *HE*, V.20 (pp. 530–1).

so presumably had a vested interest in sustaining the rhetoric surrounding his teacher's universal archdiocese. Emphasis on the 'omnis Anglorum ecclesia' seems very likely to have originated in that arena.

In much the same way, the occurrence of 'ecclesia Anglorum' in *HE*, II.4 probably derived from a passage written initially at Canterbury; it comes immediately after a short extract from Archbishop Laurence's letter to the Irish, and in the context of Bishop Mellitus's visit to Rome to 'confer with Pope Boniface about the needs of the English Church'.[43] So too does the occurrence of the same phrase in IV.1, since it comes in the description of Wigheard's unsuccessful attempt to gain papal recognition and subsequent efforts to organize a replacement for him.[44] Likewise, the appearance of the phrase 'Anglorum ecclesia' in IV.18(16) alongside notice of a synod at Rome attended by 105 bishops seems likely to have derived from a written source, although in this case this may well have been internal to Wearmouth/Jarrow, since Benedict Biscop was an agent in this story, but he was also heavily implicated in Theodore's project.[45]

Detailed examination, therefore, suggests that the phrase 'ecclesia Anglorum' normally, if not invariably, became incorporated in Bede's *Historia Ecclesiastica* from materials which emanated from Rome, from Canterbury, or (less probably) from some other related source. It does not seem to have been a phrase which Bede himself was inclined to use of his own volition when composing *de novo*; nor does it seem to ever derive from a provincial source, and certainly not a Northumbrian one, with the possible exception of one instance which may have come from Theodore's close associate, Benedict Biscop. It is perhaps worth noting that Bede failed to use 'ecclesia' in this sense in any other context: he does not, for example, refer to an 'ecclesia Scottorum', or an 'ecclesia Pictorum', or an 'ecclesia Francorum', or even an 'ecclesia Brittonum'. The majority of his uses of the term refer either to the universal church, or to specific churches; mentions of the church of a people or a region are far from common.

While there is no reason to doubt, therefore, Bede's own commitment to and recognition of the current structure in 731 of an English church centred on Canterbury, he was at the same time aware and supportive of the Gregorian vision of a dual archdiocesan structure, albeit still at the head of a single English church. The current situation was apparently, in Bede's view, better than that which had prevailed until the 660s, when the English church was divided, but there remained considerable room

---

[43] *HE*, II.4 (pp. 146–9).
[44] *HE*, IV.1 (pp. 328–9).
[45] *HE*, IV.18(16) (pp. 388–9).

for improvement. There is no sign of enthusiasm for the present situation among the majority of his informants, who were Northumbrians;
neither they nor he seem to have owned the rhetoric associated with a
single English church; rather, the 'ecclesia Anglorum' seems primarily,
in the present and recent past, a project centred on Canterbury and, in
more distant times, on Rome. Bede's inclusion of Gregory's plan for the
twin archdioceses presumably reflects his own preference for the dual
model. Although he particularly acknowledged in his Preface all the help
he had received from Canterbury in writing his *Historia Ecclesiastica*,
the underlying agenda was clearly his, not that of Abbot Albinus, and
his vision of English Christianity was always coloured at least as much
by his Northumbrian interests as by those of the archdiocese centred
so far to the south. In practice, Gregory's plan posed real dangers to
Canterbury's supremacy, preferring as it did a revolving leadership of
archbishops centred at London and York, and the more politically adept
sections of Bede's Northumbrian audience presumably recognized very
quickly just how implementation of the plan might benefit themselves.
Both Ceolwulf and Ecgberht presumably drove forward the elevation
of York to archdiocesan status, which was finally achieved in 735. That
Bede provided the key impetus seems logical, and his preference was
probably for a single English church led in tandem by two archbishops,
one in the north and one in the south, as Gregory had proposed, once
he had read the letter which set out this arrangement. The language of a
single English church does appear in his work and he was supportive of
the general concept, but the rhetoric seems to have been taken over by
those committed to the single archdiocese established by Theodore, and
it appears here primarily in material derived from Canterbury. This was
not so much Bede's language, therefore, as Albinus's, and Bede arguably
had other agendas in this work which his southern correspondents did
not share; his was an alternative, more plural vision of the one English
church, as part of the universal world of Christendom. This to an extent
cut across Canterbury's interests, which were badly served by the full
execution of Gregory's original plan.

# 2

# Archbishop Ecgberht and his *Dialogus*

## MARTIN J. RYAN

> Tempora tunc huius fuerant felicia gentis,
> quam rex et praesul concordi iure regebant:
> hic iura ecclesiae, rex ille negotia regni.
> Hic ab apostolico humeris fert pallia missa,
> ille levat capiti veterum diademata patrum.
> Fortis hic, ille pius; hic strenuus, ille benignus,
> germanae pacis servantes iura vicissim,
> ex alio frater felix adiutus uterque.
> Rexit hic ecclesiam triginta et quatuor annis,
> ille annis tenuit ter septem sceptra parentum;
> ambo felices meritis in pace sepulti.[1]

SO Alcuin assessed the central years of the episcopate of Ecgberht of York (bishop *c*. 732–5, archbishop 735–66) in his *Versus de patribus, regibus et sanctis Euboricensis ecclesiae*.[2] For all Alcuin's praise of him, Ecgberht remains a little-studied figure. He fits into an obscure and seemingly undistinguished interlude between the Venerable Bede and Alcuin himself and, indeed, Ecgberht is most often explored by scholars only as an adjunct to these two giants of the Anglo-Saxon church; rarely is he considered in his own right. Yet Ecgberht's episcopate was one of the longest of the Anglo-Saxon period and one that saw the re-elevation of York to metropolitan status more than a century after it had first lapsed.

---

[1] 'These were fortunate times for the people of Northumbria, ruled over in harmony by king and bishop: the one ruling the church, the other the business of the realm. On his shoulders the one wore the *pallium* sent by the pope, on his head the other bore his ancestors' ancient crown. The one was powerful and energetic, the other devout and kindly, both lived in peace together as kinsmen should: two brothers helping one another gladly. For thirty-four years the one ruled the church, the other wore his ancestors' crown for twenty-one years; both, happy in their achievements, were buried in peace': *Alcuin: The Bishops, Kings, and Saints of York*, ed. Peter Godman (Oxford, 1982), p. 101, lines 1277–87.

[2] Dates taken from *HBC*, p. 224. The date of Ecgberht's receipt of the *pallium* – the symbol of his archiepiscopal status – is provided by *ASC* D, E and by the continuations to the chronological recapitulation of Bede, *Historia Ecclesiastica*.

Ecgberht himself was a correspondent of Bede and St Boniface and was remembered in England and on the Continent as an expert on canon law and ecclesiastical legislation. Moreover, he was responsible for the early education of Alcuin at York and if he was not the founder of the cathedral school there then at the very least he made it into the kind of institution capable of producing an Alcuin. As Henry Mayr-Harting has stated, Ecgberht 'must be regarded as one of the great architects of the English church in the eighth century'.[3]

This chapter seeks to explore the episcopate of Ecgberht through the one text that can reasonably be assumed to have come from his pen, the so-called *Succinctus dialogus ecclesiasticae institutionis*, henceforth the *Dialogus*.[4] Ecgberht's episcopate coincided with a period of Northumbrian history that, although in many ways better documented than that which had gone before, nevertheless remains in important respects fundamentally obscure. Although Bede's *Historia Ecclesiastica* continues up to the early 730s, its focus is predominantly the seventh century and its coverage of the eighth century is patchy and, at times, opaque.[5] In the absence of charters or royal law codes, the history of Northumbria in the eighth century has to be constructed through a number of disparate and not altogether satisfactory sources: continuations to the chronological recapitulations of Bede's *Historia*; letters, particularly those of Boniface and Alcuin; annals preserved in post-Conquest sources, such as the *Historia Regum* attributed to Simeon of Durham; the *vitae* of Anglo-Saxons active on the Continent; poems, such as those by Alcuin and Æthelwulf; and texts connected with the cultivation of liturgical *memoria*.[6] To this written

---

3  Henry Mayr-Harting, 'Ecgberht (d. 766)', *ODNB* <http://www.oxforddnb,com/view/ article/8580>.

4  *Councils and Ecclesiastical Documents Relating to Great Britain and Ireland* ed. Arthur West Haddan and William Stubbs, 3 vols. (Oxford, 1869–78), III.403–13. All subsequent references to the *Dialogus* will be to this edition, cited via question number.

5  As noted, for example, by Walter Goffart, *The Narrators of Barbarian History (A.D. 550–800): Jordanes, Gregory of Tours, Bede, and Paul the Deacon* (Princeton, NJ, 1988), p. 253.

6  The best general guide is David Rollason, David Gore, and Gillian Fellows-Jensen, *Sources for York History to AD 1100* (York, 1998). For continuations to the *Historia Ecclesiastica* see Joanna Story, 'After Bede: continuing the Ecclesiastical History', in *Early Medieval Studies in Memory of Patrick Wormald*, ed. Stephen Baxter, Catherine Karkov, Janet L. Nelson and David Pelteret (Farnham, 2009), pp. 165–84 and for the post-Conquest annals, Joanna Story, *Carolingian Connections: Anglo-Saxon England and Carolingian Francia, c. 750–870* (Aldershot, 2003), pp. 116–33. For the poetry see Michael Lapidge, 'Aediluulf and the School of York', *Anglo-Latin Literature 600–899* (London, 1996), pp. 381–98. The key liturgical source, the Durham *Liber Vitae*, is explored by the essays in *The Durham Liber Vitae and its Context*, ed. David Rollason, A. J. Piper, Margaret Harvey and Lynda Rollason (Woodbridge, 2004). For a sample of the other liturgical material see Jan Gerchow, *Die Gedenküberlieferung*

evidence may be added the material sources: numismatics; archaeology – particularly that of York; and the surviving ecclesiastical architecture and artwork.[7]

Given the problems presented by the sources, it is surprising that the *Dialogus* has not been used more widely by scholars and that only scant attention has been paid to the circumstances of its production and the sources that it was drawing on.[8] This chapter is, therefore, intended to offer an introduction to the *Dialogus*, exploring issues of form, context, and sources and suggesting the kinds of information about the Northumbrian church and Northumbrian society in the eighth century that may be gleaned from it.[9]

### The Writings of Ecgberht of York

A number of works have been attributed to Ecgberht in the medieval and modern periods, though in the majority of cases erroneously. By the end of the eighth or early ninth century, a Latin penitential was ascribed to him, though the versions of it that now survive contain little if any material that can be definitely assigned to his authorship.[10] One manuscript of the Old English text known as the *Scriftboc* or *Confessionale (Pseudo-)Egberti* claims it to be a translation from Latin made by Ecgberht but the work is a product of the late ninth or tenth centuries.[11] Likewise, the

*der Angelsachsen: mit einem Katalog der libri vitae* (Berlin, 1988), particularly pp. 199–217; Winfried Böhne, 'Das älteste Lorscher Kalendar und seine Vorlagen', in *Die Reichsabtei Lorsch*, ed. Friedrich Knöpp, 2 vols. (Hess, 1973–7), II. 171–222; and Michael Lapidge, 'A Tenth-Century Metrical Calendar from Ramsey', *Anglo-Latin Literature 900–1066*, pp. 343–86, at pp. 344–9.

7    For the coinage, see Elizabeth J. E. Pirie, *Coins of the Kingdom of Northumbria c.700–867* (Llanfyllin, 1996); for a survey of the archaeology see David Rollason, *Northumbria, 500–1100: Creation and Destruction of a Kingdom* (Cambridge, 2003), chs. 4–5. For recent excavations in York see Cecily A. Spall and Nicola J. Toop, 'Before Eoforwic: New Light on York in the 6th–7th Centuries', *Medieval Archaeology* 52 (2008), 1–25 and J. McComish, *Roman, Anglian and Anglo-Scandinavian Activity and a Medieval Cemetery on Land at the Junction of Dixon Lane and George Street, York*, The Archaeology of York, Web Series 9 (York, 2010) <http://www.iadb.co.uk/i3/item.php?ID=IADB:1307:U71>. For a sample of the art and architecture, see Michelle Brown, *The Lindisfarne Gospels: Society, Spirituality, and the Scribe* (London, 2003).

8    Donald Bullough, *Alcuin: Achievement and Reputation* (Leiden, 2004), p. 135.

9    A more detailed examination of the source materials and content of the *Dialogus* is in preparation.

10   Allen J. Frantzen, 'The Penitentials Attributed to Bede', *Speculum* 58 (1983), 573–97.

11   Allen J. Frantzen, *The Literature of Penance in Anglo-Saxon England* (New Jersey, 1983), pp. 133–41 and *idem, The Anglo-Saxon Penitentials: A Cultural Database* <http://www.anglo-saxon.net/penance/index.html>. See also Catherine Cubitt, 'Bishops, Priests, and Penance in Late Saxon England', *Early Medieval Europe* 14 (2006), 41–63, at 53.

so-called *Pontificale Egberti* found in Paris, Bibliothèque Nationale, MS. lat. 10575 was probably compiled in Wessex in the tenth century and its attribution to Ecgberht was due to the inclusion of the Latin penitential ascribed to him.[12] The *Excerptiones Ecgberhti*, a compilation of church canons surviving in a number of manuscripts, is now seen as substantially the work of Archbishop Wulfstan of York and the connection of the whole collection with Ecgberht was not made during the Anglo-Saxon period, though Wulfstan may have believed some of the canons he included to be the work of Ecgberht.[13]

The one surviving work whose attribution to Ecgberht is generally – though not universally – accepted is the text now known as the *Succinctus dialogus ecclesiasticae institutionis*.[14] This is a set of sixteen questions with answers by Ecgberht on a range of topics relating to ecclesiastical discipline and the relationship of the church to the secular world, accompanied by a short Preface.

## Manuscripts and Dating

In its entirety, the *Dialogus* survives only in one manuscript: BL, Cotton Vitellius A. xii, fols. 4v–8r. In its current form, Vitellius A. xii is a composite manuscript, but the first section, fols. 4–71, comprises a collection of computistical texts, copied by a single scribe in the late eleventh century, probably at Salisbury.[15] The *Dialogus* was presumably selected for inclusion in this computistical compendium because of the final question, which concerns the instigation and observation of the Ember Days and so pertains to the liturgical year. Teresa Webber has speculated that the exemplar for parts of the first section of Vitellius A. xii may have been a Sherborne manuscript, noting that there is a good case for Exeter Cathedral MS. 3507 – a manuscript that contains effectively the same texts, though in different order, as Vitellius A. xii, fols. 10v–65 – having been copied at Sherborne.[16] Whether Sherborne might also have been the source for the *Dialogus* is unknowable.

---

[12] *Two Anglo-Saxon Pontificals (The Egbert and Sidney Sussex Pontificals)*, ed. H. M. J. Banting, HBS 104 (London, 1989), xxxvi.

[13] *Wulfstan's Canon Law Collection*, ed. J. E. Cross and Andrew Harmer (Cambridge, 1999), p. 5.

[14] For doubts see *Sacrorum conciliorum nova et amplissima collectio*, ed. Joannes Dominicus Mansi, 31 vols. (Florence, 1758–98), XII (1766), cols. 411–12, though this is based on a comparison of the *Dialogus* with one of the pseudo-Ecgberht penitentials.

[15] Teresa Webber, *Scribes and Scholars at Salisbury Cathedral, c. 1075–c. 1125* (Oxford, 1992), p. 41.

[16] Webber, *Scribes*, p. 69. See also N. R. Ker, 'Salisbury Cathedral Manuscripts and

In addition to the text in Vitellius A. xii, both CCCC 265 and Bod, Barlow 37 – manuscripts of the so-called 'Commonplace Book' or 'Handbook for a Confessor' probably compiled by Archbishop Wulfstan of York – contain questions one and twelve from the *Dialogus*. That Wulfstan also held the see of Worcester and that a number of Salisbury manuscripts share exemplars with manuscripts from Worcester[17] might suggest Worcester as a possible source of the text of the *Dialogus* in Vitellius A. xii. However, as may be seen in the Appendix, below, CCCC 265 contains some significant variant readings from the text in the Cotton manuscript, though no printed edition has yet collated these.

The text of the *Dialogus* provides no clear indication of its date of composition. Though the title given in Vitellius A. xii is now largely illegible, seemingly the result of the Cotton Library fire of 1731, James Ware's *editio princeps* in 1664 gives the title as *Succinctus dialogus ecclesiasticae institutionis a Domino Egbherto, Archiepiscopo Eburacae civitatis conpositus* as does Smith's 1696 catalogue of the Cotton Library.[18] If this title does reflect in any way the circumstances of composition, then the text must have been written after 735, when metropolitan status was restored to the see of York. Such a possibility is strengthened by the wording of question sixteen that talks of all of Ecgberht's sees (*sedes*), phrasing that would make sense only if Ecgberht were of archiepiscopal rank.

Donald Bullough noted what he believed to be Ecgberht's use of a number of letters of Gregory the Great in answers fourteen and fifteen and so suggested that the *Dialogus* should be dated after 746/7, when the Continental missionary Boniface had sent Ecgberht a collection of Gregory's correspondence.[19] However, the parallels which Bullough noted are by no means compelling. The key phrase from Gregory's letters that Bullough identified, 'poenitentiam vel curiae aut cuilibet conditioni obnoxium' is certainly similar to Ecgberht's 'si poenitentiam publicam non gessit, nec ulla corporis parte vitiatus apparet; si servilis aut ex origine non est conditionis obnoxius, si curiae probatur nexibus absolutus' in response to question fifteen. However, Ecgberht's inspiration –

---

Patrick Young's Catalogue', *Wiltshire Archaeological and Natural History Magazine* 53 (1949), 153–83, at 156.

[17] Webber, *Scribes* pp. 69–70.

[18] *Venerabilis Bedae epistolae duae, necnon vitae abbatum Wiremuthensium & Girwiensium accessit Egberti archiepiscopi Eboracensis Bedae aequalis dialogus, de ecclesiastica institutione* ed. James Ware (Dublin, 1664), p. 91; Thomas Smith, *Catalogus librorum manuscriptorum bibliothecae Cottoniae* (Oxford, 1696), p. 82. This is also the title given on the contents page of the manuscript itself.

[19] Bullough, *Alcuin*, p. 231.

and perhaps Gregory's – actually seems to have been a decretal of Pope
Gelasius I:

*Dialogus* 15:
Hujusmodi tunc ordinatio episcopi,
presbyteri vel diaconi, rata esse
dicetur, *si nullo gravi facinore
probatur infectus*; *si secundam
non habuit uxorem, nec a marito
relictam, si poenitentiam publicam
non gessit, nec ulla corporis parte
vitiatus apparet; si servilis aut ex
origine non est conditionis obnoxius,
si curiae probatur nexibus absolutus,
si assecutus est litteras,* hunc elegimus
ad sacerdotium promoveri.

Pope Gelasius I:
[…] *vel si nullo gravi facinore
probatur infectus, si secundam
non habuit* fortassis *uxorem, nec a
marito relictam* sortitus ostenditur, *si
poenitentiam publicam* fortassis *non
gessit, nec ulla corporis parte vitiatus
apparet, si servili, aut originariae
non est conditioni obnoxius, si curiae
jam probatur nexibus absolutus, si
assecutus est litteras,*[…][20]

Although Bullough's reasoning appears to be problematic, as will be
suggested below, there are some reasons to suppose that he was correct
in dating the *Dialogus* to the period after 747. However, in the absence
of other conclusive dating mechanisms, the *Dialogus* can ultimately be
assigned only to the period of Egcberht's archiepiscopate.

*Form and Audience*

There was a long tradition of presenting ascetic and monastic teachings
as the written record of a dialogue. Most notably the *Conlationes* of John
Cassian, probably written in the 420s, purport to record the conversations
that Cassian and his companion Germanus had with a number of ascetic
experts in the Egyptian deserts.[21] Likewise, it might be noted that the
*Regula Sancti Benedicti* is presented as the spoken word; the opening of
its Prologue (in allusion to Proverbs)[22] runs 'Obsculta [*or* ausculta], o fili,
praecepta magistri, et inclina aurem cordis tui'.[23] Closer to the time of
Ecgberht and in an English – and probably Northumbrian – context, the
penitential of Archbishop Theodore is described as comprising the answers
given by Theodore to questions asked by the otherwise unknown priest

---

[20]  *Decreta Gelasii papae, PL* 67 (1848), cols. 302–3.
[21]  Cassian, *Conlationes*, ed. M. Petschenig, CSEL 13 (Vienna, 1886).
[22]  Cf. in particular Prov. I.8 and VI.20.
[23]  'Listen carefully, my son, to the Master's instructions, and attend to them with the ear
      of your heart'. Benedict, *Regula*, ed. R. Hanslik, 2nd edn CSEL 75 (Vienna, 1977);
      trans. *RB1980: The Rule of St Benedict in Latin and English with Notes*, ed. Timothy
      Fry (Collegeville, Minn., 1981), p. 157.

Eoda.[24] The closest parallel to and perhaps the model for the *Dialogus* is, however, the so-called *Libellus Responsionum* of Gregory the Great, his answers to written questions asked of him by Augustine of Canterbury. Not only is the question and answer format of the majority of the manuscript witnesses of the *Libellus* similar to that of the *Dialogus* but the range of subject matter is likewise comparable, covering both strictly ecclesiastical issues and the relationship of the church with wider society. Though there has been some considerable controversy about whether the *Libellus* is authentically Gregorian, at least in the form that it has been preserved, Ecgberht is most likely to have encountered the work in the question and answer format transmitted in Bede's *Historia Ecclesiastica*.[25]

Whether Ecgberht was, like Gregory, responding to specific questions that had been asked of him or was simply couching his pronouncements in the question and answer format of the *Libellus Responsionum* is difficult to determine. That Ecgberht did not fully answer a number of the questions – he does not specify the weight of the oath of a bishop in his answer to question one, for example – suggests the former but certainty is impossible. The lack of information about the intended recipient or audience of the *Dialogus* adds to the difficulties here. The information that can be determined comes predominantly from the short Preface to the work – assuming this Preface has not been added by Ecgberht when sending a copy of an already existing work to a correspondent.[26] Ecgberht asks that his unnamed addressee receive the work he is sending with a gracious spirit and with charity and that, if any of the judgements in the text seem worthy to him, may they be strengthened by his writing. If anything does not meet with the addressee's approval, he is to insert more useful material. The Preface ends with the hope that through the exchange of letters the two of them may be bound together with the bonds of charity. That Ecgberht on occasion terms his addressee 'brother' suggests him to be a fellow bishop, as does the fact that the judgements contained in the text are said to concern 'pontificalem providentiam' – assuming, of course, that the adjective *pontificalis* here refers to the episcopal office rather than the priestly one.

Two letters to Ecgberht from the Continental missionary Boniface may shed further light on the context of the *Dialogus*. The first, dating from around 746, concerns the letter of exhortation that Boniface and a number

---

[24] Theodore, *Iudicia*, in *Die Canones Theodori Cantuariensis und ihre Überlieferungsform* ed. P. W. Finsterwalder (Weimar, 1929).

[25] For the authenticity of the *Libellus*, see Paul Meyvaert, 'Bede's Text of the *Libellus Responsionum* of Gregory the Great to Augustine of Canterbury', in *England Before the Conquest: Studies in Primary Sources Presented to Dorothy Whitelock*, ed. Peter Clemoes and Kathleen Hughes (Cambridge, 1971), pp. 15–33.

[26] Bullough, *Alcuin*, p. 230.

of other Continental bishops had sent to King Æthelbald of Mercia. Boniface writes that he has asked that Ecgberht be shown a copy of this letter
so that he might correct any errors in it and by his authority and wisdom
add strength to it.[27] The language used is different but the sentiments are
very similar to those of the Preface to the *Dialogus*. The second letter to
Ecgberht, dating perhaps a year later than the first, asks specifically for
advice concerning a priest who had performed penance after committing
fornication. Boniface was unsure whether he should have allowed this
priest and others like him to continue in their ministries and requested
written advice from Ecgberht, a subject that has clear similarities with
question five of the *Dialogus*.[28]

This is not to suggest that Boniface was the intended recipient of the
*Dialogus*. Rather, the correspondence between Boniface and Ecgberht
and the discussion therein between fellow bishops about matters of ecclesiastical discipline suggest something of the kind of context in which
the *Dialogus* might have been produced. Indeed, it seems most probable
that the *Dialogus* was intended for an insular Anglo-Saxon audience. A
number of the answers make reference to established decrees or practices
with the assumption that they would be known already to the recipient,
something unlikely if he was outside Anglo-Saxon England (and, perhaps,
outside of Northumbria). Answer twelve discusses the fine and penance
owed by someone who kills a cleric or monk and states that penance
should be carried out according to the established grades ('secundum
gradus poenitentiae constitutos') and the wergild of a bishop should be
decided by the judgement or decree – a word seems to be missing from
the text – of a general council. Likewise, answer seven states that those
who receive runaways from ecclesiastical institutions are to pay what has
been established ('quod statutum est') before enumerating these amounts,
while answer eight fines those who have fornicated with nuns double the
amount prescribed by the 'lex publica'.

The *Dialogus* might, then, be best understood as part of a correspondence between Ecgberht and one of his suffragans, though whether the
Preface was part of the original work or added later remains to be seen.
One question does, however, suggest a wider scope for the text. Question sixteen concerns the observance of the fasts of the four seasons or
the Ember Days. The questioner asks Ecgberht to explain the reason for
the institution of these fasts and when they should be observed, so that
they are performed uniformly by all 'throughout all of your sees ['sedes']
and the churches of the Angles ['Anglorum ecclesias']'. If this reference
to the 'Anglorum ecclesiae' is taken to mean all the churches of the

---

[27] Boniface, *Epistolae*, ed. M. Tangl, MGH, *Epistolae Selectae*, I (Berlin, 1916), no. 75.
[28] Boniface, *Epistolae*, no. 91.

English rather than all the churches of the Anglian Northumbrians then Ecgberht's pronouncements were clearly expected to carry some weight throughout Anglo-Saxon England. It may be significant that the canons of the 747 Council of *Clofesho* include discussion of the Ember Days, though the language in no way resembles that of the *Dialogus*.[29] Indeed, the *Clofesho* canons make reference only to fasts in the fourth, seventh, and tenth months whereas both Ecgberht and his questioner write of fasts in the first, fourth, seventh, and tenth months.[30] Whether Ecgberht offered his answer in response – requested or not – to the canons of *Clofesho*, correcting, as he would see it, their errors is not clear. The discussion of the Ember Days in the *Dialogus* is noteworthy for its repeated emphasis on the authorities that Ecgberht is drawing on, principally Gregory the Great, though also his own experiences in Rome. As Ecgberht does not cite his authorities in other answers, this may mean that the correct observance of the Ember Days was in some ways disputed and he felt the need to shore up his answer by emphasizing the authority on which it was based.

There are a few phrases that suggest Ecgberht had read the canons of the Council (or that those who composed the canons had read the *Dialogus*), in particular the opening of response fourteen – 'Quisquis vero saecularis servitium sanctae professionis subire desiderat' – which closely resembles the opening of canon twenty-four – 'Ut si quis saecularium sanctae professionis famulatum subire desiderat'.[31] It is, of course, difficult to establish precedence for such borrowings but the possibility exists that Ecgberht had access to a copy of the *Clofesho* canons and aspects at least of the *Dialogus* were intended as a response to it. The *Dialogus* may then have been intended for an Anglo-Saxon rather than simply a Northumbrian audience but it is a lot of weight to put upon two words, 'Anglorum ecclesias', and a subject shared between one of the canons and one of the questions of the *Dialogus*.

---

[29] 'Council of Clovesho, A. D. 747', *Councils and Ecclesiastical Documents*, ed. Haddan and Stubbs, III. 362–76, question 18.

[30] See Catherine Cubitt, *Anglo-Saxon Church Councils, c. 650 – c. 850* (London, 1995), p. 143, who also notes that Ecgberht's timing of the fasts agrees with the Gelasian and Gregorian sacramentaries.

[31] The other apparent borrowing is the phrase 'ex convenientia amborum', which occurs in both question thirteen of the *Dialogus* and canon twenty-nine of the Council.

*Sources and Methods*

There has been little detailed exploration of the sources that Ecgberht was drawing on in the *Dialogus* or of his methods of composition.[32] Bullough's suggestion of the letters of Gregory has already been explored and rejected – above. McNeill and Gamer saw the influence of the so-called *Canones Apostolorum* on Ecgberht's discussion of the offences that prevented a man from being ordained as a priest, but the similarities are only at a very general level and such ideas can be found in much of the ecclesiastical legislation of the late antique and early medieval periods.[33]

A detailed discussion of the sources of the *Dialogus* is beyond the scope of this chapter but a few general observations can be offered. Ecgberht tends to employ standard canon law texts, such as those collated by Dionysius Exiguus or in other late antique and early medieval canon law collections. Ecgberht's response to question five, for example, is effectively a catena of papal correspondence and decretals. The opening sentences draw on the letter of Pope Anastasius II to the Emperor Anastasius concerning the Acacian schism and, in particular, whether the ordinations made by Acacius were valid:

*Dialogus* 5:
Ministeria vero quae, *usurpato nomine sacerdotis*, non dicatus ignorante populo peregit, minime credimus abjicienda, nam *male bona ministrando* ipse sibi reus, aliis non *nocuit*.

Pope Anastasius II:
Ideo ergo et hic cujus nomen dicimus esse reticendum, *male bona ministrando*, sibi tantum *nocuit*: nam inviolabile sacramentum, quod per illum datum est aliis, perfectionem suae virtutis obtinuit. [...] quia non sine *usurpato nomine sacerdotii* adjudicatus hoc egit: in quo virtutem suam obtinentibus mysteriis, in hoc quoque aliis rea sibi persona non nocuit.[34]

Ecgberht appears to have accessed the letter via a version of the so-called *Collectio Hispana*, for this collection includes the variant reading 'usurpato nomine sacerdotii' that seems to have influenced Ecgberht's wording of

---

32  Bullough, *Alcuin*, p. 231.
33  John T. McNeill and Helena M. Gamer, *Medieval Handbooks of Penance: A Translation of the Principal* Libri poenitentiales *and Selections from Related Documents* (New York, 1938), p. 240.
34  *Epistola papae Anastasii urbis Romae ad imperatorem Anastasium*, PL 84 (1850), cols. 807–15.

his response. The second recension of the *Collectio Dionysiana* and other collections have 'usurpatione sacerdotii'.[35]

Egcberht then draws on a letter of Pope Innocent I to the Macedonian bishops and deacons, though altering the order of the information:

| *Dialogus* 5: | Innocent I: |
|---|---|
| Scienti autem causas minime detersas, *et qui tamen particeps factus est damnati, quomodo* tribuitur ei perfectio quae *in dante* non *erat*, quam ipse *accipere potest damnationem, utique* qui per quod *habuit per prava officia dedit*, ut ejus particeps similem sortiatur excommunicationis sententiam. | Sed e contra asseritur eum qui honorem amisit, honorem dare non posse, nec illum aliquid accepisse, quia nihil *in dante erat* quod ille *posset accipere*. Acquiescimus et verum est: certe quia quod non habuit, dare non potuit; *damnationem utique*, quam *habuit per pravam* manus impositionem *dedit*: *et qui particeps factus est damnato, quomodo* debeat honorem accipere invenire non possum.[36] |

Ecgberht may also have drawn on the *Regula Sancti Benedicti* in this section, for his 'similem sortiatur excommunicationis sententiam' would seem to echo the 'similem sortiatur excommunicationis uindictam' of chapter twenty-six of the *Regula*. Ecgberht then returns to an earlier part of the letter of Pope Anastasius II:

| *Dialogus* 5: | Pope Anastasius II: |
|---|---|
| Sed hoc de baptismo accipi fas non est, quod iterari non debeat: reliqua vero ministeria *per indignum data*, *minus firma videntur*. | Nam secundum Ecclesiae catholicae consuetudinem sacratissimum serenitatis tuae pectus agnoscat, quod nullum de his, vel quos baptizavit Acatius, vel quos sacerdotes, sive levitas, secundum canones, ordinavit, ulla eos ex nomine Acatii portio lesioni attingat, quo forsitan per iniquum tradita sacramenti gratia *minus firma videatur* […] Nam et Judas cum fuerit sacrilegus atque fur, quidquid egit inter apostolos pro dignitate commissa, beneficia *per indignum data* nulla ex hoc detrimenta senserunt, declarante hoc ipsum Domino manifestissima voce […] |

---

[35] For information on these collections, see Lotte Kéry, *Canonical Collections of the Early Middle Ages (ca. 400–1140): A Bibliographical Guide to the Manuscripts and Literature* (Washington, DC, 1999).

[36] *Decreta Innocentii papae, PL* 67 (1848), col. 259.

As well as papal letters and decretals,[37] Ecgberht draws on other texts concerned with ecclesiastical and monastic observances. Question fifteen, concerning the crimes which disqualify a man from ordination, draws on sermon forty-five of the so-called Eusebius Gallicanus collection,[38] a compilation of fifth-century Gallic sermons, probably by a number of different authors, assembled in the sixth century:

*Dialogus* 15:
Pro his vero criminibus nullum licet ordinari; sed promotos quosque dicimus deponendos. Idola scilicet adorantes; *per aruspices et divinos atque incantatores captivos se diabolo tradentes*; *fidem suam falso testimonio expugnantes*; homicidiis vel fornicationibus contaminatos; furta perpetrantes; *sacrum veritatis nomen perjurii temeritate violantes.*

Eusebius Gallicanus:
Si uero quisque, conscientiam suam intus interrogans, facinus aliquod capitale commisit, aut *si fidem suam falso testimonio expugnauit* ac prodidit, *ac sacrum ueritatis nomen periurii temeritate uiolauit,* si <ni>ueam baptismi tunicam et speciosam uirginitatis holosericam caeno commaculati pudoris infecit, si in semetipso nouum hominem nece hominis occidit, si *per augures et diuinos atque incantatores captiuum se diabolo tradidit*: haec atque huiusmodi commissa expiari penitus communi et mediocri uel secreta satisfactione non possunt; <u>sed graues causae grauiores et acriores et publicas curas requirunt,</u> ut, qui cum plurimorum destructione se perdidit.[39]

Ecgberht also appears to have borrowed from this sermon for answer eight, whose phrase 'quia graves causae graviores et acriores quaerunt curas', echoes the words underlined in the above extract.

For answers that relate specifically to the Anglo-Saxon situation, Ecgberht's borrowing from other authorities is far less extensive and tends to be limited to biblical references, both direct and indirect. Question two concerns whether priests or deacons can witness deathbed testaments, to which Ecgberht answers:

---

[37]  Other examples include the use of the letter of Pope Siricius to Himerius of Tarragona in question eight and the letter of Gelasius to the bishops of Lucania, Calabria, and Sicily in question fifteen, referred to above.

[38]  For discussion see Lisa Bailey, 'Building Urban Christian Communities: Sermons on Local Saints in the Eusebius Gallicanus Collection', *Early Medieval Europe* 12 (2003), 1–24 and *eadem*, 'Monks and Lay Communities in Late Antique Gaul: The Evidence of the Eusebius Gallicanus Sermons', *Journal of Medieval History* 32 (2006), 315–32.

[39]  Eusebius 'Gallicanus', in *Collectio homiliarum*, ed. Fr. Glorie, CCSL 101, 101A & 101B (Turnhout, 1970–1), homily 45.

Assumat etiam secum unum vel duos: ut in ore duorum vel trium testium stet omne verbum, ne forte sub praetextu avaritiae propinqui defunctorum his contradicant quae ab ecclesiasticis dicuntur, solo presbytero vel diacono perhibente testimonium.[40]

Ecgberht is drawing here on Matt. XVIII.16, 'si autem te non audierit, adhibe tecum adhuc unum, vel duos, ut in ore duorum, vel trium testium stet omne verbum',[41] a passage that itself draws on Deut. XIX.15, 'Non stabit testis unus contra aliquem, quidquid illud peccati, et facinoris fuerit: sed in ore duorum aut trium testium stabit omne verbum'.[42] The succeeding passages in Matt. XVIII make it clear that Ecgberht is not simply offering practical advice with an impeccable biblical pedigree, for Christ later states 'Ubi enim sunt duo vel tres congregati in nomine meo, ibi sum in medio eorum'.[43]

## *The* Dialogus *and the Northumbrian Church in the Eighth Century*

If the attribution to Ecgberht is accepted, then the *Dialogus* is precious evidence for the Northumbrian church – and, indeed, for Northumbrian society as a whole – in the eighth century. Moreover, the *Dialogus* sheds significant light on aspects of the relationship between the church and the secular world that are not dealt with by other texts from elsewhere in Anglo-Saxon England in this period. In comparison with texts produced by the south-Humbrian church in the eighth and early ninth-century, the specific subject matter of the *Dialogus* is in many ways distinctive. The *Dialogus* shows little concern for the secularization of monasteries and churches, for those kinds of issues that occupied the bishops at *Clofesho* in 747 and Chelsea in 816. There are no condemnations of excessive displays of wealth, no condemnations of feasting and drunkenness, no concern for monastics wearing suitable attire. Whilst considerable atten-

---

[40] 'He is to take with him one or two, that in the mouth of two or three witnesses every word may stand; so that the relatives of the deceased do not, on account of avarice, contradict what is said by these ecclesiastics, [as might happen] with only a priest or deacon giving testimony.'

[41] 'And if he will not hear thee, take with thee one or two more: that in the mouth of two or three witnesses every word may stand'.

[42] 'One witness shall not rise up against any man, whatsoever the sin or wickedness be: but in the mouth of two or three witnesses every word shall stand'.

[43] Matt. XVIII.20: 'For where there are two or three gathered together in my name, there am I in the midst of them'. Ecgberht may also be drawing here on 1 Thess. II.5, for although the standard Vulgate reading is 'Neque enim aliquando fuimus in sermone adulationis, sicut scitis: neque *in occasione avaritiæ*: Deus testis est', the *Nova Vulgata* reads 'Neque enim aliquando fuimus in sermone adulationis, sicut scitis, neque *sub praetextu avaritiae*, Deus testis'; I have not been able to determine a manuscript source for this reading.

tion is paid to the crimes of the clergy, there is no discussion of the problems posed by poorly educated or poorly trained clergy, though Ecgberht does state that priests should be literate.[44] Lay-controlled monasteries are mentioned, but in passing and not in any way that suggests they were necessarily worse than monasteries in ecclesiastical hands.[45]

The absence of such discussions should not be taken as evidence of the absence of such problems in Northumbria, especially given that Bede raised many of these issues in his *Epistola ad Ecgberhtum* of 734 and some of them would again be raised by the report of the Papal legates in 786.[46] Rather, it seems that the majority of the questions in the *Dialogus* were about a specific set of problems; as Mayr-Harting has stated, the subject matter of the *Dialogus* is best defined as the attempt 'to fix the clerical order into society'.[47] That is, how should the legal status of clergy and monastics be determined and what was the relationship between ecclesiastical and secular jurisdictions.

Such concerns are apparent from the very first question. Ecgberht is asked to establish the weight of oaths that can be sworn by bishops, priests, deacons, and monks. Ecgberht sets the weight of oaths by priests, deacons, and monks at 120, 60, and 30 hides respectively – he does not supply the weight of the oath of a bishop. He then makes a distinction that does not seem to be made elsewhere in the corpus of Anglo-Saxon legal texts; the weight of oaths he has specified applies only in a criminal case ('criminali causa'), for disputes arising about the boundaries of lands ('de terminis agrorum') the oath of three monks, two deacons, or one priest are sufficient to transfer one hide into the right of the church ('in jus transferre æcclesiæ'). Though the phrasing 'jus ... æcclesiæ' is reminiscent of the language used by Latin charters to refer to bookland, such as *ius ecclesiasticum* or *ecclesiastico jure*,[48] the *Dialogus* would seem here to mean simply swearing that the land in question belongs to the church rather than witnessing to the land's conversion into bookland. Presumably, the intention behind such a judgement was to avoid confusion between the use of the hide as a measure of a person's status and use of the hide as a measure of land. That is, the weight of a person's oath in hides did not equate to the number of hides of land they could swear into someone's possession.

---

[44] Dialogus 15.

[45] Dialogus 7.

[46] Bede, *Epistola ad Ecgbertum* in *Venerabilis Baedae Opera Historica*, ed. C. Plummer, 2 vols. (Oxford, 1896), I. 405–23 and George of Ostia, *Epistola ad Hadrianum*, ed. E. Dümmler, MGH Epistolae 4 (Berlin, 1895), 19–29.

[47] Mayr-Harting, 'Ecgberht (d. 766)'.

[48] For a discussion of the different terms used, see Eric John, *Land Tenure in Early England: A Discussion of some Problems* (London, 1964), pp. 4–11.

Similar concerns about the legal status of members of the church can be found in question twelve which discusses the wergild that must be paid for the killing of a cleric or monk. After stipulating that the wergild should be paid to the church of the man killed – presumably rather than to his kinsmen – and setting out the relevant tariffs for bishops, priests, deacons, and monks, Egcberht states that if the churchman's status due to his birth would require a greater wergild than that set out for his ecclesiastical grade then the higher wergild is to be paid. Given that the upper echelons of the Northumbrian church were dominated by the nobility, such a judgement is likely to have been necessary to ensure that churchmen were not seen as inexpensive targets in aristocratic feuds and dynastic infighting. Likewise, that a number of Northumbrian nobles and kings, including Ecgberht's own brother Eadberht, are known to have retired, freely or otherwise, to monasteries, maintaining monks' and clerics' wergilds at the level they had been in the secular world is likely to have been a necessary protective measure.

Ecgberht's answer to question twelve also reveals another aspect of the wergild system; if the murderer does not have the wealth to pay the wergild, then he is to be given over to the king for punishment. The punishment is not specified but given that the person is handed over to the king it seems likely that corporal or capital punishment is envisaged, though penal slavery is another possibility.[49] The *Dialogus*, then, is a reminder that behind the long lists of monetary fines in the Anglo-Saxon law-codes lay the potential for far more violent outcomes. Answer twelve also suggests the possibility that wergilds – or at least those of the upper ranks of society – could be the subject of negotiation. The wergild of a bishop is stipulated by Ecgberht to be 'secundum universalis consilii', the precise meaning of which is unclear and at least one word would seem to be missing.[50] One reading of this phrase has already been suggested, namely that a 'universalis consilium' issued a decree specifying the wergild of a bishop, but it could also be understood to mean that a council would be convened to arrive at appropriate restitution on a case-by-case basis.[51]

---

[49] For capital punishment and mutilation in the Anglo-Saxon laws and other literature, see Andrew Reynolds, *Anglo-Saxon Deviant Burial Customs* (Oxford, 2009), pp. 23–9. For the loss of freedom as a secular punishment in the *Dialogus*, see Bullough, *Alcuin*, p. 138.

[50] This is one of the sections where the reading in Cotton Vitellius A. xii differs significantly from that in CCCC 265, so it is not possible to restore the original reading. See, below, Appendix.

[51] Giorgio Ausenda has suggested that wergilds should not be seen as fixed tariffs but 'as a level of departure for discussion'; cited in the discussion to Patrizia Lendinara, 'The Kentish Laws', in *The Anglo-Saxons from the Migration Period to the Eighth Century* ed. John Hines (Woodbridge, 1997), pp. 211–43, at p. 233. By the later Anglo-Saxon period, specific amounts had been established for the wergilds of archbishops and

This is certainly the case for abbots not in holy orders; Ecgberht assigns to them the wergild of a priest but envisages that a synod might decide a higher or lower figure. Given the apparent rarity of the murder of bishops in pre-Viking England,[52] the usual mechanisms of restitution may have been felt inadequate. It is also possible that circumstances surrounding the killing of a bishop would be sufficiently grave – serious civil unrest or invasion – that peace could only be restored through the holding of a council, the negotiations of which could have included the question of compensation and restitution. There may be parallels here with the aftermath of the Battle of the Trent in 679, where the Mercians killed Ælfwine, brother of King Ecgfrith of Northumbria. Although, according to Bede, the Mercians eventually paid 'debita solummodo multa pecuniae', this was after the intervention of Archbishop Theodore who offered both sides his salutary advice ('salutifera exhortatione').[53]

The respective authority and jurisdiction of the ecclesiastical and secular powers are also explored in a number of the answers. Answer eight asserts, claiming apostolic authority, the right of priests to adjudicate in all ecclesiastical cases. However, if a churchman commits any crime among the laity, such as homicide, fornication, or theft, then they may be seized ('occupari') by those they have offended against – and so presumably be subject to secular justice – unless the church is minded to make restitution on their behalf. Likewise, answer ten stipulates that any monk or nun who relies on secular power and violence rather than the judgement of the leaders of the church to reclaim property, ought to lose what they had claimed and be expelled from the church. After the death of the excommunicant, the parties to the dispute should be assembled and the opinion of the old and the truthful ('antiquitas aut veritas') be sought, with the judgement being left to the bishops.[54] Delaying judgement until after the death of the monk or nun was presumably to ensure that even if their claim had merit, they would not have restored to them property they had originally claimed through secular power and influence. Nevertheless, as Ecgberht makes clear in his answer, he had no desire to disadvantage the church and so an investigation of the rights and wrongs

---

bishops, see *Norðleoda laga* in *Gesetze der Angelsachsen*, ed. F. Liebermann, 3 vols. (Halle a. S., 1903–16), I. 458–60.

[52] For general discussion, see Paul Fouracre, 'Why Were so Many Bishops Killed in Merovingian Francia', in *Bischofsmord im Mittelalter*, ed. Natalie Fryde and Dirk Reitz (Göttingen, 2003), pp. 13–35, at pp. 28–9.

[53] *HE*, IV.21(19); Colgrave and Mynors, p. 400.

[54] The phrasing of this part of the answer owes much to the letter of Pope Innocent I to Bishop Florentius, see *Innocentii papae ad Florentium episcopum Tiburtinensem*, *PL* 84 (1850), col. 656.

of the case had to take place, but only at such a time as the excommunicant could no longer gain benefit from it.

Significant sections of the *Dialogus*, therefore, offer ways of integrating
the church, its institutions, and its members into the existing legal structures and institutions of Northumbrian society. In the *Dialogus*, Ecgberht
is grappling with the consequences of the Christianization of Anglo-
Saxon England and the attendant growth of the institutional church. If the
specific problems dealt with in the *Dialogus* are different from those that
concerned the south-Humbrian bishops at *Clofesho* in 747, they nevertheless stem from the same root. By the middle of the eighth century,
the church was wealthy and aristocratic but its very success brought into
sharper relief the tensions inherent in its relationship with the secular
world. Ecgberht thus sought to define more precisely where the jurisdiction of the church lay and what secular legal statuses were accorded to
clerics and monks. These are not, of course, the only concerns of the
*Dialogus* – fasting, fugitive monks, and the ministries of corrupt priests
are amongst the other subjects discussed    but they are focused on sufficiently to suggest that they were of especial concern to Ecgberht and his
unidentified interlocutor.

This chapter has suggested that the *Dialogus* represents the correspondence between Ecgberht and one of his suffragan bishops and can probably
be dated to the middle years of the eighth century. Though the majority
of the questions seem to relate solely to a Northumbrian context, question sixteen may have been asked with the canons of the 747 Council
of *Clofesho* in mind. In composing his answers to the questions asked
of him, Ecgberht drew extensively on earlier writings, particularly papal
correspondence, and much of the *Dialogus* is simply a patchwork of
quotations; the source of Ecgberht's authority is here clearly his knowledge of canon law. However, for those answers that consider the relationship of the church to the secular laws and society of Northumbria,
the source of Ecgberht's judgements and the basis of his authority are
less clear. In question one, for example, is Ecgberht confirming existing
law about the weight of the oaths of churchmen and monks or establishing these specific weights for the first time and, if the latter, what is
his authority for so doing? What is clear, though, is that the *Dialogus* has
considerable potential for deepening understanding of the nature of episcopal authority in pre-Viking England. Given the ongoing debates about
the character – monastic or episcopal – of the Anglo-Saxon church in
this period the *Dialogus* is likely to reward further study.[55] The *Dialogus*
may be expected, on the basis of its author, to especially emphasize

---

[55]  Compare, for example, John Blair, *The Church in Anglo-Saxon Society* (Oxford, 2005)

potential episcopal power, and Ecgberht's own situation as archbishop of York was a distinctive one – his brother, Eadberht, was king of Northumbria for much of his episcopate.[56] Nevertheless, the *Dialogus* offers hitherto underexploited insights into how one bishop conceived of his own authority and how he viewed the relationship between his church and the wider world.

and Catherine Cubitt, 'The Clergy in Anglo-Saxon England', *Historical Research* 78 (2005), 273–87.

[56] Rollason (*Northumbria, 500–1100*, p. 205), has also plausibly suggested that York may have been an 'ecclesiastical city ruled by its archbishop', which would further extend the exceptional nature of Egcberht's status.

## *Appendix*

## *Collation of Two Manuscript Versions of Ecgberht's* Dialogus, *questions 1 and 12*

| | |
|---|---|
| BL, Cotton Vitellius A. xii (as printed in *Councils and Ecclesiastical Documents*, ed. Haddan and Stubbs, III.403–13) | CCCC 265, pp. 99–100 (Punctuation modernized and abbreviations expanded) |

I. *Interrogatio.*
Si necessitas coegerit, in quantum valet juramentum Episcopi, presbiteri, vel diaconi, sive monachi?

Interrogatio. Si necessitas cogerit in quantum ualet iuramentum episcopi, presbyteri, diaconi, monachi?

*Responsio.*
Ordines supradicti, secundum gradus promotionis, habeant potestatem protestandi: presbiter secundum numerum CXX. tributariorum; diaconus vero juxta numerum LX. manentium; monachus vero secundum numerum XXX. tributariorum sed hoc in criminali causa. Cæterum si de terminis agrorum oritur altercatio, presbitero liceat juramenti sui adtestatione terram videlicet unius tributarii in jus transferre æcclesiae. Duobus quoque diaconis id ipsum conceditur. Testificatio vero trium monachorum in id ipsum sufficiat.

Ordines supradicti secum [*sic*] gradus promotionis habeant et postestatem protestandi. Presbyter secundum numerum cxx tributariorum. Diaconus iuxta numerum lx manentium. Monachus numerum xxx tributariorum. Sed hoc in criminali causa. Ceterum si de terminis agrorum oritur altercatio, presbytero liceat iuramenti sui adtestatione terrarum uidelicet unius tributarii in ius transferre ęcclesię. Duobus quoque diaconis, id ipsum conceditur. Testificatio uero trium monachorum in id ipsum sufficiat.

XII. *Interrogatio.*
Quod si quis ex laicis clericum vel monachum occiderit, utrum precium sanguinis, secundum legem natalium parentum, propinquis ejus reddendum sit, an ampliori pecunia senioribus suis satisfaciendum sit, Vestra Unanimitas sanciat ?

Interrogatio. Quod si quis ex laicis clericum uel monachum occiderit, utrum pretium sanguinis, secundum legem natalium parentum propinquis eius redditurum sit, an ampliore pecunia senioribus suis satisfaciendum sit, uestra unanimitas sanciat?

*Responsio.*

Quicunque vero ex laicis occiderit Episcopum, presbiterum, vel diaconum, aut monachum, agat pœnitentiam secundum gradus pœnitentiæ constitutos, et reddat precium æcclesiæ suæ; pro Episcopo secundum universalis consilii, pro presbitero octingentos siclos, pro diacono sexingentos, pro monacho vero quadringentos argenteos; nisi aut dignitas natalium, vel nobilitas generis majus reposcat precium. Non enim justum est, ut servitium sanctæ professionis in meliori gradu perdat quod exterior vita sub laico habitu habuisse jure parentum dinoscitur. Cui vero non est substantia, ut redimat se a perpetrato homicidio, regi dimittendus est ad puniendum, ne interfectores servorum Dei se putent impune posse peccare. Haec vero vindicta, quam de homicidiis presbiterorum percensuimus, mancat erga abbates, qui sunt sine ordine; nisi aliquem ex his sinodale collegium altiori consilio aut superiorem aut inferiorem judicaverit.

Quicunque ex laicis occiderit episcopum, presbyterum, diaconum, uel monachum, agat penitentiam secundum grados [sic] penitentię constitutos et reddat pretium sanguinis ęcclesię sue ut suprascriptum est; nisi aut dignitas natalium uel nobilitas generis maius reposcat pretium. Non enim iustum est ut seruitium sanctę professionis in meliore gradu perdat quod exterior uita sub laico habitu habuisse iure parentum dinoscitur. Cui uero non est substantia, ut redimat se a perpetrato homicidio, regi dimittendum est ad puniendum, ne interfectores seruorum dei se putent inpune posse peccare. Hęc uero uindicta, quam de homicidiis presbyterorum percensuimus, maneat erga abbates, qui sunt sine ordine; nisi aliquem ex his sinodale collegium altiore consilio aut superiorem aut inferiorem iudicauerit.

# 3

# Abbatial Responsibility as Spiritual Labour: Suckling from the Male Breast

## CASSANDRA RHODES

ANGLO-SAXON church leaders contributed widely to the scholar-ship, government, art and architecture of the Anglo-Saxon church. However, their immediate influence was most keenly felt within their own monastic communities, and impacted largely on the spiritual family of monks and/or nuns in their care. These church leaders were removed from the experiences and realities of lay domesticity and often from biological family ties. At least as they are represented in extant texts, they transferred this experience into the spiritual realm, nurturing the spir-itual development and Christian integrity of the men and women in their community, as parents would their offspring. Whilst these leaders did not physically create and give birth to their progeny, it was their labour which inspired in their children the creation and growth of Christian faith. I will here focus on three texts which employ the language of mother-hood in portrayals of three different church leaders, Æthelthryth, Leoba and Wilfrid.[1] I will examine how and perhaps why, through the use of this lexis and imagery, the individual contributions of these leaders to the development and recognition of their monastery and their influence on the monks and nuns beneath them, was manipulated by the authors.

Before doing so, it is important to outline the semantics of the terms 'motherhood' and 'mothering' in the context of this chapter. When consid-ering motherhood or mothers, it is a natural reaction to think only of a woman who has carried through pregnancy and given birth to a child. However, many investigations into medieval and modern motherhood

---

[1] The texts used here are: *Ælfric's Lives of Saints,* ed. and trans. Walter W. Skeat, EETS os 76, 82, 94, 114 (Oxford, 1881–1900, reprinted in 2 vols, 1966), I; Rudolf, 'The Life of Saint Leoba', trans. C. H. Talbot in *Soldiers of Christ: Saints and Saints' Lives from Late Antiquity and the Early Middle Ages*, ed. Thomas F. X. Noble and Thomas Head (University Park, PA 1995), pp. 255–77; and Aldhelm, 'Letter XII: To the Abbots of Wilfrid', in *Aldhelm: The Prose Works*, trans. Michael Lapidge and Michael Herren (Ipswich, 1979), pp. 168–70.

reveal this to be a dramatic oversimplification. Scholars such as Mary Dockray-Miller, John Carmi Parsons, Bonnie Wheeler, Evelyn Nakano Glenn and Sara Ruddick amongst others have argued convincingly that 'mothering' is an 'activity' rather than a fact rooted in biological connection.[2] This of course makes perfect sense – think of foster, adoptive and step-parents – men and women who choose to mother and father children not biologically their own. Further to this, these scholars have noted that 'mothering' is culturally specific, constructed in what particular cultures consider to be specifically maternal practices. Dockray-Miller has convincingly argued that in Anglo-Saxon England this 'maternal work', as she describes it, was forged through the conscious actions of protection, nurture and training.[3] The notion that actions of protection, nurture and training are behavioural identifiers of 'mothers', and therefore that one does not need to have given birth to be a 'mother', are certainly borne out in Anglo-Saxon religious texts, which are peppered with the lexicon of domesticity and familial relations in non-biological contexts.

Whilst the Bible and the writings of the Church Fathers do place contradictory values on the maternal role, biological motherhood is often denounced as being located in carnality and female flesh. The biblical warning 'woe to them that are with child, and that give suck' (Matt. XXIV.19 and Mark XIII.17) is frequently cited by Church Fathers such as Tertullian and Jerome in texts praising virginity.[4] Motherhood is often considered a distraction from spiritual pursuits and the process of giving birth deemed a corrupting force at odds with ideals of chastity. However, the church itself is often personified in hagiographic literature

2   See Mary Dockray-Miller, 'Maternal Sexuality on the Ruthwell Cross', in *Sex and Sexuality in Anglo-Saxon England: Essays in Memory of Daniel Gilmore Calder*, ed. Carol Braun Pasternack and Lisa M. C. Weston (Tempe AZ, 2004), pp. 121–46 at pp. 122–5; John Carmi Parsons and Bonnie Wheeler, 'Medieval Mothering, Medieval Mothers', in *Medieval Mothering*, ed. John Carmi Parsons and Bonnie Wheeler (New York, 1996), pp. ix–xvii; Evelyn Nakano Glenn, 'Social Constructions of Mothering: A Thematic Overview', in *Mothering: Ideology, Experience and Agency*, ed. Evelyn Nakano Glenn, Grace Chang and Linda Rennie Forcey (London, 1994), pp. 1–29; Sara Ruddick, 'Thinking Mothers/Conceiving Birth', in *Representations of Motherhood*, ed. Margaret Honey, Donna Bassin and Meryle Mahrer Kaplan (New Haven, CT, 1994), pp. 29–45.

3   Mary Dockray-Miller, *Motherhood and Mothering in Anglo-Saxon England* (New York, 2000), p. 2.

4   Tertullian comments, 'Why did our Lord prophesy, Woe to those that are with child and that give suck, if he did not mean that on the day of our great exodus children will be a handicap to those who bear them?': Tertullian, 'To His Wife', in *Treatises on Marriage and Remarriage*, trans. William P. Le Sant (Westminster, 1951), p. 17. Jerome argues 'Woe to those who are with child, or have infants at the breast on that day' and condones the abandonment of children in spiritual pursuit: Jerome, 'Against Helvidius', in *Saint Jerome: Dogmatic and Polemical Works*, trans. John N. Hritzu, Fathers of the Church 53 (Washington, DC, 1965), 42.

as a mother, providing nourishment to her spiritual children through the milk from her virginal yet maternal breast. As Caroline Walker Bynum argues, this metaphor 'expressed so perfectly the nature of an entity withdrawn from the world (virgin) yet expanding and converting (mother)'.[5] 'Ecclesia' is personified in this way in Ælfric's homily 'On the Nativity of Holy Virgins', where he posits that 'seo gelaðung is ure modor and clæne mæden for ðan þe we beað on hire geeadcynnede to godes handa'.[6] Aldhelm describes how Eugenia 'ran to the maternal bosom of the holy church'.[7] He further links the church to maternal qualities of conception, birth and nourishment in his life of Chrysanthus, commenting that 'having been conceived in the womb of regenerating grace and having been brought forth by the fertile delivery of baptism, he was nourished in the reverend cradle of the church'.[8] The rite of baptism is figured as Christian birth, and the Christian faith as fruitful, productive and restorative.

In other Anglo-Saxon religious writings the vocabulary of family life, seemingly incompatible with a Christian ethic which demanded chastity, is repositioned to locate the relationship between church leaders and their pupils. To give one example of many, in the eleventh-century Winteney version of the *Regula Sancti Benedicti*, which is apparently tailored to a female monastic context through a use of feminine pronouns and female titles, abbesses are specifically given the appellation 'mother'.[9] Such titles and imagery had been used in monastic contexts since the late fourth century. The Christian perception of good motherhood sees maternal responsibilities relocated, and given higher status and esteem, in the care of spiritual rather than bodily children.

Of the three texts considered here, two are hagiographic and, perhaps predictably, describe female Anglo-Saxon sainted abbesses. Imagery of motherhood was an appropriate motif in Anglo-Saxon hagiography, as many of the female saints from the period were abbesses, involved in a spiritually maternal role, if not one which was also maternal physically,

---

[5] Caroline Walker Bynum, *Jesus as Mother: Studies in the Spirituality of the High Middle Ages* (Berkeley, CA, 1982), p. 127.

[6] 'The church is our mother and a pure maiden because we are in her born again to God's hand': Ælfric, 'On the Nativity of the Holy Virgins', *Ælfric's Catholic Homilies: The Second Series,* ed. Malcolm Godden, EETS ss 5 (Oxford, 1979), 327–34, at 330. The translation is from *The Homilies of the Anglo-Saxon Church: The First Part containing the Sermones Catholici or Homilies of Ælfric,* ed. Benjamin Thorpe (London, 1846), pp. 562–75, at p. 567.

[7] Aldhelm, '*De Virginitate*', in *Aldhelm: The Prose Works,* trans. Lapidge and Herren, p. 110.

[8] Aldhelm, '*De Virginitate*', in *Aldhelm: The Prose Works,* trans. Lapidge and Herren, p. 96.

[9] *abbodesse, þat is modor genemned* ('abbess, that is named mother'). *Die Winteney-version der Regula S. Benedicti,* ed. Arnold Schroer, reprinted with supplement by Mechthild Gretsch (Tubingen, 1978), p. 15.

since many aristocratic widows became abbesses.[10] Ælfric's eleventh-
century life of Æthelthryth, an Anglo-Saxon royal abbess who died in
679, is sourced closely from Bede's *Historia Ecclesiastica*.[11] She is not a
virgin martyr, so her *vita* stands out starkly against Ælfric's more typical
female lives. Æthelthryth was one of a proliferation of royal Anglo-
Saxons around whom cults developed during the period. Married twice,
first to Ealdorman Tondberht and then to Ecgfrith, king of Northumbria, she managed to retain her virginity throughout both relationships
as a signifier of her devotion to God. With the permission of her second
husband she became a nun and was subsequently made an abbess. Her
major distinction as a saint was not her period of church leadership but
her perpetually incorrupt corpse.

Rudolf of Fulda's account of St Leoba shows a similar path to sanctity. Rudolf wrote the account 'shortly before the translation of Leoba's
remains in 837 or 838', for a female religious figure called Hadamout
at the request of his abbot Hrabanus Maurus.[12] We learn that Leoba was
an English virgin nun who worked as a missionary in Germany during
the period of conversion. She was given abbatial responsibilities by the
martyr and missionary Boniface and successfully ruled a large community of nuns at the monastery of Bischofsheim.[13]

Through imagery of motherhood, both of these women are located as
emulators of the Virgin Mary, conceiving and producing a new generation
of Christians without bearing the stain of bodily corruption. In language
taken almost directly from Bede, Ælfric describes how Æthelthryth was
made abbess 'ofer manega mynecena and heo hi modorlice heold mid
godum gebysnungum to þam gastlican life'.[14] Leoba is not explicitly
described as a mother, but the *vita* opens with the actions of her own

---

[10] See Dockray-Miller, *Motherhood and Mothering*, for an examination of matrilineal
genealogy in Anglo-Saxon nuns and abbesses. See also Barbara Yorke, 'Sisters Under
the Skin? Anglo-Saxon Nuns and Nunneries in Southern England', *Reading Medieval
Studies* 15 (1989), 95–117 and Clare A. Lees and Gillian R. Overing, 'Before History,
Before Difference: Bodies, Metaphor and the Church in Anglo-Saxon England', *Yale
Journal of Criticism* 11 (1998), 315–34.

[11] *HE*, IV.19(17)–20(18); ed. and trans. Colgrave and Mynors, pp. 390–401.

[12] Stephanie Hollis, *Anglo-Saxon Women and the Church: Sharing a Common Fate*
(Woodbridge, 1992), p. 271.

[13] The Latin text can be found in *Vita Leobae abbatissae Biscofesheimensis auctore
Rudolfo Fuldensi*, ed. G. Waitz, MGH, *Scriptores*, 15: 1 (Hannover, 1887), 118–31.

[14] 'over many nuns, whom she trained as a mother by her good example in the religious
life': *Ælfric's Lives of Saints*, ed. and trans. Skeat, I. 434–5. Bede (*HE*, IV.19(17);
Colgrave and Mynors, pp. 392–3) describes how 'post annum uero ipsa facta est
abbatissa in regione quae uocatur Elge, ubi constructo monasterio uirginum Deo
deuotarum perplurium mater uirgo et exemplis uitae caelestis esse coepit et monitis'
('a year afterwards she was herself appointed abbess in the district called Ely, where
she built a monastery and became, by the example of her heavenly life and teaching,
the virgin mother of many virgins vowed to God').

'spiritual mistress and mother', Tette, abbess of Wimborne.[15] According
to Rudolf, Leoba's birth was the result of a miraculous conception to her
elderly barren parents after her mother experienced a portentous dream.
The dream is interpreted by her mother's old nurse as prophesying the birth
of a daughter who must be consecrated to God for a life of virginal Christian devotion. Aware of her daughter's connection to God, Leoba's biological mother willingly passes her daughter to 'Mother Tette' for a spiritual
upbringing. It is here that Leoba's Christian wisdom is born and grows.
This structure conforms to Clarissa Atkinson's claim that 'in almost all
early medieval lives of female saints, monastic authors presented "real" or
significant motherhood as a spiritual rather than a biological relationship'.[16]
Rudolf locates Leoba as the product of a matriarchal lineage, which priori-
tizes the production of Christian faith over ties of kinship. Tette teaches
Leoba to follow her example exactly, and by mimicking Tette's actions
Leoba becomes a spiritual mother in her own right.

However, the similarities in the portrayals of these abbess mothers
largely end here. In his Life of Æthelthryth, Ælfric barely acknowledges
the sainted abbess's contribution within the church as community leader
and does not detail her motherly work of nurturing, protecting and training
her spiritual offspring. We are informed that she trains others through her
good example, but the minutiae of her achievements are absent. Ælfric
gives even less detail than his source Bede, who does, albeit briefly,
mention that Æthelthryth 'built a convent' at Ely which she then led 'by
the example of her heavenly life and teaching'.[17] Ælfric simply states that
Æthelthryth was instituted as abbess at Ely, neglecting to mention her
responsibility for founding the community and so minimising her role as
maternal spiritual producer.[18]

In a historicist reading of Bede's account of Abbess Hild, Clare Lees
and Gillian Overing have examined how Bede's usage of metaphors of
motherhood similarly elides Hild's significant ecclesiastical power.[19]
They note that historical scholars have supplemented Bede's account of
Hild with other sources to build a portrait of the abbess as highly influential, with a central role in the Synod of Whitby and important strategic
relationships with Anglo-Saxon royalty.[20] They have argued that in Bede's

[15]  Rudolf, *Vita Leobae*, trans. C. H. Talbot, p. 259.
[16]  Clarissa W. Atkinson, *The Oldest Vocation. Christian Motherhood in the Middle Ages*
      (New York, 1991), p. 94
[17]  *HE*, IV.19; Colgrave and Mynors, p. 393.
[18]  *Ælfric's Lives of Saints*, ed. and trans. Skeat, I. 434–5.
[19]  Clare A. Lees and Gillian R. Overing, 'Birthing Bishops and Fathering Poets: Bede,
      Hild and the Relations of Cultural Production', *Exemplaria* 6 (1994), 35–65.
[20]  As a key text of this sort they point to Peter Hunter Blair, 'Whitby as a Centre of
      Learning in the Seventh Century', in *Learning and Literature in Anglo-Saxon England*:

account Hild's role in politics, social development and cultural production was ignored.[21] As they remark, 'Bede effectively "gets the birth out" of this construction of maternity, removing the specifics of female presence and experience, and sterilizing it, as it were, for clerical metaphorical use'.[22]

Ælfric follows a similar line in his depiction of Æthelthryth. Her specific actions as virgin mother are conspicuous in their absence from the narrative. All of Æthelthryth's actions within the *vita* are inward looking, rather than those of someone taking active charge of a community. They all concern herself and her own ascetic daily routine of eating little and bathing rarely. Throughout Ælfric's text, Æthelthryth has only one small passage of direct or indirect speech and it concerns neither her abbatial influence nor her responsibilities to others, but a tumour on her neck.[23] Her speech is directed not to her spiritual offspring, but to God, offering thanks for this tumorous growth. For someone in a role where communication is key, this lack of speech is telling. In Ruth Waterhouse's examination of Ælfric's use of discourse in saints' lives, she records in tabular form the percentages of discourse, indirect speech and direct speech within each of Ælfric's Lives.[24] She finds that Æthelthryth has the lowest percentages in all three categories.[25] Admittedly, Ælfric was largely only following the example of his source, but when the level of speech in this *vita* is compared to the heroic speeches of his virgin martyrs, Æthelthryth is effectively silent and silenced.[26]

We are told nothing of Æthelthryth's relationship with the men and women of her double monastery, only facts about the culturally influential men who aid her in her spiritual journey – her husband who 'permits' her to enter the monastic world, and Bishop Wilfrid who gives her the nun's veil.[27] Æthelthryth holds a position of considerable power and influence, yet textually her leadership is nominal and the potency of her

---

*Studies Presented to Peter Clemoes,* ed. Michael Lapidge and Helmut Gneuss (Cambridge, 1985), pp. 3–32.

[21] Lees and Overing, 'Birthing Bishops', p. 46.

[22] Lees and Overing, 'Birthing Bishops', p. 45.

[23] *Ælfric's Lives of Saints*, ed. and trans. Skeat, I. 434–6.

[24] Ruth Waterhouse, 'Ælfric's Use of Discourse in Some Saints' Lives', *ASE* 5 (1976), 83–103.

[25] Waterhouse (pp. 89–90) shows that 10.4% of Æthelthryth's *vita* is discourse, 4.8% direct speech and 5.5% indirect speech. She deems Ælfric's minimisation of discourse in his sources to heighten our attention on the saint herself, since most of the omitted direct speech is spoken by others anyway.

[26] It is true that Leoba also has very little direct speech in Rudolf's *vita.* However, stylistically, the piece as a whole is a descriptive third person narrative focusing on events and containing very little reported speech and less direct speech. As such, lack of speech does not silence Leoba in the same way as Æthelthryth.

[27] *Ælfric's Lives of Saints*, ed. and trans. Skeat, I. 435.

maternal guidance and instruction remains unexplored. It is notable that Æthelthryth is at her most visible in this text only after death. Here, her incorrupt virginal body is an emblem of her purity, enclosed in a white marble sarcophagus, which miraculously mimics the shape of her body. She becomes a monument 'mannum to wundrunge'.[28] In death she is rendered paradoxically both a spectacle and a sight hidden from view just as, in life, her influence and agency is hinted at, yet minimized.

Rudolf's depiction of Leoba is an entirely different employment of the imagery and practices of motherhood in relation to a church leader. Leoba is required as a mother by both the chaste women and lay people in her community and is given some maternal agency. We are told that Leoba trains her nuns 'ad exemplum beatae magistrae'.[29] She controls their daily regime, leading through her own example, and she is vocal in the behaviour that she expects from her spiritual daughters. Leoba sets standards in her monastery through disciplinary rules, never letting the nuns stay up late as she considers it to dull the mind and requiring the nuns to read the Scriptures to her even whilst she sleeps. She creates an exemplary spiritual family defined 'orationibus atque ieiuniis caste viventium'.[30] Her nuns progress under her tutelage – many, we are informed, become abbesses at other convents. Her mothering is productive and begets tangible results, creating a new generation of chaste devotees of Christ.

Leoba is unequivocally needed by her spiritual offspring for protection and guidance. When the nuns under her care are suspected of engaging in fornication and infanticide, Leoba comes to their rescue. She clears their names and the name of the monastery by ordering the nuns to go to chapel and entreat God's help by singing the entire Psalter with their arms extended in the form of the cross.[31] In performing miracles, Leoba's concern is to protect her spiritual family. Again, this is shown to have tangible results, stimulating faith in those who witness them. Her sphere of influence is not confined to the monastery, but extends to lay society. Christians from nearby villages also call upon Leoba in times of need and she is shown to bolster their faith. When Leoba saves a local village from fire, the crowd of villagers stood 'adtonita, ad laudem Dei convertitur'.[32] Leoba also nurses a sick nun to recovery, sending to the monastery for her

---

[28] 'for men to marvel at': *Ælfric's Lives of Saints*, ed. and trans. Skeat, I. 438–9.
[29] Rudolf, *Vita Leobae*: ed. Waitz, p. 126; trans. Talbot, p. 266, 'according to her principles'.
[30] 'by prayers, fasting and chaste lives'. Rudolf, *Vita Leobae*: ed. Waitz, p. 127; trans. Talbot, p. 267.
[31] Rudolf, *Vita Leobae*: trans. Talbot, pp. 268–9.
[32] 'stood amazed and broke out into the praise of God'. Rudolf, *Vita Leobae*: ed. Waitz, p. 128; trans. Talbot, p. 270.

own spoon from which she pours milk into the nun's mouth.[33] Leoba nour-
ishes her spiritual child with milk which, whilst not physically from her
own breast, has been blessed with the maternal protection of her Christian
love. As a result, religious feeling in her community increases. She is also
described as influential at court, with Pepin, king of the Franks, with his
sons and with Queen Hildegard.[34]

Through the focus on culturally specific practices of motherhood,
Rudolf evidences Leoba's creation of Christian unity and community
amongst various strata of society, including consecrated nuns, the lay
population and the royal court. She is highly active in the ecclesiastical
sphere and the wider community and crucially, like all good spiritual
mothers, her work as protector and nurturer leads not simply to love for
her, but is transformed into love for God. As such, her role and influence
in the expansion of Christian ideals at the time of conversion is presented
as prominent. Rudolf, writing at a time of Benedictine monastic enclo-
sure and gender segregation, may have worried about aspects of Leoba's
life linked to interaction with, and conversion of, the lay population.[35]
Stephanie Hollis has argued that Rudolf focuses on normative and acceptable aspects of Leoba's life, 'concentrating on her devotion to the contemplative life and the virtuous example that she set for her community'.[36]
Whilst free interaction with men and the laity would no doubt have been a
cause of anxiety for Rudolf who was apparently polemically dedicated to
monastic segregation, I would argue against Hollis's claim. The lengthily-
described maternal action of her miracles and the reaction of her spiritual
and secular children mean that Leoba is allowed access and influence
within both her own monastery and the wider social and political community, but crucially without focusing attention too deeply on everyday interaction. One of Lees and Overing's main complaints of Bede's portrayal
of Abbess Hild is that he finds her to be 'mother, founder, educator, *not*
principal actor'.[37] In Rudolf's *vita,* Leoba is the principal actor, and it is
through her maternal practices that she becomes so.

In both texts, these sainted abbesses are presented through the filter of
two male, orthodox writers, both writing in the context of Benedictine
cloistered segregation, about an earlier period where women were granted
a freedom of influence no longer available to them. Julia Kristeva has
argued that the figure of the maternal is appropriated by male Christian
figures in a way that denigrates and obscures actual maternity and female

---

[33]  Rudolf, *Vita Leobae*: trans. Talbot, p. 271.
[34]  Rudolf, *Vita Leobae*: trans. Talbot, p. 273.
[35]  Hollis, *Anglo-Saxon Women and the Church*, p. 280.
[36]  Hollis, *Anglo-Saxon Women and the Church,* p. 279.
[37]  Lees and Overing,'Birthing Bishops and Fathering Poets', p. 46.

relationships.[38] She questions whether this Christian reduction 'represents no more than a masculine appropriation of the Maternal'.[39] Certainly Ælfric's portrayal of Æthelthryth's abbatial motherhood as purely titular could be interpreted in this way. The tenth-century Benedictine reform brought rules about contact between the male and female religious and, in accordance with the *RSB*, double monasteries were divided into single-sex institutions. It is therefore unsurprising that Ælfric does not mention that Æthelthryth was abbess over monks as well as nuns and remains largely silent, even more so than Bede, on her actual contribution to the church. It is significant that Ælfric takes exactly the same line in his representation of another mother abbess, St Basilissa.[40]

Æthelthryth's cult was promoted during the Benedictine reform. Peter Jackson notes that her cult remained relatively undeveloped until Bishop Æthelwold refounded Ely as a male monastery in 970 and translated Æthelthryth's body again, using the saint and her relics to forge a link with the past and encourage aristocratic patronage.[41] Perhaps Ælfric's orthodox Christian concerns and the social concerns of the families who supported aristocratic abbatial cults led to the need to reinscribe female kinship, power and influence within an acceptable patriarchal model, one which disempowered motherhood.[42] Anomalous to this is of course the *vita* of Leoba, written by Rudolf, a writer as concerned with orthodoxy as Ælfric in his own quieter way. Lees and Overing have noted that Rudolf's life is largely a 'pastiche of earlier hagiographic motifs, most often associated with male saints'.[43] Perhaps this is why Leoba slips through the net of maternal silence to be presented as an active spiritual mother, labouring hard and consequently influential in the process of building the reputation and power of her community.

Discussion of the final text has been left until now as it differs in both genre and subject. It comes from the late seventh- / early eighth-century

---

[38] This aspect of Kristeva's text is noted in Lees and Overing, 'Birthing Bishops', p. 62.

[39] Julia Kristeva, 'Stabat Mater', in *The Kristeva Reader*, ed. Toril Moi (Oxford, 1986), pp. 160–86, at p. 163.

[40] *Ælfric's Lives of Saints*, ed. and trans. Skeat, I. 90–115.

[41] Peter Jackson, 'Ælfric and the Purpose of Christian Marriage: A Reconsideration of the Life of Æthelthryth', *ASE* 29 (2000), 235–60, at 252–3. See also Susan J. Ridyard, *The Royal Saints of Anglo-Saxon England: A Study of West Saxon and East Anglian Cults* (Cambridge, 1988), p. 194, which Jackson cites. Mechthild Gretsch confirms the late flourishing of the cult, noting that Æthelthryth appears in only one early kalendar, a lost fragment connected with Northumbria (Munich, Hauptstaatsarchiv, Raritatenselekt 108; s. viii), where she is not represented as a saint, see Mechthild Gretsch, *Ælfric and the Cult of Saints in Late Anglo-Saxon England*, CSASE 34 (Cambridge, 2005), 163 and *eadem*, 'Æthelthryth of Ely in a Lost Calendar from Munich', *ASE* 35 (2006), 159–77.

[42] See Lees and Overing, 'Birthing Bishops', pp. 60–2.

[43] See Lees and Overing, 'Birthing Bishops', pp. 62, note 53.

personal correspondence of Aldhelm rather than hagiography and applies the imagery of spiritual motherhood not to an abbess but to a male bishop, Wilfrid. Since mothering has here been separated from birthing and theorized as a behavioural construction involving practices of nurture, protection and training, it becomes open not only to women, but also to men. As Ruddick remarks, 'mothering *work* is no longer distinctly feminine. A child is mothered by whoever protects, nurtures, and trains her. Although it is a material, social, and cultural fact that most mothers are now women, there is no difficulty in imagining men taking up mothering as easily as women – or conversely, women as easily declining to mother.'[44]

Ruddick's work considered concepts of motherhood today. However, the application of maternal imagery to males and to the male God is certainly a recognized literary *topos* during parts of the medieval period, particularly in the writings of twelfth-century Cistercian monks. Here imagery of male church leaders as both spiritual mother and father is frequent. The application of maternal imagery to males has its foundations in the Old Testament, patristic works and apocrypha, where God is frequently termed 'mother'.[45] Caroline Walker Bynum argued that during the Gregorian reform, figures of ecclesiastical authority became ambivalent and anxious about their place in the world. These Cistercian monks and abbots felt a conflict between a desire to preach and a sense of the cloister as segregated from the outside world.[46] It is Walker Bynum's theory that in their writings, the male religious apply imagery of motherhood to their own position in order to enter into discussions about the nature of authority and spiritual dependence, and it certainly appears that they do. However, she goes on to remark that 'with the exception of Bede's references to God's wisdom as feminine, the theme is unimportant in the early Middle Ages'.[47]

---

44  Ruddick,'Thinking Mothers/Conceiving Birth', p. 35.
45  Walker Bynum (*Jesus as Mother*, pp. 125–6) points to Ecclus. XXIV.24–6, where God describes Himself as mother, and asserts that the apocryphal Acts of Peter, as well as Clement, Origen, Irenaeus, John Chrysostom, Ambrose and Augustine, describe God as mother. She argues that it was particularly the Greek Fathers, especially those who were influenced by Gnostic theory, who made greater use of imagery of motherhood in relation to God. See also E. H. Pagels, 'What Became of God the Mother: Conflicting Images of God in Early Christianity', *Signs* 2 (1976), 293–303; Pamela Sheingorn, 'The Maternal Behaviour of God: Divine Father as Fantasy Husband', in *Medieval Mothering*, ed. Parsons and Wheeler, pp. 77–99; and for other examples of biblical maternal imagery, see Patricia Ann Quattrin, 'The Milk of Christ: Herzeloydë as Spiritual Symbol in Wolfrom von Eschenbach's *Parzival*', in *Medieval Mothering*, ed. Parsons and Wheeler, pp. 25–38.
46  See Walker Bynum, *Jesus as Mother* and *eadem*, 'Jesus as Mother and Abbot as Mother: Some Themes in Twelfth-Century Cistercian Writing', *Harvard Theological Review* 70 (1977), 257–84.
47  Walker Bynum, *Jesus as Mother*, p. 126. Alongside this assertion, Walker Bynum

Walker Bynum's statement is in need of some qualification. Certainly, nowhere in the Anglo-Saxon canon do we find the consistent application of maternal imagery to church leaders that is apparent in twelfth-century writings, though a few Anglo-Saxon texts do describe both Jesus and male religious figures in the lexis of motherhood.[48] In fact this example from Aldhelm's correspondence is very unusual. However, the complexity of the image that Aldhelm provides and the nuanced meaning is strikingly similar to the Cistercian writers that Walker Bynum has examined. Aldhelm's letter concerns Wilfrid, saint and bishop, who was expelled by King Ecgfrith from Northumbria, whose church the bishop had controlled in its entirety. He writes to the abbots beneath Wilfrid entreating them not to abandon their leader and 'devoted master' to solitary exile, since he 'nourished and raised' them. Aldhelm's letter engages in a debate regarding the authority, influence and role of one church leader, using imagery of motherhood to appeal to the abbots' dependence upon spiritual community, in a bid to help Wilfrid in his political plight.[49] The letter is designed to persuade, and one of his rhetorical tactics is to locate Wilfrid in the role of loving mother. He writes:

> Quis enim, quaeso, tam durus atroxve labor existens ab illo vos antistite seperans arceat, qui vos ab ipso tirocinio rudimentorum et a primaeva tenerae aetatis infantia usque adultae pubertatis florem nutriendo, docendo, castigando paterna provexit pietate et quasi nutrix gerula dilectos alumnos extensis ulnarum sinibus refocilans sic caritatis gremio fotos clementer amplexus est?[50]

Aldhelm's letter presents Wilfrid as giving birth to these abbots as spiritual beings through his motherly love. They are the result of his spiritual and physical labour. The letter depicts Wilfrid as tender, gentle and

---

does give a couple of passing references to male religious figures and Christ being termed mother in Continental texts. She points to Paschasius Radbertus, *Vita Sancti Adalhardi*, *PL* 120, cols. 1507–56 at col. 1543D; Hincmar, *Opusculum LV Capitulorum adversus Hincmarum Laudunensem*, *PL* 126, cols. 79–648 at col. 488; and Hincmar, *De praedestinatione Dei ei libero arbitrio, posterior dissertatio*, *PL* 125, cols. 65–474, at col. 357.

48   See below, pp. 73–4.

49   Aldhelm, 'Letter XII', in *Aldhelm: The Prose Works*, trans. Lapidge and Herren, pp. 168–70.

50   Aldhelm, 'Letter XII': Latin text from *Aldhelmi opera*, ed. Rudolfus Ehwald, MGH, Auctores antiquissimi XV (Berlin, 1919), p. 501. 'What harsh or cruel burden in existence, I ask, would separate you and hold you apart from that bishop, who like a wet-nurse gently caressed you, his beloved fosterchildren, warming you in the folds of his arms and nourishing you in the bosom of charity, and who brought you forward in his paternal love by rearing, teaching, and castigating you from your very first exposure to the rudiments (of education) and from your very early childhood and tender years up to the flower of your maturity?': *Aldhelm: The Prose Works*, trans. Lapidge and Herren, p.169.

warm as he nurses his offspring with his breast, nourishing them as a wet-nurse would her 'children'. Anglo-Saxons routinely utilized wet-nurses and fostered out royal children and Aldhelm engages with this domestic imagery in order to glean an emotional response from the abbots. His aim is political, but his method for achieving it is to appeal to the abbots' dependence upon Wilfrid's guidance by evoking a loving bond between them and their leader. To portray Wilfrid as spiritual mother was intended perhaps to encourage these abbots to envisage an emotional bond more readily than if only typically masculine imagery were used.

Interestingly, the paternal aspect of Wilfrid's relationship with these men is not ignored. In fact it is given separate attention, exploring his fatherly contribution to the lives of these men not as compassionate nurturer, but as disciplinarian teacher, castigating the men from their childhood onwards and encouraging their tender spiritual maturity. In Anglo-Saxon texts, descriptions of male church leaders as mothers are rare. More typical are references to abbots and bishops as 'father'.[51] Spiritual fatherhood often incorporates a different set of behaviours from motherhood. Paternal identifiers seem related to the greater degree of freedom that men were granted, certainly in the Benedictine context, while interacting with the laity and official church rites, particularly those of conversion and baptism. Ælfric's St Mark, to give just one example, is officially inaugurated into the Christian church by his 'fulluht-fæder' ('baptismal father') Peter.[52]

Spiritual fatherhood, as in Aldhelm's letter, was also often associated with discipline, sometimes of a physical nature. As McLaughlin has argued, 'once entered into – either through the celebration of the sacraments or through holy example – the role of spiritual father entailed many of the same obligations as that of a secular father. Most obviously, the *paterfamilias* was expected to discipline his offspring'.[53] In *The Old English Martyrology* Abbot Benedict of Nursia is depicted as so strict that the brethren under his tutelage want to poison him. He becomes abbot at a different monastery where one monk frequently leaves church at prayer time, a small black boy pulling him by his habit. Benedict's response is to 'sloh þone broðor mid gyrde'.[54] Physical discipline is absent in the maternal behaviour of female abbesses, but it is clearly successful as a paternal behavioural trait, since the demon causing the monk to err is

[51] For the paternal etymology of 'abbot', see above, Introduction (Rumble), p. 14.
[52] *Ælfric's Lives of Saints,* ed. and trans. Skeat, I. 330–1.
[53] Megan McLaughlin, 'Secular and Spiritual Fatherhood in the Eleventh Century', in *Conflicted Identities and Multiple Masculinities: Men in the Medieval West*, ed. Jacqueline Murray (New York, 1999), pp. 25–43, at p. 31.
[54] 'hit the brother with a rod': *An Old English Martyrology,* ed. and trans. George Herzfeld, EETS os 116 (London, 1900), 44–5.

ejected from the monastery.[55] In Aldhelm's letter, Wilfrid's mothering complements his fathering in a way which considers the responsibilities and contribution of church leaders in a persuasive and nuanced manner.

It is interesting to consider Aldhelm's usage of maternal imagery in light of both the later hagiographic representations of Æthelthryth and Leoba, and the metaphor of the breast as the site of faith which is found in other Anglo-Saxon texts. In Ælfric's *passio* of Agatha, the saint explicitly pronounces that the amputation of her breast fulfils her own desire. Agatha argues that by cutting off her breast, her adversary removes nothing but an external signifier. The more important breast is that of her soul, where her Christian knowledge and virginal identity rests; 'ic habbe mine breost on minre sawle ansunde mid þam ðe ic min andgit eallunga afede'.[56] In this *passio,* her torturer misreads the symbol of her breast, believing that her faith literally lies there, cutting it from her body in a failed attempt to sever her connection with God and Christian wisdom.[57]

The church leaders examined here feed their offspring with their spiritual wisdom. However, by far the most explicit usage of this metaphor occurs in the presentation of the male Wilfrid as a wet-nurse, providing spiritual nourishment and physical comfort to his foster children from the cradle of his arms and the milk of his charitable bosom. When we then turn to these female abbess mothers, and perhaps might expect imagery of breast-feeding, we do not find it. Leoba nurses a sick nun, but with milk from a spoon, not from her lactating breast, and whilst she advises her nuns with kindness and humility, she does not caress or warm them in her arms. Æthelthryth apparently has little or no interaction with her community at all. So, the imagery of breast-feeding is far more explicit when applied to this male church leader.

In Anglo-Saxon texts the male Christ is at times linked very explicitly with motherhood through imagery of breast-feeding. We are told in the *Old English Martyrology* that throughout the year of Christ's birth many people 'seah meoloc rinnan of heofonum',[58] associating the virgin birth of

---

55 Fatherly discipline and the submission of the child are found in the bible (Heb. XII. 9): 'We had earthly fathers and paid due respect to them; should we not submit even more readily to our spiritual father, and so attain life?'

56 'I have my breast sound in my soul, with which I shall at any rate feed my understanding': *Ælfric's Lives of Saints,* ed. and trans. Skeat, I. 202–3.

57 Gulley notes that 'for Quintianus, even as he might be getting his sexual kicks, Agatha's breast houses her faith, so that when he attempts to turn her from Christ through torture, he fixates on this physical symbol as the means to success. But because he understands only the physical nature of her faith, he misses what Agatha, and a Christian audience, sees': A. Gulley, 'Suffering and Salvation: Birthing Pains in Ælfric's *Life of Agatha*', *Medieval Perspectives* 17 (2002), 105–20, at 114.

58 'saw milk flowing from heaven': *The Old English Martyrology*, ed. and trans. Herzfeld, pp. 2–3.

Christ with nourishing all with the maternal milk of faith.[59] The metaphor
of Christian wisdom as nourishment is taken to its logical conclusion in
both the *Old English Martyrology* and Ælfric's *Lives of Saints*, where the
relationship between Christ and John the Evangelist is that of a mother
nursing a son. The *Old English Martyrology* states that John

> wæs Criste leof ofer ealle oðre men þe he on middangearde gemette, ond
> he wæs him swa leof, þæt he æt gereordum hlenode on þæs hælendes
> bearme ond ofer his breost[60]

and Ælfric similarly describes how John

> wæs criste swa leof þæt he hlynode uppan his breoste on ðam þe wæs
> behyd [eall] se heofonlica wisdom swylce he of ðam drunce þa deopan
> lare.[61]

Neither these portrayals nor that of Wilfrid attempt to reduce the
maternal bond to metaphor. Rather, they link Christ's and Wilfrid's role as
influential church leader with motherhood through overt images of breast-
feeding. One cannot imagine a more explicit image of Christ passing onto
John his spiritual wisdom than the fully grown Evangelist sitting upon his
'mother's' lap at mealtimes, not eating food like the rest of the disciples,
but drinking the sustaining goodness of milk from Christ's own breast.
Both Christ and Wilfrid are depicted as mothering their offspring out of a
desire to teach love of Christianity. Christ and Wilfrid are, like all 'good'
Anglo-Saxon mothers, nurturers, protectors, and teachers.

Through a comparative reading of these three texts, one conclusion that
can be drawn is that to constrain the fecundity and productivity inherent to
maternity, to make it nominal or metaphorical and to remove motherhood
from physical metaphors of maternity, was considered more necessary in
descriptions of women than men. Aldhelm's depiction of Wilfrid is unde-
niably atypical. However, it may indicate that describing the influence of
church leaders through a lexis of motherhood that fused visible and potent
cultural production with bodily nourishment and physical love was a far
more threatening presence in writings about women than in writings about
men. Walker Bynum noted that in twelfth-century writings, references to
breasts provided an opportunity to discuss the burdens of abbacy, where

---

[59] The imagery of Christ as mother is of course biblical and so would not be deemed as
potentially unsettling as non-biblical male mothers.

[60] 'was dear to Christ more than all other men that he met on earth, and he was so dear
to him, that at meals he rested in the lap of the Saviour and on his breast': *The Old
English Martyrology*, ed. and trans. *Herzfeld*, pp. 8–9.

[61] 'was so dear to Christ that he leaned upon His breast in which was hidden the heavenly
wisdom, as if he thence might drink the deep learning': *Ælfric's Lives of Saints*, ed.
and trans. Skeat, I. 330–1.

breasts were linked to preaching in some physically explicit imagery.[62] If, in this description of Wilfrid, this link between nourishment from the breast and the preaching of Christian wisdom is, as it seems, also present, then no wonder we do not see such things in the lives of Æthelthryth and Leoba. In the context of the Benedictine reform, female preaching would certainly not be approved of, encouraged, or described.

The three texts examined here, the *vitae* of Æthelthryth and Leoba and Aldhelm's letter describing Wilfrid, offer increasingly explicit portrayals of the contribution of these leaders to the Anglo-Saxon church through imagery of spiritual motherhood. These mothers, in depictions composed progressively further back in time, move from having their influences consistently underplayed, to being generative within their community, to actually physically passing on their spiritual wisdom to their children. Somewhat unexpectedly though, in early medieval descriptions of the labour of being a church leader, a mother to the flock, we are more likely to find the religious suckling from the male breast than from the female.

[62] Walker Bynum, *Jesus as Mother*, pp. 115–24.

# 4

# Understanding the Earliest Bishops of Worcester
## c. 660–860

### ALLAN SCOTT McKINLEY

WORCESTER is the best evidenced of all the early Anglo-Saxon bishoprics, with a substantial collection of material on which to construct narratives. Yet this has rarely been done, perhaps because of the difficulty of ascertaining which charters are reliable.[1] This is a pity, for Worcester is unparalleled in the opportunities it presents to scholars seeking to understand the development of a church and its relationship with its landscape. The way in which the bishops of Worcester built up the power of their church can be at least dimly discerned in this material, and the effort of determining how the bishops did this and in what circumstances is worthwhile, as it presents an alternative perspective on parts of Anglo-Saxon history where existing narratives are focused on secular leaders, not churchmen.[2]

---

[1] Until the forthcoming volumes in the AS Charters series appear, there exists no particularly comprehensive discussion of the earliest charters in the Worcester archive, which tend rather to have been treated piecemeal. Some helpful discussion can be found in Anton Scharer, *Die angelsächsische Köningsurkunde im 7. und 8. Jahrhundert* (Vienna, 1982); Patrick Sims-Williams, *Religion and Literature in Western England 600–800* (Cambridge, 1990); and Allan Scott McKinley, 'Church-Patron Relationships amongst the Anglo-Saxons and Franks, c. 650–860', Ph.D thesis (University of Birmingham, 2002), pp. 302–406. The actual history of the archive at Worcester is better served: N. R. Ker, 'Hemming's Cartulary: A Description of the Two Worcester Cartularies in Cotton Tiberius A.xiii', in *Studies in Medieval History Presented to Frederick Maurice Powicke,* ed. R. W. Hunt, W. A. Pantin and R. W. Southern (Oxford, 1948), pp. 49–75; and Francesca Tinti, 'From Episcopal Conception to Monastic Compilation: Hemming's Cartulary in Context', *Early Medieval Europe* 11 (2003), 233–61.

[2] In this respect, this chapter takes a lead from Nicholas Brooks' excellent account of Anglo-Saxon history from the perspective of Christ Church, Canterbury: *The Early History of the Church of Canterbury: Christ Church from 597 to 1066* (London, 1984). A different approach to West Midlands history based on alternative sources of evidence, albeit one which still started with a traditional description of kingdoms and political units, has been provided by Sims-Williams, *Religion and Literature.*

**Table 4.1.** Recorded bishops of Worcester before 900 AD, with location of information about activities prior to becoming bishop

| bishop | dates of episcopate | Bede, *HE* | John of Worcester | *Annales prioratus de Wigornia* | charter evidence | other |
|---|---|---|---|---|---|---|
| Tatfrith | died before consecration | monk of Whitby | | | | |
| Bosel | 680–91 | | | | | |
| Offor | 691–3 | monk of Whitby; lived in diocese | | | | |
| Egwine | 693×699–717 | | | | | (association with Powys) |
| Wilfrid | 718–743×745 | | | | | |
| Milred | 743×745–775 | | | | | culted at Berkswell, Warwickshire |
| Wærmund | 775–7 | | | | | |
| Tilhere | 777–81 | | abbot | abbot of Berkeley | | |
| Hathored | 781–798×800 | | | | family connections in south of diocese | |
| Deneberht | 798×800–822 | | | | | |
| Heahberht | 822–845×848 | | | | | |
| Ealhhun | 845×848–869×879 | | from cathedral community | | | |
| Wærfrith | 869×879–907–915 | | | | | |

A key problem with studying the early bishops of Worcester is that they are faceless historical individuals; unlike the other subjects of this volume, the predecessors of Bishop Wærfrith (see Table 4.1) have not left a legacy of writings or controversies but, at most, a few charters which, in the current state of knowledge, may tell us more about the donors than the bishops. Understanding individual bishops' roles in history and contextualizing their few identifiable actions is, therefore, nigh on impossible. But this is not to say that there is nothing to be gained through study of those who led the episcopal church of Worcester through its first two centuries: what might appear as isolated and unconnected facts about members of the Worcester episcopate can, when the bishops are studied as a group, reveal interesting patterns. This is because although the bishops of Worcester may be names without personae, they are not in general names without any context. It is possible to identify, with varying degrees of confidence, where the vocation of a number of the early bishops of Worcester had been played out before they rose to the episcopate, and to speculate about the origins of a couple more.

Bede mentions that the first bishop-elect Tatfrith, who died before consecration, and the second consecrated bishop, Oftfor, were both formerly monks of Whitby and presumably, therefore, Northumbrians.[3] Oftfor had in fact lived in the *prouincia* of the Hwicce before his election as bishop, but owed his appointment to the precept of King Æthelred of Mercia.[4]

Less certain, but still credible, is the fourteenth-century tradition that Tilhere, bishop from 777 to 781, was previously an abbot of Berkeley.[5] It is difficult to see any benefit to a Worcester source in inventing this fact, as Worcester never seems to have made any claim to Berkeley, and Berkeley never seems to have had any particular prestige, for all its large estates; by the time the tradition was recorded, Berkeley was an established priory of Reading Abbey by gift of Stephen's Queen Adeliza and the Empress Mathilda, separately, and not noted for any particular holiness.[6] A Tilhere attests charters of the last Hwiccan kings

---

[3] *HE*, IV.23; Colgrave and Mynors, pp. 408–9.

[4] *HE*, IV.23; Colgrave and Mynors, pp. 408–11. It is tempting to suggest that Oftfor originally arrived in the diocese along with Tatfrith.

[5] *Annales prioratus de Wigornia*, s.a. 778: *Annales monastici*, IV, ed. Henry Richard Luard, RS 36 (London, 1869), 355–564, at 366

[6] *Reading Abbey Cartularies*, I, *General Documents and Those Relating to English Counties other than Berkshire*, ed. B. R. Kemp, Camden 4th ser. 31 (London, 1986), no. 268, pp. 225–6; *Regesta Regum Anglo-Normannorum 1066–1254, III, Regesta Regis Stephani ac Mathildis Imperatricis ac Gaufridi et Henrici Ducum Normannorum*, ed. H. A. Cronne and R. H. C. Davis (Oxford, 1968), no. 702, p. 259. On Berkeley, the historical information is gathered and the received history set out by C. S. Taylor, 'Berkeley Minster', *Transactions of the Bristol and Gloucestershire Archaeological Society* 19 (1894–5), 70–84. Emphasis on its position as a centre of secular (queenly)

as an abbot,[7] whilst the twelfth-century account of John of Worcester also mentions he was previously an abbot, although without specifying where;[8] this may show some continuation of memory about the origins of at least some of the early bishops at Worcester, picked up both by John and by the author of the *Annales prioratus de Wigornia*. Furthermore, the *Annales* record a similar tradition for Æthelhun, bishop from 907×915 to 915×922,[9] which perhaps bolsters the credibility of Tilhere's attribution to Berkeley, both by reinforcing the likelihood that Berkeley could provide bishops and by suggesting that origins of bishops, or at least those connected with Berkeley, were noted in some form accessible to the annalist.[10]

More tenuous connections can also be made. Thus, Bishop Hathored (781–798/800) is described as *propinquus* 'kinsman' to Headda, an abbot and priest whose patrimony lay in the south of the diocese near Dowdeswell.[11] This suggests that Hathored had a least a family connection to this area, although as so little is known of early Anglo-Saxon aristocratic family landholdings it is perhaps difficult to state with certainty that the bishop came from the south of his diocese.[12] An earlier bishop, Milred (745–774×775), is likely to be the saint whom Leland reports as

---

power in the eleventh century is set out in Pauline Stafford, '*Cherchez la femme.* Queens, Queens' Lands and Nunneries: Missing Links in the Foundation of Reading Abbey', *History* 85 (2000), 4–27, at 14–17.

[7] S 56 of AD 759; S 63 of 757 × 774.

[8] *JW,* s.a. 778; II. 212.

[9] *Annales prioratus de Wigornia*, s.a. 917; ed. Luard, p. 368. Note that an Æthelhun attests S 218 of the year 883 as abbot, in a context that implies it is all but certain that he was abbot of Berkeley. Cf. S 367a and 225, which might imply that Æthelhun (if this is the same abbot in both cases: PASE lists three different Æthelhuns for these charters, none of whom is identified with the bishop) was sometimes to be found at the early-tenth-century Mercian court, making him a likely choice for bishop.

[10] Cf. Sims-Williams, *Religion and Literature*, pp. 158–9.

[11] S 1413/BCS 283. Identification of *Tyreltune* focuses on Whittington, Gloucestershire, whilst Finberg saw *Onnandune* as covering Andoversford, Pegglesworth and Upper Dowdeswell: H. P. R. Finberg, *The Early Charters of the West Midlands*, 2nd edn (Leicester, 1972), no. 46, p. 41. Cf. A. H. Smith, *The Place-Names of Gloucestershire*, I, EPNS 38 (Cambridge, 1964), 168–9.

[12] The link between Hathored and the southern regions of the diocese of Worcester might also be strengthened by the appearance of the name *Heþeredus* in the list of early abbots of Malmesbury (edited version in Heather Edwards, *The Charters of the Early West Saxon Kingdom*, British Archaeological Reports, British ser. 198 (Oxford, 1988), 82). Whilst the list is itself probably not an accurate account of the abbots of Malmesbury, it is still significant that the only bishop of Worcester whose origins are hypothetically from the area connected to Malmesbury across the head of the Thames Valley is also the only bishop of Worcester on the list, probably drawn from a *Liber Vitae* or necrology, as suggested by Edwards, *Charters*, pp. 82–3; and *Charters of Malmesbury Abbey*, ed. S. E. Kelly, AS Charters 11 (Oxford, 2005), 106–7, 296. Cf. W. de G. Birch, 'On the Succession of the Abbots of Malmesbury', *Journal of the British Archaeological Association* 27 (1871), 314–42, 446–8, at 319.

having been culted at Berkswell, Warwickshire.[13] Berkswell shows signs that it might have been an early Anglo-Saxon church,[14] and it is conceivable that Milred had a close connection with it – perhaps as founder or as its most prominent *alumnus*; certainly Leland's synopsis of a (very probably Cambridge) manuscript whence the information comes could suggest some form of hagiography.[15] If so, Milred was another bishop who probably originated from outside the diocese of Worcester, as Berkswell lies within the presumed bounds of the Mercian diocese of Lichfield, as recorded in the later boundaries of the diocese of Coventry. A further bishop associated with a different church from Worcester is Ecgwine, the founder of Evesham. However, Evesham traditions about Ecgwine never claim that the church was his patrimony, instead emphasizing that it was a gift from King Æthelred,[16] an indication that tenth-century Evesham monks did not believe that Ecgwine had built on hereditary land. Other than this, the only hint of where Ecgwine may have originated is a late Welsh genealogy which claims him for a Powys ecclesiastical dynasty; this is likely to be a misidentification.[17] A final bishop about whose earlier career some tradition is recorded is Ealhhun (845×848–869×879), whom John of Worcester records as being brought up in the church of Worcester.[18]

It is therefore possible to make conjectures about origins for a number of bishops, and a potentially interesting pattern emerges: up until the

[13] *The Itinerary of John Leland in or about the Years 1535–1543*, ed. Lucy Toulmin Smith, 4 vols. (London, 1919), II.167. The identification is made by John Blair, 'A Handlist of Anglo-Saxon Saints', in *Local Saints and Local Churches in the Early Medieval West*, ed. Alan Thacker and Richard Sharpe (Oxford, 2002), pp. 495–565, at pp. 545–6.

[14] Steve Bassett, personal communication; it is likely that the site of the present crypt, under an earlier nave, is an indication that an earlier crypt must have existed in the same place: *Victoria County History of Warwickshire*, IV, ed. L. F. Salzman (Oxford, 1947), 30–1.

[15] Not only does the entry (*The Itinerary of John Leland*, II.167) call Milred '*S. Milredus*', suggestive of hagiography in itself, but the preceding entry in Leland's list (*Itinerary*, II.166–7) deals with the situation of the palace of King Æthelbald ('*Etheoaldi regis*') '*tempore Milredi episcopi*' ('in the time of Bishop Milred'), locating it at Stoneley near to Berkswell. All of this suggests a work of local hagiography, of the type discussed by John Blair, 'The Anglo-Saxon Church in Herefordshire: Four Themes', in *The Early Church in Herefordshire*, ed. Ann Malpas, Janet Butler, Arthur Davis, Sheila Davis, Tony Malpas and Chris Samson (Leominster, 2002), pp. 3–13, at pp. 8–9, although why this was recorded in a now-lost manuscript dealing with the pseudo-history of the University of Cambridge is unclear.

[16] Byrhtferth, *Vita Sancti Ecgwini Wigorniensis episcopi*, in *Vita quorundam Anglo-Saxonum*, ed. J. A. Giles, Caxton Society 16 (London, 1854), 349–96, at 363.

[17] *Generatio Sancti Ecguini*, in *Early Welsh Genealogical Tracts*, ed. P. C. Bartrum (Cardiff, 1966), p. 21; Michael Lapidge, 'The Medieval Hagiography of St Ecgwine', *Vale of Evesham Historical Society Research Papers* 6 (1977), 77–93 at 82.

[18] *JW*, s.a. 872; II. 298–300.

end of the long episcopate of Milred, each of the bishops of Worcester, except for Bosel, had at least plausible links to either the north of the diocese (Ecgwine and Evesham), Mercia (Milred, and through Æthelred, Oftfor) or Northumbria (Tatfrith and Oftfor). Those bishops of the later eighth century for whom we can suggest origins seem, however, to have been connected to the southern part of the diocese – Tilhere to Berkeley and Hathored to Dowdeswell. This may appear coincidental, but another interesting pattern marks out the earlier bishops from the later: the fact that there is also at least plausible evidence that bishops were appointed during the lifetime of their predecessor.[19] This applies to the same period as that during which the bishops of Worcester seem to have had more northerly origins. The most explicit example is the case of Oftfor, according to Bede appointed during his predecessor's lifetime.[20] Less reliably, John of Worcester records that Wilfrid had been elected before the death of Ecgwine;[21] it is difficult to conceive a reason why John or an earlier writer would invent this distinctly uncanonical fact. Wilfrid himself attests an originally mid-eighth-century charter alongside his successor Milred, both as *biscop/bisceop*;[22] although this may be sepa- rate attestations by successive bishops.[23] In light of attested earlier prac- tice it seems entirely possible the two attestations were made at the same time. In fact, the only early bishop for whom there is no evidence of his successor being appointed during his own lifetime is Oftfor, whose death soon after Bosel's may have been too rapid to allow for such an occasion.[24]

---

19 On the practice amongst the Anglo-Saxons of appointing bishops before their predecessor's death, see Catherine Cubitt, 'Wilfrid's "Usurping Bishops": Episcopal Elections in Anglo-Saxon England, *c.*600–*c.*800', *Northern History* 25 (1989), 18–38 and *Charters of Malmesbury*, ed. Kelly, p. 156; these do not discuss most of the Worcester evidence. For other possible examples of a seventh- or eighth-century Anglo-Saxon bishop attesting during his predecessor's lifetime: S 51/ *Charters of Bath and Wells*, ed. S. E. Kelly, AS Charters 13 (Oxford, 2007), no. 1, p. 54; S 42/ *Charters of Selsey*, ed. S. E. Kelly, AS Charters 6 (Oxford, 1998), no. 6, pp. 35–7.

20 *HE*, IV.23; Colgrave and Mynors, pp. 410–11.

21 *JW*, s.a. 717; II. 174.

22 S 98/Robertson, *AS Charters*, no. 1, p. 2. For the authenticity of this document see McKinley, 'Church-Patron relationships', pp. 340–2; *Charters of St Augustine's Abbey, Canterbury and Minster-in-Thanet*, ed. S. E. Kelly, AS Charters 4 (Oxford, 1995), lxxxv–xc.

23 Cf. S 53, where two witness-lists from different occasions can be discerned: one Hwiccan, from Oshere to Oftfor, the other relating to a council (on which see Catherine Cubitt, *Anglo-Saxon Church Councils, c. 650–850* (London, 1995), p. 259) and starting with Æthelred, in all likelihood the contemporary king of Mercia: McKinley, 'Church-Patron Relationships', pp. 309–12.

24 John of Worcester places Oftfor's death in 692, the year after Bosel's: *JW*, s.aa. 691–2; II. 154–6, with n. 3; the later priory annals of Worcester extend Oftfor's episcopate to three years, perhaps using different information (there is no significant similarity of wording): *Annales prioratus de Wigornia*, s.aa. 689, 692; ed. Luard, p. 365. The modern dating of Oftfor's death to 697×699 (e.g. Finberg, *Early Charters of the West*

However, from Milred onwards there is no evidence for the pre-humous election of a bishop's successor, matching the apparent change in origins for bishops of Worcester that becomes apparent after Milred's episcopate. It seems reasonable to state that during Milred's episcopate there was a change of conditions within the diocese of Worcester, through which an earlier pattern of what might loosely be called 'northern' bishops, often appointed during their predecessor's lifetime, was replaced by a pattern of bishops who were 'southern', at least in terms of the diocese.

To understand this change it is necessary to try and contextualize the earlier, 'northern', pattern. The fact that the first recorded bishops of Worcester tended to be from outside the diocese and seem to have been appointed in their predecessor's lifetime suggests that someone sought to keep the control of the bishopric out of the hands of those within it, or at least those in the south of the diocese. Since both Oftfor and Ecgwine are associated with Æthelred of Mercia, it appears the Mercian kings would be the most likely patrons of the early diocese of Worcester and its bishops.[25] This is in accord with Worcester traditions, which are almost unanimous in making Æthelred the founder of the see (or at least the king in whose reign the see of Worcester was founded).[26] Hwiccan rulers seem to have had little to do with the foundation of Worcester.

Indeed, until the middle of the eighth century (again) Hwiccan rulers seems to have had little to do with Worcester at all, at least that can be evidenced. The basis for this statement is directly linked to charters: of fourteen charters supposedly issued by Hwiccan royalty, only five are

---

*Midlands*, p. 32; Sims-Williams, *Religion and Literature*, p. 102, n. 62) depends upon accepting S 76 as an authentic record, which it is clearly not, being a later composition demonstrably based upon S 77, itself a (probably ninth-century) forgery: Scharer, *Die angelsächsische Königsurkunde*, pp. 153–4; McKinley, 'Church-Patron Relationships', pp. 313–20. Although the exact basis of John of Worcester's and the priory annals' dating is uncertain, there seems no reason to discard them in favour of a date based purely on the historicizing tendencies of a later forger (on the tendency for historicizing features to occur in forgeries first witnessed in *Liber Wigornensis* see Julia Barrow, 'The Chronology of Forgery Production at Worcester from *c*.1000 to the Twelfth Century', in *St Wulfstan and his World*, ed. Julia S. Barrow and N. P. Brooks (Aldershot, 2005), pp. 105–22, at pp. 113–14); therefore, it is entirely possible that Oftfor's episcopate only lasted one year. The Evesham Chronicle reference to Ecgwine being consecrated in 698/699 is probably not relevant here, as the date of Oftfor's death is not mentioned; see *Chronicon abbatiae de Evesham*, ed. William Dunn Macray, RS 29 (London, 1863), 70.

25  Compare the similar pattern at another strategic Mercian-controlled bishopric, Canterbury: Cubitt, 'Wilfrid's "Usurping Bishops"', p. 28.

26  *JW*, s.a. 680 (and s.a. 679 for the repeat of the same basic facts in John's later recension); II.136–8. *Annales prioratus de Wigornia*, s.a. 680; ed. Luard, p. 365. *The Cartulary of Worcester Cathedral Priory (Register I)*, ed. R. R. Darlington, Pipe Roll Society n.s. 38 (1968 for 1962–3), 1.

supposedly in favour of Worcester, and three of these are later forgeries.[27] Of the remaining two, one might equally well be an altered foundation charter for Tredington whilst the other relates to the settlement of a dispute over Fladbury.[28] Neither is therefore unequivocal evidence of an established relationship between the bishops of Worcester and the kings of the Hwicce. Furthermore, all five charters are attributed to the reigns of Uhtred, Eanberht and Ealdred (*c.* 757–80), the brothers who were the last Hwiccan rulers with any pretence of independence from the kings of Mercia.[29] Despite a diplomatic tradition that starts eighty years before these siblings took up the reins of power, there is no evidence for Hwiccan patronage of Worcester until after 757.

This goes against what we would expect from analogous situations. By 750 we can be certain that West Saxon rulers had patronized the Old Minster, Winchester, with gifts of land;[30] East Saxon kings had given land to St Paul's, London;[31] and Kentish royalty had endowed Rochester as well as, probably, Christ Church, Canterbury.[32] Even amongst the South Saxons, where marriage to a daughter of the Hwiccan king was part of the conversion process, local rulers can be seen endowing the local bishopric at Selsey.[33] In every other area where there is any sort of substantive survival of Anglo-Saxon diplomas prior to 775, kings can be seen establishing a relationship with their local bishoprics. Hwiccan rulers are conspicuously different.

---

[27] S 55/BCS 183; S 59/BCS 202; S 60/BCS 203 (granting the same estates as S59); S 61/BCS 204; and S 62/BCS 238. The forgeries are the nearly contemporary S 59 (see Patrick Wormald, 'Charters, Laws and the Settlement of Disputes', *Legal Culture in the Early Medieval West: Law as Text, Image and Experience* (London & Rio Grande, 1999), pp. 290–311 and *idem, How Do We Know So Much about Anglo-Saxon Deerhurst?*, Deerhurst Lecture 1991 (Deerhurst, 1993), pp. 20–2); and S 60–1, two charters written to create title to estates for St Mary's, Worcester, a church not founded until the tenth century (see McKinley, 'Church-Patron Relationships', pp. 360–2).

[28] Fladbury: S 62 (on its authenticity, see McKinley, 'Church-Patron Relationships', pp. 367–8). Tredington: S 55 (discussed with too much scepticism by McKinley, 'Church-Patron Relationships', pp. 347–54, which fails to consider the possibility that this was the transfer of a complete 'minster' church estate to Worcester).

[29] Finberg, *Early Charters of the West Midlands*, p. 178.

[30] S 259/BCS 180 (definitely) and S 258/BCS 179 (probably). Note that the records from Sherborne do not contain any authentic charters prior to 774: *Charters of Sherborne*, ed. M. A. O'Donovan, AS Charters 3 (Oxford, 1988), 1–5.

[31] S 1787/ *Charters of St Paul's, London*, ed. S. E. Kelly, AS Charters 10 (Oxford, 2004), no. 6, pp. 145–7.

[32] S 27/ *Charters of Rochester*, ed. A. Campbell, AS Charters 1 (London, 1973), no. 3, pp. 3–4; and possibly S 30/*Charters of Rochester*, ed. Campbell, no. 4, p. 5 if the conventional redating to 747 (from 762) is accepted. The early archive of Christ Church, Canterbury is missing prior to 798, when it is assumed to have suffered some disaster: Brooks, *Early History*, p. 121.

[33] S 42; *Charters of Selsey*, ed. S. E. Kelly, AS Charters 6 (Oxford, 1998), no. 6, pp. 35–7. For the dynastic marriage, see *HE*, IV.13; Colgrave and Mynors, p. 230.

Hwiccan rulers did patronize churches, just not Worcester: Fig. 4.1 shows a number of churches that can be identified as likely recipients of Hwiccan gifts.[34] However, an interesting pattern emerges here: almost all these churches are within, or just outside, the area of the Ferding of Winchcombe within Gloucestershire, the area where Bassett located the heartland of the earliest Hwiccan kings.[35] Only Gloucester and Bath seem to lie clearly away from this area: what might be significant is that these are two of the three major Roman, and probably sub-Roman, centres of the region, probably being heads of ferdings on their own account.[36] Almost no historical evidence remains for the third centre, and head of the last ferding, Cirencester, but it would be unsurprising if the archaeologically-attested large ninth-century Anglo-Saxon church located there had a predecessor that was also a recipient of Hwiccan generosity.[37] The picture painted by Hwiccan patronage of the church is of a focus on churches around the edges of a coherent block of territory and of important institutions in the area to the south. Interestingly, the area to the north is a blank.

Indeed, it might be asked why the bishopric of the Hwicce was at Worcester, a minor Roman site, probably abandoned after the Roman occupation.[38] The tendency of most Anglo-Saxon bishoprics outside the Lindisfarne tradition to be built at or near Roman sites would have

[34] For the evidence for associating these churches with the Hwiccan kings, see McKinley, 'Church-Patron Relationships', pp. 114–16.

[35] Steven Bassett, 'In Search of the Origins of Anglo-Saxon Kingdoms', in *The Origins of Anglo-Saxon Kingdoms*, ed. *idem* (London, 1989), pp. 3–27, at pp. 6–17.

[36] Barry C. Burnham and John Wacher, *The 'Small Towns' of Roman Britain* (London, 1990), pp. 165–76; John Wacher, *The Towns of Roman Britain*, 2nd edn (London, 1992), pp. 162–3; H. P. R. Finberg, Appendix to C. S. Taylor, 'The Origin of the Mercian Shires', in *Gloucestershire Studies*, ed. H. P. R. Finberg (Leicester, 1957), p. 47; Della Hooke, *The Anglo-Saxon Landscape: the Kingdom of the Hwicce* (Manchester, 1985), pp. 76–7. For the continued importance of these centres in the sub-Roman period *ASC* 577 is suggestive of continuing importance, although it must be remembered this may be a late-ninth-century perspective; *The Anglo-Saxon Chronicle MS A*, ed. Janet Bately, The AS Chronicle: A Collaborative Edition, ed. David Dumville and Simon Keynes, 3 (Cambridge, 1986), 26.

[37] David J. Wilkinson and Alan D. McWhirr, *Cirencester Anglo-Saxon Church and Medieval Abbey*, Cirencester excavations 4 (Cirencester, 1998). On Cirencester as a probable regional centre, see Finberg, Appendix, pp. 45–6; Hooke, *Anglo-Saxon Landscape: The Hwicce*, pp. 75–6. What is known for certain about Cirencester is summed up by John Blair, 'Cirencester', in *The Blackwell Encyclopaedia of Anglo-Saxon England*, ed. Michael Lapidge, John Blair, Simon Keynes and Donald Scragg (Oxford, 2001), p. 105.

[38] Burnham and Wacher, *The 'Small Towns'*, pp. 232–4; Martin Carver, 'An Archaeology of Worcester, 680–1680 A.D.', in *Medieval Worcester: An Archaeological Framework*, ed. *idem*, Transactions of the Worcestershire Archaeological Society, 3rd ser. 7 (1980), 1–12, at 1–3. Hooke (*Anglo-Saxon Landscape: The Hwicce*, pp. 17–19) suggests that Worcester was selected as the seat of the bishopric due to a speculative connection with British kingdoms to the west, but it is difficult to see how this would be a positive feature for the location of an Anglo-Saxon bishopric with no known missionary links.

been better served by any of Gloucester, Cirencester or Bath. Yet this ignores one other vital rule of Anglo-Saxon bishopric location: proximity to royal patrons. Rochester and Sherborne are sited on the eastern edge of their dioceses and Leicester is at the north of what may have been a huge diocese stretching to the Thames: in each case the bishop's seat lies almost as close as practically possible to the homelands of the kings who founded it: respectively East Kent, Hampshire and eastern Dorset, and the Mercian heartland.[39] Worcester is not necessarily convenient for Hwiccan rulers but, in terms of its diocese, it was certainly about the most convenient Roman site for the other rulers with a historically-recorded interest there, the Mercians.[40]

The Mercians were still undoubtedly a force within the diocese of Worcester. This is perhaps best illustrated by control of the important salt-production site at Droitwich, where there is no evidence of Hwiccan royal involvement, but plentiful evidence for Mercian kings having an interest.[41] Indeed, Hwiccan influence in the north of the diocese of Worcester was seemingly non-existent. The only reason for assuming any connection between this area and the Hwiccan kings is that it lay within the (later-recorded) bounds of the bishopric of Worcester, sometimes called the bishopric of the Hwicce.[42]

---

[39] Alec Detsias, *The Cantiaci* (Gloucester, 1983), pp. 39–54; Nicholas Brooks, 'The Creation and Early Structure of the Kingdom of Kent', in *Origins of Anglo-Saxon Kingdoms*, ed. Bassett, pp. 55–74, at pp. 68–9; Barbara Yorke, *Kings and Kingdoms of Early Anglo-Saxon England* (London and New York, 1990), pp. 33–4 and *Wessex in the Early Middle Ages* (London and New York, 1995), pp. 57–60; Nicholas Brooks, 'The Formation of the Mercian Kingdom', in *Origins of Anglo-Saxon Kingdoms*, ed. Bassett, pp. 159–70, at pp. 160–2; Cyril Hart, 'The Kingdom of Mercia', in *Mercian Studies*, ed. Ann Dornier (Leicester, 1977), pp. 43–61; Barry Cunliffe, *Wessex to AD 1000* (London and New York, 1993), p. 306.

[40] As well as being sited on the River Severn, Worcester lies on the direct Roman road from Wall, near Lichfield, to Gloucester: Ivan D. Margary, *Roman Roads in Britain*, 3rd edn (London, 1973), pp. 287–8. The only equally suitable Roman site in the north of the diocese of Worcester would have been Droitwich, but this was probably too strategically important as a source of salt for the Mercian kings to allow an alternative centre of power to be established there, see J. R. Maddicott, 'London and Droitwich, c. 650–750: Trade, Industry and the Rise of Mercia', *ASE* 34 (2007), 7–58; Steven Bassett, 'Sitting above the Salt: The Origins of the Borough of Droitwich', in *A Commodity of Good Names: Essays in Honour of Margaret Gelling*, ed. O. J. Padel and David N. Parsons (Donington, 2008), pp. 3–27.

[41] See Maddicott, 'London and Droitwich'.

[42] Although Bede (*HE*, V.32; Colgrave and Mynors, p. 350) identifies the diocese as that of the Hwicce, prior to S 1279/BCS 580 of 899 only one document from the Worcester archive identifies the diocese thus: the unusually early lease S 1254/BCS 166, which covers what was probably perceived as the same estate as S 1279 and has some indications (anachronistic bounds; witness attestations) which suggests that the text may have been tampered with.

However, that the bishopric of Worcester could be referred to as the bishopric of the Hwicce need not mean they were the only people or political unit identifiable within the bishopric: after all, Mercian Lichfield contained at least the *Pecsætna* and *Wreocensætna*, as well as the Mercian *Tamsætna* and *Pencersætna*;[43] and East Saxon London incorporated the Middle Saxons (themselves composed of multiple different identifiable groupings) and was situated in their territory.[44] The Hwicce were the most notable group within their diocese, but this does not mean that everyone within the bishopric of Worcester was Hwiccan, nor need it mean that Worcester was located in Hwiccan territory; it simply means that as the most notable occupants of the diocese the name of the Hwicce was identified with the diocese as a whole. It is possible to name some groups who may have been non-Hwiccan but who occupied territory in the north of the diocese. The most notable of these are the *Arosæte* of the Warwickshire Arrow valley;[45] west of them lay Phepson, named from the *\*Fepsæte*.[46] The *Husmerae* are identified as living in the north-eastern corner of the diocese by charter-evidence,[47] whilst the place-names Wyre (Forest) and Worcester itself record the group called the *Wiogorna*.[48] These units had separate political identities, judging from the fact that the *Arosæte* appear alongside the Hwicce in the Tribal Hidage,[49] the fact that the *Husmerae* were seen as a *prouincia* and also the possibility that later administrative divisions reflected their boundaries.[50] Considering their locations, just south of the Mercian heartlands, it is likely that these groups were subject to Mercian hegemony in a way the Hwicce were more able to resist – the only rulers recorded acting in the territories north-east of Worcester are after all Mercian, not local or Hwiccan.

[43] David Dumville, 'The Tribal Hidage: An Introduction to its Texts and their History', in *Origins of Anglo-Saxon Kingdoms*, ed. Bassett, pp. 225–30, at pp. 226–9; S 197/ *Charters of Peterborough Abbey*, ed. S. E. Kelly, AS Charters 14 (Oxford, 2009), no. 8, p. 207; S 1272/ BCS 455; Hart, 'The Kingdom of Mercia', p. 54.

[44] Keith Bailey, 'The Middle Saxons', in *Origins of Anglo-Saxon Kingdoms*, ed. Bassett, pp. 108–22.

[45] Dumville, 'The Tribal Hidage', pp. 226–9.

[46] A. Mawer and F. M. Stenton with F. T. S. Houghton, *The Place-Names of Worcestershire*, EPNS 4 (Cambridge, 1927), 137–8; Margaret Gelling, 'The Place-Name Volumes for Worcestershire and Warwickshire: A New Look', in *Field and Forest: An Historical Geography of Warwickshire and Worcestershire*, ed. T. R. Slater and P. J. Jarvis (Norwich, 1982), pp. 59–78, at p. 69. Note that there is no reason for the *Fepsæte* to be connected to the Tribal Hidage group known as the *Færpingas* or *Feppingas* as, despite an apparent similarity, there are no elements of the names which are the same, see McKinley, 'Church-Patron Relationships', p. 229.

[47] S 89/BCS 154.

[48] Mawer and Stenton, *Place-Names of Worcestershire*, pp. 19–20.

[49] On the Hwicce (*Hwinca*) in the Tribal Hidage see J. Insley, 'Hwinca', *Reallexikon der germanischen Altertumskunde* 15 (2000), 296.

[50] Hooke, *Anglo-Saxon Landscape: The Hwicce*, pp. 77–87.

It is therefore possible to argue that Worcester was a Mercian bishopric, established as Worcester tradition states by a Mercian king, at a site convenient for Mercia, in an area of direct Mercian rule. The Hwiccan kings to the south may have been effectively independent rulers within the diocese, but Worcester was primarily a Mercian foundation. This in turn explains the recruitment pattern for early bishops of Worcester observed earlier, with outsiders being parachuted into the bishopric, generally before the death of the incumbent. This would allow Mercian rulers to ensure their choice of candidate, and provide a strong link between the Mercian court and the bishops.

This linkage can be seen in action during the reign of Æthelbald of Mercia, who made four recorded grants to Worcester, each of which seems to have had a particular purpose. Within the first year of his reign, Æthelbald exchanged salt works at Droitwich with Worcester; he later granted woodland and what was most likely sheep-grazing at Woodchester and Batsford, Gloucestershire, and a trading privilege at London.[51] By involving himself with the community's salt production, and by granting a trading privilege, Æthelbald was declaring himself protector of and provider for Worcester; the grants at Woodchester and Batsford also provided valuable resources for Worcester.[52] Essentially, as a patron of Worcester, Æthelbald was ensuring that it had resources it needed to meet its own needs, and also took steps to make acquisition of these easier. He was also tying the church to his own sphere of interest, for in order for his grants to be recognized people also had to recognize Æthelbald's authority to make these grants. It was therefore in Worcester's interest to promote their Mercian patron's authority to the detriment of other alternative sources of local power.

A diagrammatic representation of this can be seen by comparing Figure 4.2 with Figure 4.1. The former shows where Æthelbald's patronage within the diocese of Worcester was located. As can be seen, it is mutually exclusive from the area where Hwiccan rulers practised patronage as mapped on Figure 4.1. When we consider that two of those for whom Æthelbald provided land to found churches were relatives of the Hwiccan rulers, possible exiles from the courts of the Hwiccan kings,[53] this pattern begins to look quite aggressive – not only was Æthelbald emphasizing his royal power by granting land all around the Hwiccan core territory, but he

---

51   S 98/BCS 171; S 101/BCS 163; S 102/BCS 137; S 103/BCS 164.
52   McKinley, 'Church-Patron Relationships', pp. 240–3.
53   S 94/BCS 175; S 101/BCS 163. Note that this assumes that there were Hwiccan rulers contemporary with the greater part of Æthelbald's reign in Mercia, which is not actually historically attested.

was granting land to those who were potential threats to Hwiccan rulers. Worcester and its bishops were only one part in Æthelbald's schemes within the diocesan boundaries, but probably an important part.

It is likely that this situation was the norm prior to Æthelbald's death. Indeed, it is even likely that at times of Mercian weakness, Worcester's local position was threatened by Hwiccan rulers: thus during the reigns of Ceolred and Cenred of Mercia (704–16) there may have been an expansion of Hwiccan power into the Avon Valley area of Worcestershire – a sale of land at Ingon by the Hwiccan rulers Æthelheard and Æthelweard, the only recorded Hwiccan transaction north of the Worcestershire Avon, dates from this period.[54] That this expansion of power was not peaceful is suggested by a later Evesham tradition that records Æthelheard and Æthelweard seizing Stratford-upon-Avon from the bishopric of Worcester, and receiving Fladbury (also in the Avon Valley) in order to get them to relinquish the site.[55] An eighth- or early-ninth-century Worcester forgery may provide some support for this story as it purports to show Ecgwine, bishop at the time of Æthelheard and Æthelweard and, importantly, founder of Evesham, leasing Fladbury to Æthelheard.[56] This charter was forged as part of a sustained campaign to acquire Fladbury from various Hwiccan and Mercian rulers,[57] but it suggests that Fladbury may have been regarded as changing hands in the second decade of the eighth century, long before the story was recorded. That Ecgwine's construction of Evesham, another Avon Valley church, is placed in this context might suggest that Ecgwine was taking further measures to oppose Hwiccan influence in the area by constructing churches connected directly to Worcester. If any credence can be given to the papal immunity for Evesham that Ecgwine reputedly acquired, it too would fit well in this context, as Ecgwine sought to secure his foundation from Hwiccan aggression.[58]

So it is possible to sketch a picture of Worcester and its bishops dependent on Mercian support and, when this was not forthcoming, threatened by Hwiccan power. Yet this picture seems to vary after what could be regarded as momentous changes in 757, when Æthelbald was ultimately succeeded in Mercia by Offa, at best an extremely distant

---

[54]  S 1177/BCS 122. Note that S 54/BCS 116 appears to be a later forgery, and cannot be taken as evidence of a genuine grant of Æthelweard.

[55]  *Chronicon abbatiae de Evesham*, ed. Macray, pp. 71, 73.

[56]  S 1252/BCS 76 (second part).

[57]  McKinley, 'Church-Patron Relationships', pp. 315–20, 367–8, 390–2.

[58]  Jane Sayers, '"Original", Cartulary and Chronicle: The Case of the Abbey of Evesham', *Fälschung in Mittelalter, Internationaler Kongreß der Monumenta Germanicae Historica, München, 16.–19. September 1986*, Teil IV, *Diplomatische Fälschungen (II)*, Schriften der MGH 33 (Hanover, 1988), 371–95, at 374–80.

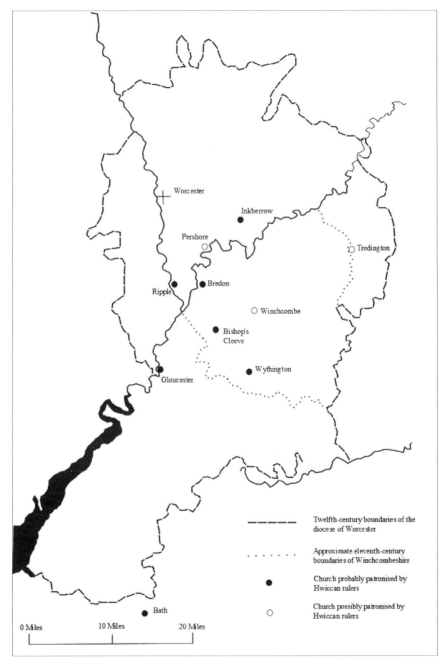

Figure 4.1. Churches probably or possibly patronised by independent (or quasi-independent) Hwiccan rulers

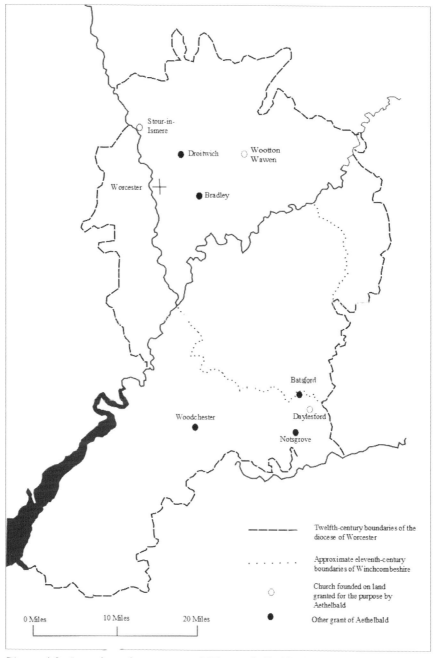

Figure 4.2.  Location of patronage of King Æthelbald of the Mercians (716–57)

kinsman to earlier Mercian kings,[59] and when Uhtred and his brothers appear as rulers of the Hwicce. The Mercian-appointed bishops are then replaced with bishops who, when their origins are apparent, were from the south of the diocese and who seem to have had more cordial relationships with the Hwiccan rulers. This appears to be something of a *volte face*, and demands some explanation.

One factor that may have changed is the nature of the Hwiccan rulers. Uhtred, Eanberht and Ealdred need not have been descendants of earlier kings of the Hwicce, a relationship which is purely modern conjecture.[60] What we do know is that S 55 records that the ruling brothers' parents were buried at Worcester, suggesting that wherever their ancestry the three ruling brothers were likely to have a much closer relationship with the bishopric than their predecessors. It should be noted that S 55 is not a charter than can be unconditionally accepted: the burial of parents is the sort of historicizing feature so beloved of forgers. Nevertheless, there need not be any particular problem with the idea that Uhtred, Eanred and Ealdred's parents were buried at Worcester.[61] Indeed, considering the increasing power and influence that Worcester could wield within the diocese as a result of Æthelbald's patronage, and perhaps as a conduit to the Mercian court, it would not be surprising if the Hwiccan kingship came into the hands of candidates well-disposed to Worcester. It would be nice to speculate on support from Worcester for the brothers' claim to the Hwiccan kingship, but this goes beyond the bounds of our evidence.

A second factor that may have forced changes was the Mercian king, Offa. Often described as predatory or aggressive, Offa certainly seems to have had problems with alternative centres of authority. He appears to have opportunistically downgraded and eliminated alternative kingships, including that of the Hwicce.[62] Furthermore, in a very Carolingian style, Offa seems to have seen the church as beholden to the king, and therefore ideally under his control, most famously perhaps in his

---

59  See the genealogies in David Dumville. 'The Anglian Collection of Royal Genealogies and Regnal Lists', *ASE* 5 (1976), 23–50, at 30–3, 36 and *ASC* 626, 716, 755: *ASC MS A*, ed. Bately, pp. 28, 34, 38.

60  Best illustrated by the conjectural history of the Hwiccan royal 'family' presented in Finberg, *Early Charters of the West Midlands*, pp. 167–80 and Smith, 'The *Hwicce*'. More judicious with the facts is J. Insley, 'Hwicce', *Reallexikon der Germanischen Altertumskunde* 15 (2000), 287–95.

61  There may be charter evidence for the burial of local notables at Worcester a generation or two later, if an argument is accepted that underlying the much reworked S 1185/ BCS 1007 is a transaction of the late eighth or early ninth century: McKinley, 'Church-Patron Relationships', pp. 376–82 (an argument which, however, regrettably fails to treat properly the names of those buried).

62  Simon Keynes, 'The Kingdom of the Mercians in the Eighth Century', in *Æthelbald and Offa: Two Eighth-Century Kings of Mercia*, ed. David Hill and Margaret Worthington, British Archaeological Reports, British ser. 383 (Oxford, 2005), 1–21, at 14.

disputes with Archbishop Jænberht of Canterbury and the elevation of Lichfield to an archbishopric.[63] Offa does not seem to have offered any actual patronage to Worcester until the middle of the 780s, some thirty years after ascending the throne; compare this with Æthelbald who made his first grant within a year.[64] This lack of support does not suggest that Worcester was a church favoured by Offa, and it may be that he saw it as a threat in his attempt to assert direct control over churches within the diocese. This is most apparent in a document deriving from the 781 Synod of Brentford, when Offa claimed possession of some six churches and their lands that were under the control of the bishopric of Worcester, represented by Bishop Hathored, a new appointment and potentially from the south of the diocese.[65] Offa's timing is significant – the disappearance of Ealdred, the last attested of the three joint rulers of the Hwicce is generally dated *c.* 780, with his last certain charter attestation being between 777 and 780.[66] It seems possible that Offa (characteristically) seized an opportunity to challenge a new bishop who could no longer draw on the support of an alternative (however subservient) ruler. Such opportunism and acquisitiveness may have given Offa a successful reign; it would also explain why Worcester might withdraw from its Mercian connection and start to focus within its own diocese, at least in terms of appointing bishops. The growing power of Worcester, changes in the Hwiccan ruling strategy and the policies of Offa would all lead the bishops of Worcester to alter the alignment of their church; despite all this, Offa increasingly attained a position in which he could make his will felt regarding Worcester's estates. It is no coincidence that only after Offa displayed his power at Brentford can we find evidence for his direct patronization of Worcester, for it was inherently unlikely that Offa would patronize a church that was not firmly under his thumb.[67]

Yet if we look at the ninth century we do not see Worcester as beholden to the Mercian court. It was neither a partner as under Æthelbald, nor a dependency such as Offa may have hoped to achieve. As a glance at the rather uncertain dates of the ninth-century episcopates will show, the ninth century at Worcester is rather less well-evidenced than the eighth;

---

[63]  Brooks, *Early History*, pp. 114–20.

[64]  S 102/BCS 137.

[65]  See above, p. 80 nn. 11–12.

[66]  The undated S 62/BCS 238. It is perhaps optimistic and very likely hind-sighted to see some significance in it being a disposal of property and an attempted resolution of the long-running Fladbury dispute which might be regarded as testimonial.

[67]  S 104/BCS 216 (dated 759 but with inconsistent witness-list) and S 107/BCS 221 (765) appear to be later forgeries relating to an estate at Pyrton in Oxfordshire. S 117/BCS 234 and S 118/BCS 235 date from 780, but are also likely forgeries, so S 120/BCS 239 of 26 December 780 (dated 781 on the charter, due to the earlier change of year) is the first charter likely to show transaction between Offa and Worcester.

enough evidence exists, however, to see a new trend, epitomized perhaps by Bishop Ealhhun, elected from within the Worcester community.[68] This is the growing power and influence of Worcester within the diocese. The bishops were able to deal with kings and ealdormen as equals, purchasing land and immunities for their estates.[69] Only Coenwulf I, the last great Mercian king, still patronized Worcester with outright gifts; his successors seem generally to have made sales.[70] The bishop could become involved in transactions outside of his own direct sphere – thus in 836, the community at Hanbury, Worcestershire, bought immunity from secular impositions; as part of the transactions associated with this grant and recorded as marginalia on the original charter the bishop paid off an ealdorman.[71] Yet the bishopric did not own Hanbury at this time – the charter is made out to Hanbury as an independent community. The bishop's interest was perhaps reforming, in that a bishop might be expected to try to minimise lay influence over churches. However, as John Blair has pointed out, it would also be to increase episcopal resources and power:[72] the bishop himself was an important political figure, and by buying out potential competitors, even the king, he was establishing a powerbase based on church estates. It is worth noting that over half of the known monastic foundations within the diocese of Worcester seem to have come into episcopal hands by the middle of the ninth century;[73] the example of Hanbury suggests that the bishop had interests in others also. Even fellow bishops were not safe – Bishop Deneberht established his rights over properties of the bishops of Hereford within the diocese.[74]

This may seem a rapid turnaround from the situation under Offa, but it is a logical corollary. Worcester became the obvious centre of local identity upon the disappearance of the Hwiccan kingdom: a powerful

---

68  *JW*, s.a. 872; II.298–300.
69  S 192/BCS 430; S 194/BCS 436; S 196/BCS 432; S 198/BCS 450; S 215/BCS 240. Cf. S 1272/BCS 455 (part 1), where King Berhtwulf leases land from Bishop Ealhhun.
70  S 182/BCS 359 of 817 is the last direct grant by a Mercian king to Worcester without mention of a counter gift (S 201/BCS 462 and S 206/BCS 541 are probably eleventh-century forgeries made out to St Mary's, Worcester, the new church built by Bishop Oswald in the tenth century; S 205/BCS 428 also does not seem authentic in its present form). This could of course reflect a change in diplomatic convention rather than the form of transactions, but tenth-century charters from Mercian centres do not conventionally imply sales or exchanges rather than gifts, suggesting that if this was a diplomatic change it disappeared surprisingly quickly, after a century of use, with the appearance of West Saxon rulers.
71  S 190/BCS 416.
72  Blair, *The Church in Anglo-Saxon Society*, pp. 131–2.
73  See the discussions in Sims-Williams, *Religion and Literature*, pp. 144–76 and Blair, *The Church in Anglo-Saxon Society*, pp. 115–16. It should be noted that minsters in the diocese of Worcester are of course often historically recognized only because they are recorded in the Worcester archive.
74  S 1431/BCS 309.

and established institution which had been acquiring lands from various rulers, and which was increasingly becoming locally connected. Towards the end of the eighth century, Worcester started visibly to benefit from the patronage of the local aristocracy, who left to it churches which their families possessed.[75] The motives for this are indeterminable, although the charters offer a hint in stating that it was for the donors' souls;[76] what it does reflect however is the improved standing of Worcester. The ninth-century bishops were in a position where they were locally powerful, often controlling local churches by tenure as well as spiritually. They had the wealth to deal with kings. They were clearly attractive patrons at a local level.

The bishops of Worcester built up a church, and a position, not through any consistent policy, but through adapting to circumstances. Although perhaps exceptional, they are unlikely to have been unique. Worcester's archives allow us to see the outlines of the processes in a way denied to us elsewhere amongst the Anglo-Saxons. From dependent agents of the Mercian court to free agents able to treat with kings, a plausible development of the evolving situation in which the often faceless bishops of Worcester found themselves can be made. This story is not complete in every detail, nor has it considered the great changes after 870 when a bishop of Worcester sought patronage from the West Saxon king,[77] nor the reforms of the tenth century. Yet hopefully this foreshortened narrative has shown how bishops could lead their communities, and be led by circumstances, and that by taking a broad view of these circumstances and of the bishops themselves, we can produce a coherent narrative into which to fit the known actions of bishops.

---

[75] S 1185/BCS 1007 (see McKinley, 'Church-Patron Relationships', pp. 376–82, for arguments regarding this as an altered essentially eighth-century record); S 1187/BCS 313.

[76] See the conclusions of McKinley, 'Church-Patron Relationships'.

[77] *Bishofs Wærferth von Worcester Übersetzung der Dialoge Gregors des Grossen*, ed. Hans Hecht, 2 vols. (Leipzig, 1900–7), p. 1; noting however that this preface may be the work of neither Werferth nor Alfred (see Janet Bately, 'The Alfredian Canon Revisited: One Hundred Years On', in *Alfred the Great: Papers from the Eleventh-Centenary Conferences*, ed. Timothy Reuter (Aldershot, 2003), pp. 107–20, at pp. 114–17), and that the translation may not have been part of Alfred's core vision (see Malcolm Godden, 'Wærferth and King Alfred: The Fate of the Old English *Dialogues*', in *Alfred the Wise: Studies in Honour of Janet Bately on the Occasion of Her Sixty-Fifth Birthday*, ed. Jane Roberts and Janet L. Nelson with Malcolm Godden (Cambridge, 1997), pp. 35–51.

# 5

# The Role of Bishops in Anglo-Saxon Succession Struggles, 955 × 978

DOMINIK WASSENHOVEN

Obiit tam inclitus rex .viii. Idibus Iulii; cuius obitu turbatus est status totius regni: commoti sunt episcopi, irati sunt principes, timore concussi sunt monachi, pauefacti populi [...][1]

WITH these words the anonymous author of the *Vita Sancti Oswaldi*, now believed to be Byrhtferth of Ramsey,[2] depicts the situation after the death of King Edgar in 975. The successions to the Anglo-Saxon kingdom in the second half of the tenth century were indeed quarrelsome. In this chapter, I will try to present the role of the bishops in these succession struggles. I focus on bishops because the organization of the church was probably more sophisticated than that of the lay magnates and the kingdom itself, and thus the bishops could possibly ensure continuity where the laity perhaps was not able to do so. Examining the bishops' activities can give insights into the scope of action they had at their disposal. Furthermore, the incentives for a bishop to decide in favour of one of the candidates will be dealt with, as well as questions such as: Did he act primarily on behalf of his own bishopric? Which factors were involved in his decision? Were some of the bishops responsible for the continuity from one king to his successor? The answers to these questions, as far as the sources provide insights into the events, should shed light on the relationship between bishop and king in Anglo-Saxon

---

[1] 'This great king died on 8 July [975]; at his death the commonwealth of the entire realm was shaken: bishops were perplexed, ealdormen were angry, monks were struck with fear, the people were terrified [...]': Byrhtferth of Ramsey, *Vita S. Oswaldi*, in *The Lives of St Oswald and St Ecgwine*, ed. and trans. Michael Lapidge (Oxford, 2009), pp. 1–203, at pp. 122–3. Cf. the earlier translation in Whitelock, *EHD*, p. 912: 'The illustrious king died on 8 July, and by his death the state of the whole kingdom was thrown into confusion, the bishops were agitated, the noblemen stirred up, the monks shaken with fear, the people terrified [...]'. I would like to thank Levi Roach for his valuable suggestions and for correcting the errors I made. I am, of course, responsible for any remaining inconsistencies.

[2] *Lives of Oswald and Ecgwine*, ed. and trans. Lapidge, pp. xxxvi–xxxviii.

England as well as on the issue of the extent to which the bishops in the latter half of the tenth century were not only leaders of the church, but also political leaders.

### Oda, Cynesige, and the situation of 955–9

The oldest *Vita Sancti Dunstani* includes a description, as famous as it is dramatic, of the feast after the coronation of Eadwig, who had become king in 955 at the age of fifteen. The anonymous author, who is only known by the first letter of his name, B., tells us how Eadwig was enticed by the noblewoman Æthelgifu and her daughter, Ælfgifu. While the nobles celebrated the anointing of the new king, Eadwig left the feast and withdrew to his chamber, together with the two women. Some time later, Oda, the archbishop of Canterbury, asked his fellow bishops and other leading men to go and bring back the king. At first, nobody reacted because of the fear of falling from the king's grace; but finally they chose Dunstan and his kinsman, Bishop Cynesige, to fetch Eadwig. When they entered the room,

> invenerunt regiam coronam, quæ miro metallo auri vel argenti gemmarumque vario nitore conserta splendebat, procul a capite ad terram neglegenter avulsam, ipsumque more maligno inter utrasque, velut in vili suillorum volutabro, creberrime volutantem.[3]

The two clerics asked the king to come back to the feast but, as he refused, Dunstan raised the king up, restored the crown to his head and brought him back to the royal assembly – ignoring the women's reluctance.

Though this episode is well-known, it is nevertheless worthwhile to take a closer look at some of the actors in this scene. In doing so, we have to keep in mind that B.'s report of the events is biased, since he wants to show Dunstan in a favourable light; but Dunstan was later exiled by Eadwig, so B., writing retrospectively, deprecates the king. The dropped crown seems to be a symbol for Eadwig not being the right man on the throne, but that is of course a later interpretation by the author. It is highly

---

[3] 'they found the royal crown, marvellously worked with gold, silver and gems, carelessly thrown down on the floor, far from his head, and the king repeatedly wallowing between the two women, in evil fashion as if in a vile sty': *Vita Sancti Dunstani, Auctore B*, in *Memorials of Saint Dunstan, Archbishop of Canterbury*, ed. William Stubbs, RS 63 (London, 1874), pp. 3–52, at ch. 21, pp. 32–3; Whitelock, *EHD*, p. 901. See also Nicholas Brooks, 'The Career of St Dunstan', in *St Dunstan: His Life, Times and Cult*, ed. Nigel Ramsay, Margaret Sparks and Tim Tatton-Brown (Woodbridge, 1992), pp. 1–23, at pp. 14–15.

questionable whether the incident happened as B. has described it, but in any case his account shows the attitudes of some of the persons involved.

Dunstan was still abbot of Glastonbury at the time Eadwig was consecrated. As in this chapter the focus is on bishops, I will now turn to Oda and Cynesige. The latter became bishop of Lichfield in 949 at the latest. He attested several charters of King Eadred, Eadwig's uncle and predecessor: four in 949, one in 950, two in 953 and another five in 955.[4] In the first year of Eadwig's reign, he appears also in the witness lists of three (or maybe four) of Eadwig's charters (if the fourth one is to be regarded as genuine).[5] But we have to bear in mind that no less than sixty charters issued by Eadwig in that same year, 956, are extant. This is an extraordinarily large number of charters issued within one year. And as Simon Keynes has shown, Cynesige seems to have been excluded from the group of the king's counsellors, the *witan*, for about one year, probably not long after the coronation feast.[6] Afterwards, he only appeared in one of Eadwig's charters, in 957.[7] From this documentary evidence we can assume a breach between Eadwig and Cynesige, at least a temporary one. The question of whether B.'s report of the events is accurate remains unanswered, but the fact that Cynesige did not support Eadwig seems to be attested.

What were the reasons for this discord? One possible factor is that many of the protagonists were related. As Nicholas Brooks argued, 'there is an obvious possibility' that Dunstan had already been in conflict with Ælfgifu's kin.[8] Ælfgifu's brother was most likely Æthelweard, who was later ealdorman of the western shires of Wessex. Thus, Ælfgifu seems to originate from western Wessex, as does Dunstan. He had once been driven out of Glastonbury as a boy, which may be a hint of an earlier conflict. B. calls Cynesige Dunstan's *consanguineus*, that is his blood relative. So maybe the underlying cause – or at least one of the causes – for the conflict between Dunstan, Cynesige and probably some others, who do not appear in the sources, on the one side and King Eadwig, his later wife Ælfgifu and her mother Æthelgifu on the other side can be found in a family dispute. I would like to emphasize that this is just a conjecture, because we do not have indisputable evidence that Dunstan and Cynesige were related, nor for the kinship of Ælfgifu and Æthelweard. But I think, nevertheless, it is a likely conjecture, and one that fits the pattern of the

4    S 544, 546, 549–50, 552a, 560–1, 563–6, 569.
5    S 582, 597, 605, 629. The possible forgery is S 605.
6    Simon Keynes, *The Diplomas of King Æthelred 'the Unready' 978–1016: A Study in their Use as Historical Evidence* , Cambridge Studies in Medieval Life and Thought, 3rd ser., 13 (Cambridge, 1980), p. 49.
7    S 646.
8    Brooks, 'Career of St Dunstan', p. 15.

early years of Eadwig's reign, because Eadwig seems to have attempted governance largely independent of the advisers who had served his father and his uncle. Dunstan and Cynesige obviously belonged to a group at court not in favour with the new king, or not favouring the new king nor, especially, his designated wife.

If we follow B.'s account, the factions at court could have led to the division of the kingdom, though Dunstan's biographer does not explicitly say so. However, he depicts a Mercian rebellion: Eadwig was despised by the northern people

> quoniam in commisso regimine insipienter egisset [...] Sicque universo populo testante publica res regum ex diffinitione sagacium sejuncta est, ut famosum flumen Tamesæ regnum disterminaret amborum.[9]

That the division of the kingdom should have been the result of a Mercian rebellion is not reflected in other early sources. Two versions of the Anglo-Saxon Chronicle just state 'Her Eadgar Æþeling feng to Myrcna rice'.[10]

We do not know what Cynesige did nor where he stayed during his exclusion from the *witan*. As already mentioned, he witnessed one of Eadwig's charters in 957, on 9 May, to be precise, in which the king made a grant of 40 hides at Ely to archbishop Oda.[11] This charter is also witnessed by Edgar. The division must have taken place afterwards, in the summer of 957, and it is striking that Cynesige attested seven of the eight charters which Edgar issued in 958.[12] And what is more, he subscribed in the third to fifth position, in one occasion even in the second position, before the bishops Oskytel of York and Dunstan. Thus Cynesige could be regarded as one of Edgar's most prominent supporters at the beginning of his reign.

The division of 957 seems to have been, above all, a territorial one: the bishops north of the Thames witnessed Edgar's charters, whereas the southern bishops stayed with Eadwig.[13] However, there could be some

---

9    'because he acted foolishly in the government committed to him [...]. And thus in the witness of the whole people the state was divided between the kings as determined by wise men, so that the famous River Thames separated the realms of both.': *Vita Sancti Dunstani*, ed. Stubbs, ch. 24, pp. 35–6; Whitelock, *EHD*, p. 901. Cf. *JW, s.a.* 957; II.406.

10   'In this year the atheling Edgar succeeded to the kingdom of the Mercians': *ASC* 957 BC: *Two of the Saxon Chronicles Parallel,* ed. Charles Plummer (Oxford, 1892–9), I.113; Whitelock, *EHD*, p. 225.

11   S 646/BCS 1347.

12   S 674–6, 676a, 677–9. From then onwards, Cynesige is a frequent witness to Edgar's charters: S 681 (959), S 684 (960), S 691, 694 (961), S 705 (962), S 712, 712a, 713, 723 (963).

13   Simon Keynes, 'Edgar, *Rex Admirabilis*', in *Edgar, King of the English 959–975: New Interpretations*, ed. Donald Scragg (Woodbridge, 2008), pp. 3–58, at p. 8: 'Significantly, if perhaps not unexpectedly, bishops and ealdorman whose areas of responsibility lay

interesting deviations from this general scheme: Oda, for example, 'ceased attending the royal court in the course of the year 957', as we, again, can learn from the charter witness lists.[14] This could have been due to an illness preventing him from travelling to the court. But it is possible that Oda withdrew his backing for Eadwig during the crisis of that year, since it is known that in the following year he separated Eadwig and Ælfgifu, because they were supposed to be too closely related.[15] And if we recall the account of the coronation feast cited earlier, B. depicted the position taken by Oda as not entirely opposed to Eadwig, but more or less neutral.

Oda does not witness any of Edgar's charters up to his death in June 958, and there is only one hint in the sources that he may have supported the younger brother. In the *Vita Sancti Dunstani* written by Adelard of Ghent at the beginning of the eleventh century, so only a few years after B., the consecration of Dunstan in 958 is undertaken by Archbishop Oda – which would mean that Oda had crossed the Thames and come into Edgar's territory.[16] At first sight, this seems to be very odd. One would expect the northern archbishop of York to consecrate Dunstan, since his see was situated in Edgar's territory. However, there could be a reason why the archbishop of Canterbury took over. The archbishopric of York was held by Oskytel, who formerly had been bishop of Dorchester. He was translated to York in 956, but in all his subsequent attestations – at first for Eadwig and after the division for Edgar – he appears as 'episcopus', not as 'archiepiscopus'. He refused to call himself archbishop until he could travel to Rome and get the *pallium*. From 959 onwards, he subscribes as 'archiepiscopus'.[17] Thus, it is also possible that he in 958 refused to act as archbishop and instead sent for Oda, who was not only of Danish origin as Oskytel himself, but also his relative. The earlier *Vita Dunstani* by B., however, does not mention Oda in connection with Dunstan's consecration. And the later version by Adelard was drawn up in order to be read as twelve lections to the Christ Church community and was dedicated to the archbishop of Canterbury (Ælfheah, 1006–12), so he could have included the participation of Oda with his Canterbury audience in mind. To sum up, we cannot conclude whether Oda was a

north of the Thames, or in East Anglia, disappear from view' in Eadwig's charters after the division of 957.

[14]  Nicholas Brooks, *The Early History of the Church of Canterbury: Christ Church from 597 to 1066* (Leicester, 1984), p. 224.

[15]  *ASC* 958 D: *Two Chronicles*, ed. Plummer, I.113: 'Her on þissum geare Oda arce biscop to twæmde Eadwi cyning 7 Ælgyfe. forþæm þe hi wæron to gesybbe'. Cf. Brooks, *Early History*, pp. 224–5.

[16]  *Epistola Adelardi ad Elfegum archiepiscopum de Vita Sancti Dunstani*, in *Memorials of Saint Dunstan*, ed. Stubbs, pp. 53–68, at *lectio* vii, p. 60.

[17]  There is one exception (S 684/BCS 1056), dated 960, where Oskytel and Dunstan both subscribe as *episcopus*.

loyal but critical counsellor of King Eadwig or whether he decided to opt for a new prospect, namely Edgar.[18]

After Oda's death on 2 June 958, succession to the archbishopric of Canterbury provides some interesting details concerning the two kingly brothers. At first, Eadwig appointed Ælfsige, bishop of Winchester, to the metropolitan see. Ælfsige was probably one of the king's most reliable supporters and had witnessed nearly all of his numerous charters. Still in 958, Ælfsige made for Rome to fetch the *pallium*, but on the way – in early 959 – he encountered extreme weather and died crossing the Alps.

When Eadwig heard of Ælfsige's death from the fellow travellers who had returned, he elevated a certain Byrhthelm to the vacant archbishopric.[19] There is a strange coincidence of bishops with the name Byrhthelm during the years 956 to 959. All in all, there might have been up to five bishops with that name in these few years. The name is connected with the sees of London, Selsey, Sherborne, Wells, and Winchester. However, no bishops with that name are known at other times during the Anglo-Saxon period. Thus, it seems unlikely that there were as many Byrhthelms around and in office during these few years, particularly since no more than two bishops named Byrhthelm witnessed one charter at a time. I shall not go into the details of this riddle,[20] but it can be regarded as a fact that the Byrhthelm who was appointed to Canterbury had previously held the see of Wells because, after Eadwig's death, Edgar did not hesitate to remove Byrhthelm from Canterbury and send him back to Wells, installing Dunstan instead; this is pointed out by B. in his *Vita Dunstani*.[21] Edgar could do this easily, since Byrhthelm had not received the *pallium*, and he did it for political reasons, even though B. tries to explain that Byrhthelm was incapable of administering the archbishopric. And the most probable solution to the 'Byrhthelm riddle' is that the bishop of Wells previously had been bishop of London until the division of the kingdom in 957.[22] After this division, the bishop of London seems to have supported Eadwig, in spite of the fact that his see was situated in Edgar's dominion. If this interpretation is correct, it is not very surprising that Edgar decided to send Byrhthelm back to Wells immediately after Eadwig's death. However, this incident also indicates that not everyone must have agreed to the territorial segmentation of 957.

---

[18] Cf. Brooks, *Early History*, p. 227.

[19] *Vita Sancti Dunstani*, ed. Stubbs, ch. 26, pp. 37–8; cf. Brooks, *Early History*, pp. 237–8.

[20] See instead Patrick Wormald, 'The Strange Affair of the Selsey Bishopric, 953–963', in *Belief and Culture in the Middle Ages*, ed. Richard Gameson and Henrietta Leyser (Oxford, 2001), pp. 128–41.

[21] *Vita Sancti Dunstani*, ed. Stubbs, ch. 26, p. 38; cf. Brooks, *Early History*, p. 239.

[22] Wormald, 'Strange Affair', p. 137.

*Sidemann, Æthelwold, and the situation of 975–8*

The quotation at the beginning of this chapter from the *Vita Sancti Oswaldi*, composed between 997 and 1002 by Byrhtferth, a monk at Ramsey,[23] is an impressive report of the situation after Edgar's death in 975. Byrhtferth continues by describing the so called anti-monastic reaction,[24] and later adds:

> [...] dissensio et tribulatio undique aduenire, quam nec presules nec duces ecclesiasticarum et secularium rerum poterat sedare.[25]

The bishops were agitated, says Byrhtferth, but they could not resolve the conflicts. Unfortunately, the author gives no further details concerning the role of bishops except for the general remark that they incited the people.[26] Apart from that, he only mentions Sidemann of Crediton incidentally, because he was Edward's tutor. This Sidemann occurs regularly in the witness lists of Edgar's charters, at first as abbot[27] of St Peter in Exeter then, from 972, as bishop[28] of Crediton. Especially in the last years of Edgar's reign, in 974 and 975, he is quite often to be found at court. On that score it is astonishing that he does not subscribe a single charter issued by Edward, all the more since two of them, dated 976 and 977, might have been written at Crediton.[29] But we have to bear in mind that the charters are not as relevant for the years 975–8 as they are for the events of 955–9, for two reasons. First, there are only five of Edward's charters extant, so that the evidence we can obtain from them is rather limited. Second, Æthelred naturally did not issue charters before he became king;

---

[23] *Lives of Oswald and Ecgwine*, ed. and trans. Lapidge, p. xxxviii.

[24] See Shashi Jayakumar, 'Reform and Retribution: The "Anti-Monastic Reaction" in the Reign of Edward the Martyr', in *Early Medieval Studies in Memory of Patrick Wormald*, ed. Stephen Baxter, Catherine Karkov, Janet L. Nelson and David Pelteret (Farnham, 2009), pp. 327–52.

[25] 'there came [...] dissension and trouble, which neither the bishops nor the leading men in ecclesiastical and secular affairs were able to assuage': Byrhtferth, *Vita S. Oswaldi*, ed. and trans. Lapidge, pp. 136–7 . Cf. Whitelock, *EHD*, p. 914: 'there began to approach on all sides dissension and tribulation, which neither bishops nor leaders in ecclesiastical and secular affairs could allay'.

[26] '[...] episcopum instigat aduersus populum et plebem contra pastorem sibi prelatum.' ('[...] provokes bishop against people and people against the shepherd chosen for them'): Byrhtferth, *Vita S. Oswaldi*, ed. and trans. Lapidge, pp. 448–9: this part was not translated in Whitelock, *EHD*.

[27] S 668, 771, 786, 788, 805, 807.

[28] S 671, 751, 794, 794a, 795, 799–801, 803.

[29] S 830 (dated 976) and S 832 (dated 977); cf. Cyril Hart, *The Early Charters of Northern England and the North Midlands* (Leicester, 1975), p. 26 with n. 4. Regarding charter production at Crediton and Exeter, see Charles Insley, 'Charters and Episcopal Scriptoria in the Anglo-Saxon South-West', *Early Medieval Europe* 7 (1998), 173–97.

his first charter is dated to 979. This is a different situation compared to the mid tenth century where two kings were both issuing charters. Thus, we cannot conclude from Sidemann's absence from Edward's charters that he did not support his former pupil. Also Sidemann died in 977, as the B and C versions of the Anglo-Saxon Chronicle report in a quite elaborate fashion:

> In this year was the great assembly at Kirtlington, after Easter, and Bishop Sideman died there by a sudden death on 30 April. He was bishop of Devonshire, and he had wished his burial to be at Crediton at his episcopal see. Then King Edward and Archbishop Dunstan ordered that he should be conveyed to St Mary's monastery which is at Abingdon, and this was done, and he is also honourably buried at the north side in St Paul's chapel.[30]

It is remarkable that Sidemann's death gets so much attention in the Anglo-Saxon Chronicle, especially as this is the only reference to Crediton in the whole source. It is particularly notable that Edward and Dunstan buried the bishop at Abingdon and not at Crediton. What were the reasons to act against Sidemann's own wish? The most obvious solution would be a spatial one: the proximity. Kirtlington is about 20 miles north of Abingdon, whereas Crediton is more than 150 miles away. Another answer could be that Sidemann was of such importance for Edward that he wished his former tutor to be buried in one of the kingdom's leading houses. This could also explain why the incident is reported in the Chronicle in such detail. Apart from that, the relevance to Abingdon itself (where versions B and C were written) could give cause for this verbose note.

However, there is something else to be learnt from this annal, namely that Dunstan obviously supported Edward. If we look at the few charters once more, this is backed by the fact that Dunstan witnessed every single charter that Edward issued. But again, the charter evidence is ambiguous for Edward's reign: the only other bishop who subscribed all of Edward's charters which are still available is Æthelwold, the bishop of Winchester and former abbot of Abingdon. However, it has been stressed more than once that Æthelwold probably supported Æthelred, Edward's younger half-brother. Æthelred, who in 975 cannot have been older than nine years, was promoted by his mother Ælfthryth, Edgar's third wife. And as Barbara Yorke has shown, there was a long and, as it seems, close collaboration between Æthelwold and Ælfthryth.[31] The most striking evidence for this alliance is recorded in a grant of privileges by Edgar for the

---

[30] *ASC* 977 BC: *Two Chronicles*, ed. Plummer, I.122; Whitelock, *EHD*, p. 230.
[31] Barbara Yorke, 'Æthelwold and the Politics of the Tenth Century', in *Bishop Æthelwold: His Career and Influence*, ed. *eadem* (Woodbridge, 1988), pp. 65–88, at pp. 81–6.

New Minster at Winchester.[32] It was presumably composed by Æthelwold and contains a witness list where Edmund, the first son of Edgar and Ælfthryth, is listed as 'clito legitimus prefati regis filius', that means as legitimate ætheling, whereas Edward, his elder brother, signs as 'eodem rege clito procreatus', that is as the offspring of the aforementioned king, Edgar. Barbara Yorke concluded:

> At Winchester, a distinction seems to have been made between Edmund and Edward. Both were sons of Edgar, but only Edmund was *legitimus*, and his mother was Edgar's *legitima coniunx*.[33]

However, this charter dates from 966, and we cannot automatically conclude that later, after the death of the ætheling Edmund in 970 or 971,[34] Æthelwold still supported Ælfthryth and her claim for her second son Æthelred to be elected as king. As a matter of fact, there is no such evidence for the period of Edward the Martyr's reign. Only from 980 onwards do we learn from several sources that Æthelwold supported Ælfthryth again,[35] but that does not mean inevitably that he also supported her son Æthelred during Edward's reign.

What is more, in one of Æthelred's charters, issued between 999 and 1006, the king claims that Edward was elected unanimously by all the leading men, both lay and ecclesiastic.[36] This seems odd in an Æthelredian text, since he clearly had – or rather was made out to have – opposed Edward. But on the other hand, this phrase could also be propaganda, focusing on Æthelred's integrity and on the legitimacy of his succession. Be that as it may, there is a hint in the Anglo-Saxon Chronicle concerning Æthelwold's behaviour in 975. The D version reads as follows:

> In [Edward's] days because of his youth, the adversaries of God, Ealdorman Ælfhere and many others, broke God's law and hindered the monastic life, and destroyed monasteries and dispersed the monks and put to flight the servants of God, whom King Edgar had ordered the holy Bishop Æthelwold to institute […][37]

---

[32] S 745. For an edition, translation and discussion, see Rumble, *Property and Piety*, no. IV.

[33] Yorke, 'Æthelwold and the Politics', p. 83.

[34] *ASC* 970 DE, 971 G, 972 BC: *Two Chronicles*, ed. Plummer, I.118–19.

[35] Yorke, 'Æthelwold and the Politics', p. 85.

[36] S 937; *Charters of Abingdon Abbey*, ed. S. E. Kelly, AS Charters 7–8 (Oxford, 2001), no. 129 (p. 503): '[…] dum pater meus rex EADGAR, uniuerse terre uiam ingrediens, senex et plenus dierum migrauit ad Dominum, quod uidelicet omnis utriusque ordinis optimates ad regni gubernacula moderanda fratrem meum Eadwardum unanimiter elegerunt […]'.

[37] *ASC* 975 D: *Two Chronicles*, ed. Plummer, I.121; Whitelock, *EHD*, p. 229.

This annal was probably written by Wulfstan, archbishop of York, at the beginning of the eleventh century, as it is in his style, but the E and F versions have a shorter annal with roughly the same statement and also naming Æthelwold:

> And Ealdorman Ælfhere caused to be destroyed many monastic foundations which King Edgar had ordered the holy Bishop Æthelwold to institute.[38]

Since Ælfhere is in other sources characterized as a leader of the so called 'anti-monastic reaction' and, in the cited passage, is said to have destroyed monasteries Æthelwold was connected with, one could assume that Æthelwold himself would be on Edward's side, not on Æthelred's. But, sure enough, the division between an anti-monastic group on one side and a group loyal to the king on the other was not as clear as some later sources delineate it. Different scholars have made the observation that there was not one unitary anti-monastic party struggling against the beneficiaries of Edgar's reign.[39] It is even doubtful if there was any connection between the activities against monasteries and the struggle for the kingship at all. It is more likely that some magnates who were disadvantaged during the process of reforming the monasteries in Edgar's reign exploited the unstable situation after his death in order to recover what they saw as their own property.

So how then should we handle the different and incongruous sources concerning Æthelwold's position during Edward's reign? I would like to propose two possibilities. The first one is that Æthelwold did not support Æthelred at all. A conceivable explanation for this position could be that a young king would weaken the state of the kingdom. But this is not very plausible, since Æthelred was backed by Ælfthryth, and Æthelwold's connection to her could guarantee him some influence. Also, Ælfthryth later collaborated with Æthelwold again, as I have said already. The second option is that Æthelwold first backed Æthelred and Ælfthryth, but later submitted to the majority which had chosen Edward. This would explain why we find Æthelwold among the witnesses of Edward's charters. This option is more likely in my opinion, though owing to the scarcity of sources it is unlikely that we will ever find conclusive proof of Æthelwold's position.

Finally, I would like to take a step back and see if it is possible to determine the role of some of the bishops in tenth-century succession struggles. I can here only give some preliminary considerations which will need to be further examined. One element that was very significant during

---

[38] *ASC* 975 EF: *Two Chronicles*, ed. Plummer, I.119, 121; Whitelock, *EHD*, p. 229.
[39] See Jayakumar, 'Reform and Retribution', esp. pp. 348–52.

the 955–9 struggle and, to a lesser extent, also during that of 975–8, was that of interconnection. While it is obvious that personal relationships play a major role in disputed successions, especially in a community where orality and symbolic communication are far more important than the written word, the ties of kinship between several of the persons involved – including bishops – seem to have been very strong, and often lasted several decades. It is therefore important to keep in mind that the bishops, or nearly all of them, stemmed from the nobility (even if there is not proof in every case) and were thus not a group separated from, but heavily intertwined with, the lay magnates.

Unfortunately, it is not possible to determine explicitly why a bishop decided to support a particular royal candidate. This is due to the scarcity of sources, which yield few references to the role of the bishops. One could cautiously draw the conclusion that the bishops did not provide continuity, but that they took wider and longer-term considerations into account. I am aware that these arguments need more backing and thus further research.

At the beginning of the eleventh century the bishop was depicted by Wulfstan of York in his *Institutes of Polity* as a central figure in society, and as a teacher and herald of God's law,[40] but the ultimate power on earth belonged to the king, not to the bishop.[41] The question is whether this depiction accords with the deeds of the bishops a few decades earlier – and with Wulfstan's own activities as well, since he witnessed the struggle for the throne in the years 1013–16. But this question cannot be answered here and has to be left to future research. At least, Wulfstan's representation of a bishop is in accordance with the activities of the bishops that have been analysed in this chapter, since the impression gained from the few sources is that the bishops merely conducted the process of royal succession rather than taking the lead in it.

[40] *Die 'Institutes of Polity, Civil and Ecclesiastical': Ein Werk Erzbischof Wulfstans von York,* ed. Karl Jost, Schweizer anglistische Arbeiten 47 (Bern, 1959), 62: 'And bisceopas syndon bydelas and Godes lage lareowas […]'. See further, Introduction (Rumble), above, pp. 10–12.

[41] This can be deduced from a small text by Wulfstan called *Incipit de synodo,* see *Councils & Synods,* ed. Whitelock, no. 54, pp. 406–13, at pp. 412–13: 'Bisceopum gebyreð þæt hi mid geþylde geþolian þæt hi sylfe gebetan ne magan, oð þæt hit þam cyncge gecyþed weorðe; 7 bete he syððan Godes æbylhþe þær bisceop ne mæge, gif he Godes willan rihte wylle wyrcean 7 his agene cynescype rihtlice aræran' ('It befits bishops that they endure with patience what they themselves cannot amend, until it is announced to the king; and he is afterwards to amend the offence against God where the bishop cannot, if he wishes to do God's will aright and rightly to exalt his own royal dignity.'). *Incipit de synodo* can also be found in *Institutes of Polity,* ed. and trans. Jost, pp. 210–16. See further, Introduction (Rumble), above, pp. 12–13.

# 6

# Image Making:
# Portraits of Anglo-Saxon Church Leaders

GALE R. OWEN-CROCKER

WHEN I imagine St Cuthbert, I draw on two unrelated pictures. The first is of the hermit saint described in Bede's near-contemporary *Historia Ecclesiastica* and the *Vitae* of St Cuthbert. I thus see him as emaciated from a diet consisting, in his last days, entirely of raw onions; and in the boots which he wore day and night, only removing them for the Maundy footwashing ceremony at Easter, when the calluses from constant friction were revealed. I visualize him in simple undyed clothes, blending in with the wild seas and bleak landscape of my native Northumberland. The folk memory of the area softens the image slightly: legends of Cuthbert communing with seals, which still inhabit the waters around Lindisfarne, the familiar naming of the wild birds as 'Cuddie ducks', or 'St Cuthbert's ducks', and the local pronunciation of the place-name: not 'Lindisfarne' or, as the tourist would read it off the map, '*Holy* Island', but 'Holy *Island*', which takes for granted the palpable sanctity the place still manifests.

My second image is of a kind of silken cocoon. The saint's body, possibly embalmed but increasingly desiccated and skeletal, came to be swathed in layer after layer of precious textile, Chinese and Byzantine silks: not, on the whole, tailored garments but rather lengths of cloth, with the glint of gold from the embroidered stole, maniple and girdle which King Æthelstan probably presented to Cuthbert's shrine. Some of the textiles were older than the saint himself; but most of them, including the tenth-century embroideries, were added to his coffin centuries after his death. Like the Lindisfarne Gospels (BL, Cotton Nero D. iv), which were eventually kept in the coffin, this magnificence was posthumous tribute to the hermit saint. Only a robe which has been called a dalmatic, and the pectoral cross, found in the innermost layers of wrappings, are likely to be contemporary. The cross, made of gold and inlaid with garnets (and matching red glass – which was arguably rarer than the garnets in seventh-century England), employs the same materials as the most extravagant secular jewellery of Sutton Hoo and Kent and the jewelled hilts of the Staffordshire Hoard. Its material value and its seventh-century date are securely established by comparison with these elite artefacts. Yet Cuthbert's cross is somewhat austere in its design and, with space for a small relic behind the central setting, the quincunx of jewels representing the five wounds of Christ, and the meaningful use of twelve cloisons in each of the four arms reminding us of twelve disciples and four evangelists, it is unmistakably ecclesiastical. It demonstrates that Cuthbert, as bishop, manifested the magnificence of God's church. Yet that magnificence is humanized when we contemplate that the cross was broken and repaired; the suspension loop is a substitute and the bottom arm was broken, a point weakened perhaps by the bishop, possibly Cuthbert himself, repeatedly holding the cross up to bless and to be kissed. Many of the occasions when Cuthbert's coffin was opened are documented,[1] and some gifts, like the stole and maniple, can be plausibly dated; but the pectoral cross is not mentioned in any documents, and, hidden in textiles which were apparently not much disturbed over the centuries, it remained unknown to the later Anglo-Saxons and was only brought to light when the tomb was excavated in the nineteenth century, since when it has become an icon of Anglo-Saxon culture.

## Images in Manuscripts

When an Anglo-Saxon illuminator portrayed Cuthbert in manuscript art it was neither as hermit nor relic, but as a living ecclesiastic in vestments. In what is the earliest surviving 'portrait' in an Anglo-Saxon manuscript, King Æthelstan is depicted presenting a copy of Bede's *Vita Sancti Cuthberti* to the saint himself (see Fig. 6.1).[2] The book is thought to have been presented on the king's visit to the Cuthbert shrine at Chester-le-Street in 934.[3] The unobtrusive frame is filled with plant ornament, including the vine scroll, symbol of Christ, which had been a major feature of Northumbrian sculptural art since the seventh century, especially the inhabited vine in which naturalistic mammals and birds perch and peck, demonstrating God's creation of the world with its plants and animals. The frame

---

[1]  'Historical Introduction', in *The Relics of Saint Cuthbert*, ed. C. F. Battiscombe (Oxford, 1956), pp. 21–64.

[2]  CCCC 183, fol. 1v. According to Thomas H. Ohlgren, *Insular and Anglo-Saxon Illuminated Manuscripts: An Iconographic Catalogue c. A.D. 625–1100* (New York and London, 1986), p. 82, there is also a 'rough, drypoint sketch of the full-length saint Cuthbert' in BL, Cotton Vitellius A. xix, fol. 8v.

[3]  Mildred Budny, *Insular, Anglo-Saxon and Early Anglo-Norman Art at Corpus Christi College, Cambridge: An Illustrated Catalogue*, 2 vols. (Kalamazoo, MI, 1997), I. 164.

Figure 6.1. CCCC, fol. 1v: Bede's *Life of St Cuthbert*: King Æthelstan and St Cuthbert. © The Master and Fellows of Corpus Christi College, Cambridge. All Rights Reserved

also displays the more recent motif of the acanthus plant, a Byzantine/ Carolingian import to southern England which was to become a major feature of Winchester Style art. The frame thus brings together the tastes of Cuthbert's northern realm and Æthelstan's Wessex. Æthelstan, himself arguably a leader of the Anglo-Saxon church as benefactor and assiduous relic collector, occupies more than half of the space in the picture, and is shown against an archway with roof shingles, architecture suggesting a secular palace, sketching, in a simpler way, the kind of structure that frames King Edward the Confessor in the Bayeux Tapestry.[4] St Cuthbert emerges from an adjacent structure. Its pitched roof, with crosses, its shingles, arcading and brick or shingle and plank walls indicate that it is a church; symbolically it is perhaps The Church. The merging of the two buildings behind Cuthbert's halo and hand demonstrates the union of secular royal power and the ecclesiastical, which Æthelstan's patronage had brought; but the narrowness of the church building and the way Cuthbert is enclosed by its rectangular entrance suggest the coffin in which the saint's body was contained when Æthelstan visited him, a reliquary which still exists today in Durham Cathedral. Though the king bends in a humble way, he is crowned with gold, his cloak is purple and his hose and shoes scarlet, suggesting expensively dyed garments. There is a yellow-coloured border to his tunic, and yellow dotted decoration at wrist and shoulder, which may indicate that his garments are embroidered with gold, perhaps even jewelled. It is the same blend of humility and royal opulence which King Edgar later achieves in the New Minster Refoundation Charter,[5] prostrating himself before Christ yet crowned and dressed in scarlet, blue and gold.

The saint raises his right hand in blessing and is vested as a bishop. It was as prior, then as bishop, of Lindisfarne that Cuthbert was a leader of the Anglo-Saxon church, in that he oversaw the absorption of Roman Christianity in the monastery that had been founded as the heart of Celtic Christianity in Northumbria. The resulting fusion of culture has left its heritage in the art of the so-called 'Golden Age of Northumbria', in which Roman naturalism, Saxon zoomorphism and Celtic ornament come together in an eclectic burst, most famously in the Lindisfarne Gospels dedicated to Cuthbert himself.

Cuthbert here is simply dressed in a white alb and a chasuble. The chasuble, though, is scarlet and the orphreys on it are painted yellow,

4  David Wilson, *The Bayeux Tapestry* (London, 1985), plate 1.
5  BL, Cotton Vespasian A. viii, fol. 2v. For the manuscript context, see Rumble, *Property and Piety*, pp. 69–72. For a liturgical reading of the miniature, see Catherine E. Karkov, 'The Frontispiece to the New Minster Charter and the King's Two Bodies', in *Edgar, King of the English 959–75: New Interpretations*, ed. Donald Scragg (Woodbridge, 2008), pp. 224–41.

suggesting gold work though not embroidery. We should not be surprised at the absence of the pectoral cross, since that had arguably been hidden since Cuthbert's death in 687 or at least since his translation eleven years later; or at the lack of a mitre, because this item of episcopal dress was not introduced until the eleventh century, and the mitre which Reginald of Durham recorded in the coffin at the saint's translation of 1104 was presumably an addition to keep the dead saint's vestments up to date.[6] What *is* surprising is that he does not wear the stole and maniple which would have been normal for bishops and priests by this time. It is entirely possible that the artist knew of Æthelstan's forthcoming gift of stole and maniple and assumed, probably correctly, that the corpse was not vested in these items already. Sarah Keefer, however, suggests that since the stole, which was placed round the shoulders of a man as he was ordained priest, represented the yoke which priest and bishop bore in caring for their flock, it is omitted because Cuthbert is now removed from the cares of this world.[7]

The artist of the tenth-century Benedictional of St Æthelwold (BL, Additional 49598) similarly manipulates vestments. In what is probably only half of the original illumination of the Choir of Confessors, SS Gregory, Benedict and Cuthbert are all depicted in full pontifical regalia, their visible garments from inner to outer being alb, stole, dalmatic, amice round the neck, chasuble and *pallium*;[8] they have crowns on their heads. The crowns are symbolic. None of these men was a king. Robert Deshman explains the crowns plausibly enough as evidence that, as saints, the figures have become 'co-rulers of the heavenly kingdom with Christ the king',[9] part of a complex crown iconography played out through the manuscript.[10] Gregory, the driving force behind the Roman mission to Kent, was pope, and so is entitled to wear the *pallium*, but it is not correct dress for either Benedict or Cuthbert.[11] Furthermore, since Benedict was neither priest nor bishop he should not be wearing ecclesiastical vestments, though as an abbot he was equivalent in status to a bishop so perhaps this justifies it.[12] Deshman explains the anomaly in the light of the Benedictine reform in England, whereby it became the

6   *Relics of Saint Cuthbert*, ed. Battiscombe, p. 42.
7   Sarah Larratt Keefer, 'A Matter of Style: Clerical Vestments in the Anglo-Saxon Church', *Medieval Clothing and Textiles* 3 (2007), 13–39, at 35.
8   Keefer, 'A Matter of Style', p. 38, where the Latin names of the vestments are used.
9   Robert Deshman, *The Benedictional of Æthelwold*, Studies in Manuscript Illumination 9 (Princeton, NJ, 1995), p. 149.
10  Deshman, *Benedictional*, pp. 117–19, 136–7,150.
11  Sarah Larratt Keefer, 'Every Picture Tells a Story: Cuthbert's Vestments in the Benedictional of St Æthelwold', *Leeds Studies in English* 37 (2007), 111–34. For the significance of the *pallium*, see above, p. 6, n. 26 (Levison and Lamb).
12  Keefer, 'A Matter of Style', p. 38, n. 88.

practice for bishops to be monks, and Æthelwold himself, the patron and user of the Benedictional, was both bishop of Winchester and abbot of the Old Minster there.[13] This strikes me as sleight of hand; the fact that it had become desirable for a bishop to be a monk does not justify representing a monk as a bishop.

Theological reasoning apart, undoubtedly the episcopal vestments gave more scope to the painter's luxuriously wide-ranging palette of colours and the swirling animation of the Winchester Style than a monochrome monastic habit would have done. All three of the main protagonists here wear different coloured chasubles; and Benedict's dalmatic is patterned in a way which could, if realistic, only have been achieved by the use of woven silk or elaborate embroidery, both opulent; and the dangling *pallia* make convenient places to write the names and offices of the three saints.

St Benedict, a popular figure in Anglo-Saxon art, rarely, if ever, appears there as a simple monk.[14] In Orléans, Bibliothèque Municipale 175, fol. 149v, he wears vestments and carries an episcopal crozier.[15] He appears again in the Benedictional of St Æthelwold, enthroned, with a circular diadem on his head, which Deshman argues 'assimilate[s] him to Christ',[16] again wearing vestments, at the benediction for the Translation of St Benedict (fol. 99v). He holds a book, presumably the *Regula Sancti Benedicti*, and a crown to be won by those who follow him in virtuous monasticism. The curtains on either side of his head indicate that he is indoors, and the arch under which he sits is flanked by towers, walls, rows of windows and roofs. Above, asymmetrical buildings fill both angles inside the frame of the picture. If this indicates a monastery, it is a very grand one indeed. Perhaps it is not; could it be the City of God? Benedict appears again, seated, crowned with a diadem, in highly emblematic illuminations in the Arundel Psalter[17] (fol. 133r) and BL, Cotton Tiberius A. iii (fol. 2v). He wears the breastplate of justice, clasping together a cape which Deshman describes as 'cope'.[18] In both cases richly patterned fabrics associated with the saint – his garment, his cushions, his breastplate – contrast with the simplicity of the monks who receive the Rule and are bound by it. Both these illuminations combine image and text: there are words dangled by the hand of God, on the saint's halo, diadem and

---

13   Deshman, *Benedictional*, pp. 172–3. See above (Rumble), pp. 21–3.
14   Possibly it is Benedict seated as a tonsured monk flanked by two others in BL, Arundel 155, at fol.10r: Ohlgren, *Iconographic Catalogue*, p.185, item 171.2; Francis Wormald, *English Drawings of the Tenth and Eleventh Centuries* (London, 1952), pl. 24b.
15   Thus Ohlgren, *Iconographic Catalogue*, p.107, item 148.1; partially shown in C. R. Dodwell, *Anglo-Saxon Art: A New Perspective* (Manchester, 1982), p. 62, pl. 11.
16   Deshman, *Benedictional*, p. 118.
17   BL, Arundel 155.
18   Deshman, *Benedictional*, p. 203.

breastplate, on books, on the girdle of the monk who kneels at Benedict's feet in the Arundel manuscript, and on the diadem and its lappets and the roll which binds the monk in the Cotton manuscript. Just as these pictures combine several levels and areas of action, so they encompass multiple times: monks, in the present of the Benedictine reform, receiving and committing to the Rule; Benedict in the past giving the Rule, but in his diadem and throne, representing Christ, in the remoter past but ever-present; and the Hand of God, eternal.

This telescoping of time is also present with the inclusion in the Bene-dictional of two English saints, Æthelthryth, who flourished in the seventh century, and Swithun, bishop of Winchester in the ninth. The cults of both were vigorously developed at the time of the Benedictine reform. Æthelthryth was celebrated by Bede in the *Historia Ecclesiastica*, in an extensive and dramatic prose narrative and a poem.[19] Twice married, she preserved her virginity, became a nun and founded the abbey of Ely, and after her death her body was miraculously preserved and the means of miracles. She appears twice in the Benedictional, first among the Choir of Virgins (fols. 1v–2r) where, together with Mary Magdalene, she is prominent and named by lettering on the book she carries, not visible in facsimiles. Curiously enough, though all the anonymous virgins in the double-page spread are crowned, Mary Magdalen and Æthelthryth are not, though Æthelthryth, through her second marriage to Ecgfrith of Northumbria, was in fact a queen, albeit a divorced one, and her royal birth and connections played a large part in the fact that she was able to train as a nun under a royal abbess and found a monastery on her own family lands. Instead of crowns the two most prominent virgins in the choir bear massive gold haloes which dwarf the crown of the third virgin with them; and they turn towards each other in apparent collaboration.

Æthelthryth appears again at the opening of the benediction for her feasts (fol. 90v; see Fig. 6.2). She has a decorated halo this time, and though she is dressed in the standard late Anglo-Saxon dress of the Virgin Mary and almost all other women in art, she has an extra bit of drapery down her back which may represent the nun's veil. Several of my students have suggested that the relative dullness of her clothing may reflect the asceticism of her life, which according to Bede was manifested in her choice of garments, and certainly her colours here lack the variety of other portraits in the book; but Deshman refers to her tunic as 'pink' and the shades may have been brighter than the brown and cream they appear today. She carries a book and a spray of flowers which Deshman relates directly to Bede's poem, which refers to her worthiness bearing

---

[19]  *HE*, IV.19(17)–20(18): ed. and trans. Colgrave and Mynors, pp. 390–401.

Figure 6.2.  BL, Additional 49598, fol. 90v: Benedictional of St Æthelwold:
St Æthelthryth. © British Library Board. All Rights Reserved

virgin flowers, and that as a nun and bride of Christ she herself flowered. Her blossoms appear to be lilies, which are biblical flowers and have come to represent the Resurrection, though I do not know if that meaning was established in the tenth century. She is surrounded by identifying text, not a background of landscape, buildings or furnishings as other miniatures have. The effect is starker, more in key with her asceticism. Outside that, is trellis opulently decorated with acanthus. She stands on the frame, enclosed by it yet firmly grounded on it. Acanthus frames were, as we have seen, not new, but this one is so prominent we cannot fail to notice it and perhaps we should question it further. Its leaves and lily-like flowers suggest the garden of Paradise, enclosing her now, as a saint, as the convent enclosed her in life. She looks out of her picture to the opposite page (fol. 91r) where Christ, her heavenly bridegroom, occupies a historiated initial at the opening of her text, which matches her background and is enclosed in a similar frame. This is not the only historiated initial in the manuscript containing Christ, but there are other large initials which are not illuminated in this way. The relationship is not chance.

A poem about the commissioning of this manuscript informs us that Æthelwold particularly requested 'many arches well adorned'.[20] The arched setting had been a feature of Anglo-Saxon manuscript art since the late antique Augustine Gospels (now CCCC 286) was brought to Canterbury with the Roman missions. In the Benedictional it reaches new heights, and we must remember that building and rebuilding were an essential part of the Benedictine reform, especially for Æthelwold who made the new shrine of St Swithun a central feature of the cult he fostered within the church he rebuilt magnificently. In the portrait (fol. 97v) which marks the feast of his deposition, Swithun is tonsured as a monk and vested as a bishop; yet more than this, he is both enclosed in the inner arch, as his body is enclosed in his shrine, and supporting it, as his holy presence supported the Old Minster and the reform movement. This inner architecture abuts and is framed by the heavy arch which is recurrent in other miniatures.[21]

We find a focus on the building yet again in the unusual miniature of a bishop pronouncing a blessing (fol. 118v; see Frontispiece). The miniature is associated with the blessing for the dedication of a church. The church is sketched in red. The external view shows it to be very large, consisting of several towers, a central belltower with three bells and two weathercocks. The interior includes a gallery from where the laity gaze down. Only the central figure and his immediate setting are coloured. The altar cloth is a rich purple, with a gold edging; the altar vessels are

[20]  Deshman, *Benedictional*, p. 148.
[21]  Deshman, *Benedictional*, p. 138.

Figure 6.3.  BL, Cotton Tiberius A. iii, fol. 2v: *Regularis Concordia*: King Edgar, Archbishop Dunstan and Bishop Æthelwold. © British Library Board. All Rights Reserved

gold. The bishop is vested in a blue chasuble with gold edging, and a gold acanthus leaf decorating the shoulder.[22] His stole and maniple are gold. This is a bishop in full magnificence. It is generally assumed to be Æthelwold himself.

We find him depicted again, posthumously, as architect of the Benedictine reform, in the frontispiece to a copy of the *Regularis Concordia* in BL, Cotton Tiberius A. iii (fol. 2v; see Fig. 6.3), a drawing which was later copied, minus the king, into what is now Durham, Cathedral Library, B.III.32. Enthroned beneath a triple arcade, the bishop on the left and the archbishop on the right – identified as such by his *pallium* – make a symmetrical group with the king, to whom they look. All three make gestures of blessing and King Edgar's sceptre takes the form of a palm. The ecclesiastics hold staffs which are tipped similarly to the palm. They hold firmly on to the parchment roll that represents the *Regula Sancti Benedicti*, and a monk below them is bound by it. Edgar no longer wears traditional secular dress as he did in the New Minster Refoundation Charter. The artist has given him the seated posture and the long robes that go with it, an emblem of authority with royal, Christological and abbatial connotations. He is Edgar, wearing the unique square crown that Dunstan is said to have made for him, but he also represents St Benedict and he represents Christ; as such, and as the Lord's anointed, he is the only one of the figures depicted full face.

None of the images I have discussed so far can be considered 'portraits' in the modern sense. Figures with identical faces are identified by their clothes and by text. The 'architects of the Benedictine reform' image, however, demonstrates more individuality than most: Æthelwold has a prominent nose, Edgar's beard is carefully drawn and Dunstan is bald. A tonsured monk would normally have a fringe of hair at the front, but the archbishop has no hair at the forehead. Sarah Keefer has raised the possibility that Dunstan wore a Celtic tonsure,[23] but I am unsure that an Anglo-Saxon would have such a thing so late in the period. There is a scatter of bald men in the illustrations of Anglo-Saxon art and it may have been remembered that Dunstan's hair was thinning at the front; but this eleventh-century picture is posthumous and was not drawn from life.

It gives an interesting insight into the psyche of the monk/bishop of the Benedictine reform that Dunstan had himself portrayed in a monastic habit at the feet of Christ in his own prayerbook.[24] If Deshman is correct

---

[22] Dodwell, *Anglo-Saxon Art*, p. 183.
[23] *Manuscripts of Durham, Ripon and York*, ed. Sarah Larratt Keefer, David Rollason and A. N. Doane, Anglo-Saxon Manuscripts in Microfiche Facsimile 14 (Tempe, AZ, 2007), 61.
[24] Bod, Auct F. 4. 32, fol. 1r.

in his identification, Æthelwold, too is portrayed as a monk, his girdle labelled 'zona humilitatis', in the Arundel Psalter (fol. 133r).[25]

'In the beginning was the Word' says St John's Gospel (I.1), and Christianity is a religion of the written word. Many of the figures depicted in Anglo-Saxon art are holding books or scrolls, presenting or receiving books, or writing them. Aldhelm, abbot of Malmesbury and bishop of Sherborne, is depicted several times, not specifically in those leadership roles but as author of the medieval best-seller, *De virginitate* 'In Praise of Virginity'. In different manuscripts he is shown in the act of writing,[26] seated by a lectern[27] and, twice, presenting his book to the nuns for whom he wrote it.[28] In Lambeth Palace 200 (see Fig. 6.4) he is tonsured and wears what looks like a cowled outer garment but he has elaborate sleeves and border to what might be a dalmatic and alb: a strange mixture. It is generally supposed that the leading female figure is Abbess Hildelith of Barking, one of the recipients mentioned in Aldhelm's preface to his work, and that the others are her nuns. However, if Scott Gwara is correct in his suggestion that the other women mentioned in the preface were not subordinate nuns but influential abbesses in their own right,[29] then it may be that in this group we have a depiction of some of the most important women of their day – royally connected West Saxon abbesses. The decoration on their clothing is unusual and suggests status. Another English author honoured by a drawing was Felix, who composed the *Vita Sancti Guthlaci*, but the drypoint sketch is incomplete and now barely visible, though Thomas Ohlgren asserts that it shows Felix offering his book to a king.[30]

St Gregory, founder of the Anglo-Saxon church, was a popular subject. He is more than once depicted with St Benedict, originator of the form of monasticism which the Anglo-Saxons eventually adopted, though they were not contemporaries. They appear together in the Benedictional (fol. 1r), with St Cuthbert; and as a pair, flanking Christ, in Orléans, Bibliothèque Municipale 175, fol. 149v, a manuscript of Gregory's homilies. Gregory also appears as recipient of a book presented by Hrabanus Maurus in Cambridge, Trinity College, B.16.3, fol. 1v. In addition, Gregory has been identified as the subject of a miniature in the form of a historiated initial which opens Book II of the St Petersburg manuscript of Bede's *Historia Ecclesiastica* (St Petersburg, National Library, lat. Q.v.I.18, fol. 26v), copied at Jarrow within a few years of the death of

---

[25] Deshman, *Benedictional*, p. 180.

[26] BL, Royal 7. D. XXIV, fol. 85v.

[27] Bod, Bodley 577, fol. 1r.

[28] London, Lambeth Palace Library, 200, fol. 68v; and Bod, Bodley 577, fol. 1v.

[29] Scott Gwara, *Aldhelmi Malmesbiriensis prosa De virginitate: cum glosa Latina atque Anglosaxonica*, CCSL 124A (Turnhout, 2001), 51*.

[30] CCCC 389, fol. 17v; Ohlgren, *Iconographic Catalogue*, p. 101 and photo 3.

Figure 6.4. Lambeth Palace 200, fol. 68v: Bishop Aldhelm and Abbess Hildelith.
© The Trustees of Lambeth Palace Library. All Rights Reserved

the author, or even during his lifetime. The identification is contentious, since the illumination is captioned 'Augustinus', but in a handwriting thought by some scholars to be an addition.[31] Since the Book opens with

---

[31]  See P. Meyvaert, *Bede and Gregory the Great*, Jarrow Lecture, 1964; and O. Arngart, 'Three Notes on the St Petersburg Bede: (i) The Augustinus Miniature', in *Names, Places and People: An Onomastic Miscellany in Memory of John McNeal Dodgson*, ed. Alexander R. Rumble and A. D. Mills (Stamford, 1997), pp. 1–7, at pp. 1–3.

an account of St Gregory, the identification with Gregory is entirely
possible, but since Bede particularly venerated Augustine of Canterbury,
the missionary whom Gregory sent to England, and since Book II of the
*Historia* includes the death of St Augustine, the interpretation indicated
by the caption, later or not, is plausible too. If so, this would be the only
known 'portrait' of Augustine of Canterbury. The figure carries a crozier
and wears vestments including a *pallium*, so could be either archbishop
or pope. His nimbus indicates that he is a saint.


## *Images in Textiles*

There is a strong tradition of figural art in English embroidery, with the
long, narrow stole and maniple providing a fertile ground for depictions
of holy figures, usually apostles and prophets. However, the silk and
gold maniple which was presented to St Cuthbert's shrine bears non-
biblical figures identified by embroidered inscriptions: two popes and
their deacons, all significant figures in the establishment of the liturgy.
One of the popes is St Gregory, here perhaps included as much for his
contribution to the revision of the Roman rite as to his establishment of
the English church. Ecclesiastical correctness is sacrificed to design here,
as it sometimes is in the Benedictional of St Æthelwold, since Gregory
both blesses and holds his maniple with the wrong arms.[32]

Athough many stole and maniple sets were embroidered with apostles
and prophets, there was evidently a tradition of including kings and saints
of English origin, usually as terminals. A set was found in Worcester
Cathedral in the nineteenth century in a tomb believed to belong to
William of Blois, bishop of Worcester from 1218 to 1236.[33] The embroideries probably date to a century before. In silk and silver-gilt, the stole
depicts the twelve apostles and the maniple almost certainly shows four
prophets. However, four wedge-shaped pieces, which were probably the
ends of the two vestments, were decorated with non-biblical figures, two
kings and two bishops.[34] One king is named as 'Adelbertvs', which is

---

[32] Christopher Hohler, 'The Stole and Maniples: (b) The Iconography', in *Relics*, ed.
Battiscombe, pp. 396–408, at pp. 401–2.

[33] A. G. I. Christie, *English Medieval Embroidery* (Oxford, 1938), pp. 53–4; Donald
King, 'Textiles and Embroideries',. in *English Romanesque Art, 1066–1200, Catalogue
of Exhibition in the Hayward Gallery, London 5 April – 8 July 1984*, ed. George
Zarnecki, Janet Holt and Tristram Holland (London, 1984), pp. 490–3, at p. 495;
H. B. Southwell, *A Descriptive Account of Some Fragments of Medieval Embroidery
Found in Worcester Cathedral* (n.p., 1914); Elizabeth Coatsworth, 'Stitches in Time:
Establishing a History of Anglo-Saxon Embroidery', *Medieval Clothing and Textiles*
1 (2005), 1–27, at 17.

[34] Possibly St Nicholas and an English saint, Thomas of Canterbury (Thomas Becket).

generally understood as a reference to an Anglo-Saxon king, Æthelberht. This 'Adelbertvs' is depicted beneath a semicircular roof with a tower projecting above it, architecture not unlike some of the architecture in the Bayeux Tapestry which is executed in the Anglo-Saxon tradition and dates to the 1080s. The position of the name is above his head and under the roof as Duke William's is in the 'Odo eps, Rotbert' inscription of the Tapestry[35] and is obviously in the same tradition. Whereas I would have assumed that 'Adelbertvs' was the King Æthelbert of Kent who received the missionary Augustine in 597, led his people in conversion and baptism, and was buried in St Augustine's Abbey, Canterbury, the pioneering expert on English medieval embroidery, Mrs Christie, considered this 'Adelbertvs', and also another on the fourteenth-century Toledo cope[36] to be St Æthelberht, King of the East Angles, who was murdered in 793 or 794 and sanctified after posthumous miracles.[37]

The tradition of commemorating native saints on embroidered vestments evidently continued into the twelfth century, though no other sets survive. The 1245 inventory of St Paul's Cathedral mentions a number of stole and maniple sets with embroidered figures, usually of apostles and prophets. Among them was a stole with St Oswald and St Nicholas on its extremities, and a maniple with SS Erkenwald and Edmund on its ends.[38] Three of these were Anglo-Saxon saints. The cathedral had the arm and a finger relic of St Oswald, the Northumbrian king, and a shrine to St Erkenwald,[39] a seventh-century bishop whose seat had been St Paul's. Edmund was king of East Anglia, martyred by the Vikings and made famous by the *vita* translated by Ælfric from Abbo of Fleury, *Passio Sancti Eadmundi*. Erkenwald appears on another stole and maniple set with a later saint, Thomas Becket, and St Paul and a Bishop Richard, while Oswald and Edmund appear on yet another set in the company of SS Thomas and Nicholas.

Another embroidered churchman is more controversial. The eleventh-century Bayeux Tapestry depicts the coronation of the short-lived King Harold II with the archbishop of Canterbury, Stigand, standing beside

---

[35] Wilson, *Bayeux,* pl. 48, right.

[36] Christie, *English Medieval Embroidery*, p. 156, pl. cix.

[37] He has thirteen churches and a cathedral dedicated to him and is named in many prayers though the information on his life comes from two fourteenth-century texts; 'St Ethelbert', *Catholic Encyclopaedia*, E <http://www.newadvent.org/cathen/05553a.htm>.

[38] W. Sparrow Simpson, 'Two Inventories of the Cathedral Church of St Paul, London, Dated Respectively to 1245 and 1402; Now for the First Time Printed, With An Introduction', *Archaeologia* 50 (1887), 439–524, at 487. Sparrow (p. 450) states that the figures of Erkenwald and Edmund were on an amice but the Latin text has 'manipuli'.

[39] Simpson, 'Inventories', p. 444.

Figure 6.5. Bayeux Tapestry: Archbishop Stigand (coronation of King Harold II).
© The City of Bayeux. All Rights Reserved

him, named (see Fig. 6.5). Both, unusually for the Tapestry, are depicted
full-face. This is unsurprising in the case of Harold, the crowned king,
since the frontal pose was usual in Carolingian and Ottonian majesty
portraits. The full-face depiction of the ecclesiastic who had evidently
crowned him is not usual. Norman historians would claim the coronation
was invalid, since Stigand was not properly consecrated. He had received
a *pallium* from the anti-pope, not the legitimate pope; English historians
would claim it was not Stigand of Canterbury but Ealdred archbishop
of York who crowned Harold.[40] The Tapestry designer, however, seems
confident of the validity of the coronation and of Stigand's authority
since Harold here and subsequently is firmly called 'Rex' and Stigand is
wearing an archiepiscopal *pallium*. It has been suggested that the letters
which prefix 'eps' with 'archi', thus proclaiming him *archi*bishop were
added by a different hand,[41] but the *pallium*, which is worked in the same
colours as the rest of the vestments, is integral to the design.

---

[40]  Barbara English, 'The Coronation of Harold in the Bayeux Tapestry', in *The Bayeux
     Tapestry: Embroidering the Facts of History*, ed. Pierre Bouet, Brian Levy and François
     Neveux (Caen, 2004), pp. 347–81. On Stigand, see below, chapter 9 (Rumble); and for
     the coronation scene, p. 176, n. 79.
[41]  English, 'The Coronation', p. 377.

Figure 6.6. Breedon-on-the-Hill, Leicestershire. The Virgin Mary or an unnamed abbess. © David Wright. All Rights Reserved

## Images in Sculpture

Stone sculptures are vulnerable to weathering and fracture. The only really probable 'portrait' of an Anglo-Saxon church leader is a damaged bust on part of a cross from Hackness, North Yorkshire. The figure is believed to be female because of the plait of hair said to be visible over the shoulder – but frankly not visible on photographs – and by Latin inscriptions on other fragments of the cross saying 'OEDILBURGA blessed forever', 'most loving mother' and 'religious abbess'. Oedilburga may be equated with Æthelburh, the Kentish princess who brought Christianity to Northumbria through her marriage to King Edwin, and who founded England's first convent in her widowhood.[42] Though this convent was far away in Kent, it is possible that her leadership was remembered by the nuns of Hackness.

---

[42] Hackness 1; James T. Lang, *Corpus of Anglo-Saxon Stone Sculpture*, III, *York and Eastern Yorkshire* (Oxford, 1991), 135–40; the carving is described by J. Higgett and R. I. Page at pp. 136–7. Carol Farr, 'Questioning the Monuments: Approaches to Anglo-Saxon Sculpture through Gender Studies', in *The Archaeology of Anglo-Saxon England: Basic Readings*, ed. Catherine E. Karkov (New York and London, 1999), pp. 375–402, at pp. 380–92. Another Anglo-Saxon St Æthelburh, sister of St Eorcenweald, seems an unlikely candidate.

No other carved figures are associated with an identifying inscription other than biblical characters. Modern scholars tend to identify the draped figures as anonymous 'ecclesiastic' or 'saint' and almost all the surviving sculptures of women are generally identified as the Virgin Mary.Where the iconic scene is recognizable, such as the Annunciation or the Visitation, this is entirely justified; but, as Carol Farr advocates, there is reason to re-think some of the images, such as the one from Breedon-on-the Hill (see Fig. 6.6), and to consider that here we might have a holy abbess.[43] The lowest scene on the Bewcastle Cross, a figure with a large bird, may represent St John the Evangelist, but it *might* be a secular patron with a hunting bird; or, given the Anglo-Saxon facility for double-speak, it might be both. Two male figures on a sculpture from the church of St Mary Bishophill Junior, York, one bearing a horn, might be secular patrons, important in their own day, but whose names are now lost.[44]

## Multiple Readings

The Anglo-Saxons adopted as icons not just Old and New Testament figures but also Pope Gregory who gave them their Church; St Jerome,[45] Cassiodorus,[46] Prudentius[47] and Hrabanus Maurus,[48] scholars who gave them their biblical texts and schoolbooks but none of whom ever set foot in the country. The Anglo-Saxons were not producing Christian martyrs and so their native saints were mostly pious royal patrons and ecclesiastics. We cannot say how many of these were once honoured with a

---

[43] Farr, 'Questioning the Monuments', p. 391.

[44] Lang, *Corpus of Anglo-Saxon Stone Sculpture*, III. 83–4, fig. 216.

[45] St Jerome appears writing in CCCC 389, fol. 1v. The manuscript contains Jerome, *Vita Sancti Pauli*. Ohlgren (*Iconographic Catalogue*, p. 269) tentatively identifies as St Jerome a figure in mass vestments under an arch in BL, Cotton Tiberius C. vi, fol. 71v. See *Francis Wormald: Collected Writings, 1: Studies in Medieval Art from the Sixth to the Twelfth Centuries*, ed. J. J. G. Alexander, T. J. Brown and Joan Gibbs (London, 1984), ill. 151.

[46] Florence, Biblioteca Medicea Laurenziana, Amiatino 1 (*Codex Amiatinus*), fol. V; a Jarrow/Monkwearmouth manuscript. The author figure is depicted in the guise of the Old Testament prophet Ezra (the caption and features of Hebrew dress establish this) but he is surrounded by, and writing, translations of the bible made by Cassiodorus. Hence the image may be interpreted as a 'portrait' of Cassiodorus. See R. L. S. Bruce-Mitford, *The Art of the Codex Amiatinus*, Jarrow Lecture, 1967.

[47] Prudentius appears at prayer several times in manuscript copies of his works in CCCC 23, part 1, fols. 4v and 40r; BL, Cotton Cleopatra C. viii, fols. 6v and 36v; and BL, Additional 24199, fols. 4r and 37v.

[48] Hrabanus Maurus appears in manuscripts of his *De laudibus sancta crucis*: in Cambridge, Trinity College, B.16.3, fol. 1v, he offers a book to Pope Gregory, and at 30v he adores the Cross. He also adores the Cross in Cambridge, University Library, Gg. 5.35, fol. 225r.

'portrait' in one of these media, now destroyed or lost in anonymity. The medieval talent for multiple readings should, however, make us question some well-known images. The interpretation of the bust on the Alfred Jewel has moved on from the simple assumption that it depicts the king who is named on it as donor, or a local saint.[49] Sophisticated comparative research now suggests plausibly that the figure represents the sense of Sight, or more than that, Insight, or Wisdom; but could it not *also* represent the donor? I am sure the owners of it, faced with the inscription 'Alfred ordered me to be made' associated the enamel bust with Alfred. Likewise, the illustration in the Vespasian Psalter (BL, Cotton Vespasian A. i, fol. 30v) is acknowledged as complex, showing the Old Testament King David as Psalmist, wearing clothing and hairstyle worn in art by Christ, and episcopal shoes and stockings, with the halo of a saint, seated on an imperial throne, playing a round lyre of Anglo-Saxon type.[50] Is it not worth considering that a Mercian king and patron of the manuscript might have seen himself in these multiple roles? I do not assert it. I merely suggest that we should be open to considering it.

In conclusion, I must mention two portraits, the identity of which must have been perfectly obvious to the artist who created them, but is not so to us. The first is the disembodied head peeping round a curtain at the Evangelist Matthew in the Lindisfarne Gospels (fol. 25v). The figure is sometimes identified as Christ, though his nimbus is not cruciform, as St Cuthbert, even as St Jerome;[51] but nobody now knows. At least the nimbus indicates that he is a saint. However, at p. 2 of Bod, Junius 11 someone has sketched a portrait bust and the name 'Ælfwine'. PASE lists 182 men with this name, so it was quite common.[52] We do not know if the artist was associated with the original text or pictures in the manuscript or if he was a later doodler. To the artist Ælfwine was important, maybe because he was the abbot or just because he, himself was Ælfwine. The artist gave us the picture and he gave us the name, but sadly, without the inclusion of an office or place-name we cannot identify him at all.

---

[49] *The Making of England: Anglo-Saxon Art and Culture AD 600–900*, ed. Leslie Webster and Janet Backhouse, British Museum Exhibition Catalogue (London, 1991), pp. 282–3.

[50] See *The Vespasian Psalter*, ed. D. H. Wright, Early English Manuscripts in Facsimile 14 (Copenhagen, 1967), 69–71.

[51] The Jerome identification is among those suggested by Ohlgren, *Iconographic Catalogue,* p. 8, item 9.9.

[52] This particular drawing is shown at the head of the PASE website.

# 7

# 'To Keep Silence Following the Rule's Command': Bishop Æthelwold, Reforming Ideology and Communication by Signs

DEBBY BANHAM

Þis sindon þa tacna þe mon on mynstre healdan sceal þær mon æfter regoles bebode swigan haldan wile and geornlice mid godes fultume begyman sceal.[1]

## Early Medieval Monastic Sign Language

THE precise importance of sign language in the Benedictine reform of the tenth century is difficult to assess. However, this aspect of the movement has received so little scholarly attention that it is surely safe to say that its role has been underestimated. The publication of Scott Bruce's *Silence and Sign Language in Medieval Monasticism* is therefore to be welcomed for placing communication by signs firmly under the gaze of the wider, especially Anglophone, academic public.[2] It is to be hoped that his work will renew analytical interest in the texts among historians and linguists, while prompting a wider debate on the role of signs in reforming life and thought. As a contribution to that debate, this chapter will look at the evidence, exiguous though it may be, for the use of signs in Anglo-Saxon reforming monasteries and will examine the possible role of one of the leading English reformers, Bishop Æthelwold of Winchester, in promoting their use.

---

[1] 'These are the signs that must be used in the monastery and diligently observed with God's help, where it is desired to keep silence following the Rule's command.' This is the OE heading at the beginning of the Anglo-Saxon list of monastic signs, see *Monasteriales Indicia: The Anglo-Saxon Monastic Sign Language*, ed. and trans. Debby Banham (Pinner, 1991), pp. 22–3; and below, pp. 131–5.

[2] Scott G. Bruce, *Silence and Sign Language in Medieval Monasticism: The Cluniac Tradition, c. 900–1200* (Cambridge, 2007), with a discussion of recent scholarly attitudes to monastic sign language at pp. 4–6.

The first thing to remark upon is that there is no evidence that manual signs were used as a substitute for speech by monks in England, or indeed on the Continent, before the reform. In England, there is no mention of them in any text earlier than Wulfstan of Winchester's *Vita Sancti Æthelwoldi*, probably completed *c*. 996.[3] On the Continent, such signs are first mentioned in the *vita* of the reforming Abbot Odo of Cluny (925–42).[4] Before this, there were certainly references in the Benedictine and other Rules to asking for things at mealtimes by knocking and other signals, but these do not necessarily imply the use of a systematic set of signs.[5] The *Regula Sancti Benedicti* (*RSB*) does however require silence at mealtimes, as well as in church and after bed-time.[6] If the *RSB* is to be observed strictly, some non-verbal means of communication is clearly required, but there is no reason to suppose it *was* observed to the letter in pre-Viking Age England. It might once have been shocking to suggest that the *RSB* was not observed strictly at the Venerable Bede's Jarrow, for instance, but more recent work has shown that a number of rules were known in early Christian England, and St Benedict's was not necessarily regarded as *the* Rule that had to be observed above all others.[7]

Bede himself provides us with unwitting testimony that sign language was not in use, or even known about, in English monasteries of the eighth century. In chapter one of his *De temporum ratione*, he details a system of finger counting, the *computatio Romana*, intended to enable the user to count, if not without difficulty, as far as a million.[8] He goes on to suggest that the same system could be used, in combination with an alphanumeric key, to convey messages without speaking. This would be a ludicrously cumbersome procedure, given the difficulties of using the *computatio* even to count from one to ten,[9] and his suggestion is almost certain proof that Bede was not familiar with a simpler and more direct method of communicating words by hand. Bede of course spent his life in one of the most rigorously Benedictine houses of his day, so we can be

---

3    *Wulfstan of Winchester: Life of St Æthelwold*, ed. and trans. Michael Lapidge and Michael Winterbottom (Oxford, 1991). Hereafter *VÆ*.
4    John of Salerno, *Vita Odonis*, PL 133 (1853), cols. 43–86, at col. 57.
5    See Bruce, *Silence and Sign Language*, pp. 60–1.
6    *La règle de saint Benoît*, ed. Adalbert de Vogüé, 7 vols., Sources chrétiennes 181–7 (Paris, 1971–2), chs. 6, 38 and 42.
7    For a recent discussion of this issue, see Sarah Foot, *Monastic Life in Anglo-Saxon England, c. 600–900* (Cambridge, 2006), pp. 48–58.
8    *De temporum ratione*, I.i: *Bedae Opera didascalica*, ed. C. W. Jones, II, CCSL 123B (Turnhout, 1971), 268–71; trans. Faith Wallis, *Bede: The Reckoning of Time* (Liverpool, 1999), pp. 11–12.
9    For some reflections on these difficulties, see Debby Banham, '"The Very Useful and Very Accessible Skill of Bending the Fingers": Finger Counting from Bede's *De temporum ratione*', in *The Body as Instrument*, ed. Anke Timmerman, Nick Jardine and Debby Banham (Cambridge, 2006), pp. 8–15, especially pp. 12–14.

fairly confident that, if sign language was not in use at Jarrow, it was not in use elsewhere in England either. It was only with the reform that the idea became current that, not only was the only real monk a Benedictine, but every word of the *RSB* had to be obeyed to the letter (even then, the *Regularis Concordia* was needed to make sure everyone obeyed it in the same way). It was in this climate of opinion that sign language recommended itself as a way of ensuring that the *RSB*'s provisions on silence could be *seen* to be obeyed.

The *Vita Odonis* says that Odo of Cluny found sign language already in use at the sister house of Baume-les-moines. However, there is no surviving list of signs from Baume. A list may have been lost, of course, but the other possibility is that signs were used quite informally there, perhaps improvised when needed. The list from Cluny is only preserved in two customaries dating from the 1070s and 1080s, that is to say, long after Odo's time.[10] It is possible that it was just the *idea* of using signs that was introduced from Baume to Cluny, and it may have been a while before conventions grew up as to *how* they should be used. Nevertheless, the list may well pre-date the customaries it appears in, because the relationships between the early sign lists makes it clear that Cluny was the original on which the others, from for instance Fleury (1087) and the German reforming house of Hirsau (also 1080s), were based.[11] The Hirsau list is by far the longest, however, containing a large number of signs not listed elsewhere, some of which may not be local inventions, nor derived from a written list, but from a wider corpus of signs in use at Cluny and not yet written down.[12]

A similar relationship exists between the Cluny list and an Old English one found under the rubric 'Monasteriales Indicia' in a mid-eleventh-century manuscript from Christ Church, Canterbury, now BL, Cotton Tiberius A. iii:[13] many of its signs are clearly translated from Cluny's Latin, others are worded differently, but describe the same gestures, while

---

[10] Those of Bernard of Cluny and Ulrich of Zell; see Walter Jarecki, *Signa loquendi: die cluniacensischen Signa-Listen eingenleitet und herausgegeben*, Saecula spiritalia 4 (Baden-Baden, 1981), 11–12. The Cluny sign list is edited by Jarecki, *Signa loquendi*, no. 1, pp. 121–42.

[11] The texts are edited by Anselme Davril OSB, 'Le langage par signes chez les moines: un catalogue de signes de l'abbaye de Fleury', in *Sous la règle de saint Benoît: structures monastiques et sociétés en France du moyen âge à l'époque moderne*, Hautes études médiévales et modernes 47 (Paris and Geneva, 1982), 51–74, and Jarecki, *Signa loquendi*, no. 3, pp. 163–230, respectively.

[12] For discussion of this point, see Bruce, *Silence and Sign Language*, pp. 114–15.

[13] Dating and origin after Helmut Gneuss, *Handlist of Anglo-Saxon Manuscripts: A List of Manuscripts and Manuscript Fragments Written or Owned in England up to 1100*, Medieval and Renaissance Texts and Studies 241 (Tempe, AZ, 2001), p. 67, no. 363. For the Old English list, see *Monasteriales Indicia*, ed. and trans. Banham.

others again are found in the Hirsau but not the Cluny list. The Old English
list forms part of a large collection of texts, most of them individually
quite short, starting with the *RSB*, glossed in Old English, together with
the *Regularis Concordia*, part of Æthelwold's translation of the *RSB* into
Old English, and various texts on the monastic life written in connection
with the Benedictine reform on the Continent (the 'Aachen group').[14]
Further on in the manuscript we have the 'Colloquy' of Æthelwold's
pupil Ælfric, written to teach monastic pupils Latin, and part of the same
author's *De temporibus anni*, his textbook on the calculation of the date
of Easter, adapted from Bede, *De temporibus*. Several other short texts
share this interest in chronology and measurement: prognostics, notes on
the Ages of the World, on the age of the Virgin and on the dimensions of
Noah's Ark, and so on. There are also an Old English 'Handbook' for a
confessor, and several homiletic and liturgical texts. Finally, the manuscript contains some medical fragments, the 'Devil's account of the next
world' and various other items of arcane knowledge.

What are we to make of this collection of material? I have in the past
characterized it as a 'manifesto of the Benedictine reform', or even a
'textbook of reformed Benedictinism', but of course the mid eleventh
century was a bit late for a manifesto of a movement launched during the
reign of Edgar (959–75), and 'a few of the texts do not seem to belong in
a teaching book'.[15] Tiberius A. iii could be a copy of a compilation made
earlier, but certainly not as early as Edgar's time, containing as it does
several pieces by Ælfric, mostly written around the millennium. Some of
its contents, such as the text on the development of the foetus, are also
more difficult to characterize as reflecting specifically Benedictine interests.[16] More recently, Tracey-Anne Cooper has argued convincingly that
the manuscript was put together for a Benedictine archbishop, combining
as it does monastic and pastoral concerns, together with a few items only
an archbishop would normally need.[17] This would also help explain its
combination of luxurious production values with often utilitarian content.

[14] The contents are listed in detail by N. R. Ker, *Catalogue of Manuscripts containing Anglo-Saxon* (Oxford, 1957), pp. 240–8 (no. 186), where he also shows that the copy of the *RSB*, beginning on fol. 116, originally stood in first place.

[15] Helmut Gneuss, 'Origin and Provenance of Anglo-Saxon Manuscripts: The Case of Cotton Tiberius A. iii', in *Of the Making of Books: Medieval Manuscripts, their Scribes and Readers. Essays presented to M. B. Parkes*, ed. Pamela Robinson and Rivkah Zim (Aldershot, 1997), pp. 13–48, at p. 15.

[16] On this text, see L. S. Chardonnens, *Anglo-Saxon Prognostics, 900–1100* (Leiden, 2007), pp. 241–4, and for an edition with translation, *idem*, 'A New Edition of the Old English "Formation of the Foetus"', *Notes and Queries* 47 (2000), 10–11. I should like to thank Conan T. Doyle for sharing his knowledge of the text with me.

[17] Notably the *Examinatio* of a bishop, discussed by Gneuss, 'Origin and Provenance', p. 36. Cooper's analysis of the manuscript is summarized in her article 'The Homilies of a

The most appropriate context for such a compilation might be the final conversion of the Canterbury cathedral community into a fully Benedictine monastery. When that took place is, of course, controversial,[18] but the existence of this book may fittingly play a part in that discussion. The collection must presumably have been put together before the Conquest; one cannot imagine Lanfranc (1070–89) having much use for the numerous vernacular items included, nor Stigand (1052–70) much sympathy with its Benedictine concerns. Cooper dates Tiberius A. iii to 1012×1023, considerably earlier than Gneuss or Ker.[19] This would place it in the archiepiscopates of the Benedictines Lyfing (1012–20) or Æthelnoth (1020–38), the latter being the only archbishop elected from within the community. It is perhaps more likely that the texts were assembled under one of these archbishops, but the surviving manuscript copied at a later date. Æthelnoth's successor was Eadsige (1038–50), a royal chaplain who was professed as a monk on his appointment as archbishop.[20] His dates fit better with the widely accepted dating of the manuscript, and his needs might have prompted the production of Tiberius A. iii.

The Old English sign list found in Tiberius A. iii is often described as the 'Canterbury List',[21] but there is no particular reason to suppose that this text, any more than the others in the compilation, had its origin where the manuscript was copied and the collection it contains drawn up. It consists of 127 signs, falling under the same basic categories (although in a different order) as in the Continental lists: for use in church, at table, in the dormitory, and for various persons, both members of the community (e.g. Sign 1 for 'abbot', see Fig. 7.1) and outsiders. The Old English list, unlike the Continental ones, has signs for 'king' and 'king's wife'

---

Pragmatic Archbishop's Handbook in Context: Cotton Tiberius A. iii', *Anglo-Norman Studies* 28 (2006), 47–64, especially 47–9, and set out at greater length in *eadem*, 'Reconstructing a Deconstructed Manuscript, Culture and Community: London, BL MS Cotton Tiberius A. iii', unpublished PhD dissertation, Boston College (2005).

[18] For a judicious appraisal of the probabilities, see Nicholas Brooks, *The Early History of the Church of Canterbury: Christ Church from 597 to 1066* (Leicester, 1984), pp. 255–60.

[19] Cooper, 'The Homilies', p. 47. Gneuss ('Origin and Provenance,' p. 13) moves to 'the middle of the eleventh century or somewhat later', while Ker, *Catalogue*, p. 240, gives 's. xi med.'. D. H. Turner in *The Golden Age of Anglo-Saxon Art*, ed. Janet Backhouse, D. H. Turner and Leslie Webster (London, 1984), p. 47, ascribes the manuscript to the second half of the century.

[20] For a summary of the careers of these late Anglo-Saxon archbishops, see Nicholas Brooks, 'The Anglo-Saxon Cathedral Community, 597–1070', in *A History of Canterbury Cathedral*, ed. Patrick Collinson, Nigel Ramsay and Margaret Sparks (Oxford, 1995), pp. 1–37, at pp. 29–33.

[21] A translation has been published by David Sherlock under the title 'Anglo-Saxon Monastic Sign Language at Christ Church, Canterbury', *Archaeologia Cantiana* 107 (1989), 1–27, and Bruce discusses the text as 'the Canterbury sign lexicon', in *Silence and Sign Language*, pp. 108–17 and table 4 on pp. 129–31.

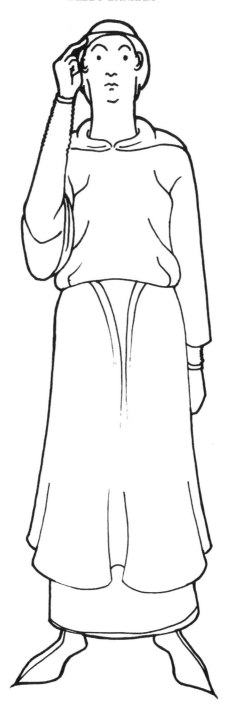

Figure 7.1. Sign for abbot as prescribed in the *Monasteriales Indicia*.
© Debby Banham. All Rights Reserved.

reflecting the vital role of royalty in promoting the English reform, but there is no sign for 'archbishop'.[22] A few other signs unique to the Anglo-Saxon text may represent differences between English and Continental reformed practice. However, most of the Continental lists are substantially longer than the Old English one, and it probably represents a selection from a broader common repertoire. One reason for its brevity might be that some aspects of Anglo-Saxon Benedictine life were more basic, less 'advanced' than was the case in the Continental houses from which it took its inspiration.[23] On the other hand, a small group of signs concerned with personal hygiene seem to be an Anglo-Saxon innovation, but this is probably not the place for an extended speculation about differing regional responses to medieval anxieties about the physical body.[24]

### The Vita Sancti Æthelwoldi

Let us turn instead to one of the leaders of the reform, and to his *vita*. Wulfstan's *Vita Sancti Æthelwoldi* is a highly polemical work. This is not meant to be a controversial statement: all saints' *vitae* are propaganda, designed to convince the audience that their protagonist is worthy of veneration as a saint.[25] In some cases, where the *vita* was written when the cult in question was securely in place, this task was not particularly urgent, but other hagiographers had a harder job, either because the cult was under threat, or because it had yet to be established. The *Vita Sancti Æthelwoldi* falls into the last category, written by one of his own disciples and close collaborators at Winchester, in the immediate aftermath of the bishop's death.[26] Within Winchester, and at Abingdon, where Æthelwold had been abbot, many people were no doubt already convinced of

---

[22] Signs 118 and 119: *Monasteriales Indicia*, ed. and trans. Banham, p. 44. Bruce, in *Silence and Sign Language*, p. 114, accounts for the absence of an archbishop by suggesting he would be addressed as 'abbot' within the community, but this seems more plausible for some archbishops than others.

[23] Bruce (*Silence and Sign Language*, p. 114) suggests that the restricted Anglo-Saxon sign vocabulary reflected an anxiety about superfluous communication, but this seems to project later reformers' concerns back into a period that regarded signs as a novel means of avoiding idle chatter.

[24] Signs 95–8: *Monasteriales Indicia*, ed. and trans. Banham, pp. 40–2. Various scholars (among them Bruce, *Silence and Sign Language*, p. 116) have linked these signs to the extensive system of waterworks shown in the plan of Christ Church in the Eadwine Psalter (Cambridge, Trinity College, R.17.1, fols. 284v–285r; s. xii med.), but there is of course no reason to suppose that these already existed in the eleventh century.

[25] *VÆ*, ed. and trans. Lapidge and Winterbottom, pp. ci–cii.

[26] Lapidge and Winterbottom (*VÆ*, pp. c–ci) argue that Wulfstan was the chief instigator of Æthelwold's cult, and certainly the author of several liturgical pieces in his honour (pp. xxiii–xxvii).

his sanctity, but in the wider world there was more work to do. Æthelwold was only one, if the most rigorous and energetic, of three leaders
of the Benedictine revival or revolution that produced such wide-ranging
changes in the English Church in the latter part of the tenth century. The
other two, Dunstan and Oswald, finished their careers as archbishops, and
both, interestingly, are still counted as saints at the present day.[27] Æthelwold is not, except in the context of the Benedictional of St Æthelwold,
the splendid manuscript made for him, probably at Winchester,[28] during
his time as bishop, and of course in his *vita*. It is not my purpose in this
chapter to speculate about why Æthelwold has not been more widely
accepted as a saint, but rather to examine some of the ways in which the
*vita* tries to convince us of his sanctity, and what role Æthelwold's status
as a leader of the reform plays in that. The association of reform and
sanctity in the *vita* no doubt helped in turn to promote the reform movement itself, bearing in mind that Æthelwold's death in 984 was followed
by what may be called an 'anti-monastic reaction'.[29]

Æthelwold's miracles, as recounted by Wulfstan, are not the conventional signs of God's favour common to many saints' *vitae*, but rather
present a picture of a man seen as saintly in his own particular way.
This means they are likely to represent genuine events from the bishop's life, rather than being derived from literary sources.[30] They begin,
if we discount the experiences of his mother during her pregnancy, with
the infant Æthelwold and his nurse being miraculously transported to
church in a rainstorm without getting wet.[31] Æthelwold's childhood and
youth were pious and attended by royal favour, but the next miracle did
not occur until he was abbot of Abingdon, following its refoundation (if

---

[27] See the collections of papers from their millennial conferences: *St Dunstan: His
Life, Times and Cult*, ed. Nigel Ramsay, Margaret Sparks and Tim Tatton-Brown
(Woodbridge, 1992); and *St Oswald of Worcester: Life and Influence*, ed. Nicholas
Brooks and Catherine Cubitt (Leicester, 1996).

[28] Andrew Prescott, *The Benedictional of St Æthelwold, A Masterpiece of Anglo-Saxon
Art: A Facsimile* (London, 2002), although it has become acceptable in recent years to
drop the 'St': see Robert Deshman, *The Benedictional of Æthelwold* (Princeton, NJ,
1995).

[29] See Simon Keynes, *The Diplomas of King Æthelred 'the Unready', 978–1016: A
Study in their Use as Historical Evidence*, Cambridge Studies in Medieval Life and
Thought, 3rd ser., 13 (Cambridge, 1980), 176–86, where it is termed 'the period of
[the king's] youthful indiscretions'. The term 'anti-monastic reaction' is normally
applied to the period after the death of King Edgar in 975: D. J. V. Fisher, 'The Anti-
Monastic Reaction in the Reign of Edward the Martyr', *Cambridge Historical Journal*
10 (1952), 254–70. Both were fundamentally periods of factional change in English
royal politics. Cf. above, pp. 103–6, the discussion by Dominik Wassenhoven of the
years 975–8.

[30] For Wulfstan's sources and influences, see *VÆ*, ed. and trans. Lapidge and Winterbottom,
pp. cv–cviii.

[31] *VÆ*, ch. 5; ed. and trans. Lapidge and Winterbottom, pp. 8–9.

refoundation it was) probably in the early 950s.[32] King Eadred, visiting with a large retinue, was invited to dine by Æthelwold. Despite the celebrations going on all day, the stocks of mead decreased by no more than a 'palm's measure' ('ad mansurum palmi').[33] Also during his abbacy at Abingdon, there occurred the notorious miracle of Æthelwold's testing the obedience of the monk, Ælfstan, in charge of food for the workmen, by commanding him to plunge his hand into a cauldron of boiling water, which Ælfstan did without question, and was not harmed by the experience.[34] Finally during the Abingdon period, according to Wulfstan, Æthelwold was saved from almost certain death when a huge post fell on him during the building works.[35]

After Æthelwold's move to Winchester in 963, God's favour to him was demonstrated, Wulfstan tells us, by his survival when he was served a goblet full of poison.[36] On another occasion, a nearly empty flask of oil, lost by one of his clerks on a preaching trip with the bishop, was retrieved full to the top.[37] Another of Æthelwold's miracles concerned one of his monks, who refused to own up to a theft: he was paralysed in his seat in the chapter-house at Æthelwold's command, and only released when he confessed.[38] A different monk, named Godus, was unharmed when he fell from the very top of the church to the ground, during renovation work.[39] Another time, a monk named Theodric sat down and tried to read a book that Æthelwold had left to deal with some important business. This 'temeritas', as Wulfstan describes it, was punished with severe eye pain, until Theodric had done penance for his presumption.[40] In another reading-related miracle, Æthelwold once fell asleep over his book, and his candle fell onto the page, but the book was unharmed (as was the bishop, presumably).[41] This was the last miracle that Wulfstan recorded for Æthelwold's lifetime, but as the hagiographer wrote 'not all his virtuous works can be related'.[42] There were also portents surrounding his death, and the obligatory healing miracles at his tomb afterwards.

Taking these miracles as a group, the first thing that stands out is the

---

[32] For the pre-Æthelwoldian history of Abingdon, see Alan Thacker, 'Æthelwold and Abingdon', in *Bishop Æthelwold: His Career and Influence*, ed. Barbara Yorke (Woodbridge, 1988), pp. 43–64, at pp. 43–51.

[33] *VÆ*, ch. 12; Lapidge and Winterbottom, pp. 22–5.

[34] *VÆ*, ch. 14; Lapidge and Winterbottom, pp. 26–9.

[35] *VÆ*, ch. 15; Lapidge and Winterbottom, pp. 28–9.

[36] *VÆ*, ch. 19; Lapidge and Winterbottom, pp. 34–5.

[37] *VÆ*, ch. 32; Lapidge and Winterbottom, pp. 48–9.

[38] *VÆ*, ch. 33; Lapidge and Winterbottom, pp. 48–51.

[39] *VÆ*, ch. 34; Lapidge and Winterbottom, pp. 52–3.

[40] *VÆ*, ch. 35; Lapidge and Winterbottom, pp. 52–5.

[41] *VÆ*, ch. 36; Lapidge and Winterbottom, pp. 54–5.

[42] *VÆ*, ch. 37; Lapidge and Winterbottom, pp. 54–5.

suspicious recurrence of attempts on Æthelwold's life. Wulfstan attributes the Abingdon incident to the 'hostis antiquus' 'the ancient enemy', but clearly he had other enemies.[43] Some of the episodes seem less miraculous than lucky (his unburned book, for instance). The hazards of early medieval building work also impress themselves on the reader, but more important than any of these is the emphasis on obedience (albeit chiefly to Æthelwold himself). As O'Brien O'Keeffe stressed in her 2009 Chadwick Lecture, obedience was an important, perhaps the most important, Benedictine virtue.[44] As Wulfstan tells us, Æthelwold

> Erat namque terribilis ut leo discolis et peruersis, humilibus uero et oboe-dientibus se quasi agnum mitissimum exhibebat, ita serpentinae prudentiae temperans seueritatem ut columbinae simplicitatis non amitteret lenitatem. Quem si quando zelus rectitudinis cogeret ut iura disciplinae subiectis imponeret, furor ipse non de crudelitate sed de amore processit, et intus paterna pietate dilexit quos foris quasi insequens castigauit.[45]

Æthelwold's 'zelus rectitudinis' ('zeal for the right') is of course seen as a virtue in itself, and independent evidence of his sanctity, but it is also an integral component of his rigour as a reformer. Wulfstan is at pains to show how important a role the *RSB* played in the life of Æthelwold's communities, and numerous episodes in the *vita* reinforce this emphasis: Wulfstan tells us how, while abbot of Abingdon, Æthelwold, who had been prevented from going overseas for his own monastic education, sent one of his monks, Osgar, to the reformed house of Fleury

> ut regularis obseruantiae mores illic disceret ac domi fratribus docendo ostenderet, quatinus ipse normam monasticae religionis secutus [...].[46]

On his appointment to Winchester, Æthelwold famously expelled the existing cathedral clergy with the assistance of royal authority (presumably military), and replaced them with monks from Abingdon.[47] He went on to

---

43 Lapidge and Winterbottom, pp. xlvi–xlvii, for some of them.

44 Katherine O'Brien O'Keeffe, *Stealing Obedience: Narratives of Agency in Later Anglo-Saxon England*, Chadwick Lecture (Cambridge, 2009).

45 'Indeed he was terrible as a lion to malefactors and the wayward; but to the humble and obedient he showed himself the meekest of lambs, tempering the severity of a serpent's cunning in such a way as to preserve the gentleness of an innocent dove. If ever zeal for what is right compelled him to impose the discipline of the law on his subjects, his very rage proceeded from love, not from cruelty, and inwardly he loved with a father's tenderness those whom he seemed on the surface to be correcting and harrying.': *VÆ*, ch. 28; Lapidge and Winterbottom, pp. 44–5.

46 'to learn there the way of life according to the Rule and show it to his brothers when he taught them back at home. Thus Æthelwold could himself follow the regulations of monastic observance [...]': *VÆ*, ch. 14; Lapidge and Winterbottom, pp. 26–7.

47 *VÆ*, ch. 18; Lapidge and Winterbottom, pp. 32–3; and *ASC* 964 A: *The Anglo-Saxon*

remove the 'canonicos' from the New Minster, replacing them with monks 'living according to the Rule' ('regulariter conversantes'), and he 'established flocks of nuns' ('mandras sanctimonialium') at the Nunnaminster.[48] Wulfstan tells us that, despite Æthelwold's frequent illness 'in his innards and legs' ('in visceribus et in cruribus'), he refused to eat meat, except when seriously ill and ordered to do so by Archbishop Dunstan.[49] This is mentioned as evidence of Æthelwold's sanctity, without an explicit reference to the *RSB*, but it is no doubt because vegetarianism was endorsed by St Benedict that it counted as a symptom of holiness. The same applies to the references to manual labour, to Æthelwold's working in the garden and kitchen and even on the construction of his church at Abingdon, and to his requiring his monks to share in the building work at Winchester. Again, the unfortunate Theodric, whose interest in Æthelwold's reading matter was rewarded with pain, is said to have come to the bishop

> [t]empore quodam hiemali, cum fratres secundum regulae edictum temperius ad uigilias surgerent ct nocturno interuallo psalmodiae et lectioni inseruirent [...].[50]

The Rule quoted here is that of St Benedict, but the quotation 'temperius ad uigilias' is embedded, interestingly, in a longer one from the *Regularis Concordia*, the customary drawn up by Æthelwold himself for the common use of English reformed houses.[51]

### Æthelwold and Sign Language

Furthermore, Theodric is said to have come to Æthelwold 'uolens indiciis de quadam necessitate ei indicare' ('wanting to tell him by signs about some important matter').[52] The signs that Theodric used to communicate with the bishop were almost certainly those listed in Cotton Tiberius A. iii or, if not those precise signs, some very like them. Although the manuscript was copied at Canterbury, and we have seen that the compilation it contains was most plausibly assembled there, the texts involved, as we have also seen, are very miscellaneous, and must have been drawn

---

*Chronicle MS A*, ed. Janet Bately, The AS Chronicle: A Collaborative Edition, ed. David Dumville and Simon Keynes 3 (Cambridge, 1986), 75.

[48] *VÆ*, chs. 21 and 22; Lapidge and Winterbottom, pp. 36–7.

[49] *VÆ*, ch. 30; Lapidge and Winterbottom, pp. 46–7.

[50] 'One winter's day, when the monks, as the Rule lays down, "rose earlier for Vigils" and gave themselves over to singing psalms and reading in the night interval [...]': *VÆ*, ch. 35; Lapidge and Winterbottom, pp. 52–3.

[51] *RSB*, ch. 11; *Regularis Concordia*, ed. and trans. T. Symons (London, 1953), ch. 29, p. 26.

[52] *VÆ*, ch. 35; ed. and trans. Lapidge and Winterbottom, pp. 52–3.

from a wide range of sources. Nevertheless, many of the items exhibit a relationship with Æthelwold.[53] As well as a portrait of him with Dunstan and Edgar (see Fig. 6.3), two very important works by the bishop, the *Regularis Concordia* and a chapter of his Old English version of the *RSB*, emphasize the seminal importance of his ideas in the English reform. A number of the liturgical pieces are also associated with Æthelwold. The works of his *alumnus* Ælfric are similarly testimony to his influence. The collection also includes the *Monasteriales Indicia*, not normally linked particularly with Æthelwold but, as we have seen, communicating with signs is mentioned in the bishop's *vita*, and, perhaps significantly, nowhere else in Anglo-Saxon literature. This may be an accident of survival but, as things stand, it constitutes a unique link between sign language and the reforming bishop of Winchester.

This dearth of references must raise the question of whether signs were genuinely used in English reformed monasteries, and the episode in the *vita* has some light to shed on this matter. The editors of Wulfstan's *Vita Sancti Æthelwoldi* have a footnote about the monk Theodric which provides some interesting information.[54] He is not listed among the Old Minster monks in the *Liber Vitae* of the New Minster (BL, Stowe 944, s. xi[1]); in fact, the only person of that name mentioned in the *Liber Vitae* is a late addition to the list of monks at the New Minster. The editors say this is unlikely to be the same monk, and they also point out that Theodric was not a common name in England at this time. It is possible then that Theodric was not after all a member of the Old Minster community, but a visiting monk. (Wulfstan only describes him as 'quidam monachus' 'a monk'.) Could he in fact have been a visitor from the Frankish realms, where the name Theodric was common? Whether member or visitor, if Theodric was Frankish, with either German or French as his mother tongue, this might explain why he was using signs, while they were not in general use at the Old Minster, at least to judge by Wulfstan's narrative. In fact there are two ways in which his nationality might account for his use of signs. In the first place, he might not have another language in common with Æthelwold, but, as reformed Benedictines, they ought both to have been fluent enough in Latin to use it for everyday conversations, and in any case, they should have been avoiding speech at night. The second possibility is that Theodric and Æthelwold were the only two people at the Old Minster who could use signs, in Theodric's case due to his Continental training, and in Æthelwold's because he was

---

[53] Indeed, Lapidge and Winterbottom (*VÆ*, p. lxxv) suggest that the manuscript had a Winchester exemplar, although its archiepiscopal content would argue against that.

[54] *VÆ*, ed. and trans. Lapidge and Winterbottom, p. 53, n. 4.

such a zealous reformer that he had learned the signs even though they were not in general use in England. A third possibility, of course, is that no-one at all at the Old Minster was using signs, and Wulfstan invented the episode in order to exaggerate the rigour of the inmates' lifestyle. If that were the case, it would be interesting that he attached his invention to a monk with what may well be a foreign name, perhaps hoping to promote Æthelwold's version of the reform by reference to its Continental source. Even if Wulfstan's story is of impeccable historical accuracy, it does not enable us to conclude that signs were in general use in English reformed monasteries in Æthelwold's time. Although the hagiographer only mentions signs in passing, it is nevertheless likely that he included them to add to the general impression of Benedictine commitment that he built up throughout his narrative. This tactic would not be effective if his audience knew that all monks used signs as a matter of course; in fact, the rarer they were in real life, the more lustre they would shed on Æthelwold in the *vita*.

There is another Æthelwoldian text that may tell us something about sign language: the *Regularis Concordia*.[55] There is no explicit mention of signs in it, but there is a considerable emphasis on silence, exceeding that of the *RSB* on which the text comments and builds. Section 56, following the list of mealtimes and duties, liturgical and otherwise, in section 55, begins:

> Ceteris enim horis secundum regulae praeceptum, quia tempus lectionis est, lectioni tantummodo uacantes, silentium diligenti cura in claustro custodiant.[56]

The chapter goes on to prescribe silence all night (from before Vespers until after Chapter), and only quiet and necessary conversation at other times. Elsewhere, silence is required on feast days[57] and when the monks were allowed to warm themselves at the fire in winter.[58] The question arises, whether the *regol* mentioned in the Old English heading to the *Monasteriales Indicia* is, as normally assumed, that of St Benedict, or whether it may in fact be the *Regularis Concordia*. However, the latter cites and quotes the *RSB* repeatedly and, as we have just seen, uses the words 'secundum regulae praeceptum … silentium … in claustro custo-

---

[55] For Æthelwold's authorship, see Michael Lapidge, 'Æthelwold as Scholar and Teacher', in *Bishop Æthelwold: His Career and Influence*, ed. Barbara Yorke (Woodbridge, 1988), pp. 89–117, at p. 98.

[56] 'At other hours let them keep silence in the monastery with diligent care, following the command of the Rule, spending their leisure only in reading, because it is the time for reading.'; *Regularis Concordia*, ed. and trans. Symons, pp. 54–5.

[57] *Regularis Concordia*, ch. 24; ed. and trans. Symons, pp. 20–1.

[58] *Regularis Concordia*, ch. 29; ed. and trans. Symons, pp. 24–5.

diant' ('let them keep silence [...] following the command of the Rule'),
the literal equivalent of 'on mynstre … æfter regoles bebode swigan
haldan' in the *Indicia* heading. Thus it seems that, in echoing the *Regularis Concordia's* wording, the *Indicia* is emulating its fidelity to the *RSB*.

It might be tempting to suggest that the *Indicia* heading was written by
the author of the *Regularis Concordia*, that is to say Æthelwold, translating
his own words into the vernacular. We know, after all, that he put the *RSB*
into English.[59] And the *Indicia* does have a sign for 'bishop', suggesting
that it comes from an episcopal community.[60] English monastic chapters
in the late tenth century comprised Winchester, Sherborne and Worcester,
but, given all the other Æthelwoldian connections of the Tiberius A. iii
collection, the first of these seems by far the most likely. However, if
Æthelwold himself had been responsible for the *Indicia*, we might expect
the Old English list to be more closely related to that from Fleury, where
he had sent a monk to learn about the regular life. In fact, none of the
'daughter' lists bear more resemblance to each other than they do to the
Cluny original, so it seems likely that each was derived independently
from that source, or rather that the use of signs was transmitted 'orally'
(or manually) from Cluny, before any of the surviving lists was written
down. There is not enough affinity between the English and the Fleury
lists, for instance, to suggest that the *Indicia* drew upon a Fleury usage
which had already diverged from that of Cluny.

### Sign Language in England after Æthelwold's Time

It seems likely that an English list only seemed necessary at a later stage
of the Benedictine reform, when signs may have begun to be used more
widely. Perhaps their use was established first at Winchester, then spread
to other reformed houses, resulting in a perceived need to standardise
practice by means of written instructions comprehensible to all. When
this stage might have been reached is hard to estimate: perhaps in the
second generation of the reform, around the millennium, in which case
Æthelwold's protégé Ælfric might have had a hand in it, or perhaps in the
third, around the time we have suggested for the compilation of the Tiberius A. iii. collection. Unfortunately, the manuscript context has no light
to shed on this issue: the sign list is detached both from the Æthelwoldian
texts in the manuscript and from Ælfric's works, and indeed from all the

---

[59]  See Mechthild Gretsch, 'Æthelwold's Translation of the *Regula Sancti Benedicti* and
its Latin Exemplar', *ASE* 3 (1974), 125–51.
[60]  Sign 120: *Monasteriales Indicia*, ed. and trans. Banham, p. 44.

other clearly Benedictine items.[61] If the list were drawn up especially for the collection, we would have to conclude that it was composed at Christ Church, but this does not seem very likely, there being no sign for 'archbishop'. Rather more plausible, perhaps, is the scenario that the Canterbury compiler borrowed the text from some more established reformed community, such as one of the Winchester houses, as a template for the newly monastic archiepiscopal community.

However, there is an argument for a Canterbury origin, arising from Lucia Kornexl's work on the interlinear Old English version of the *Regularis Concordia* in Tiberius A. iii. Here, the words 'secundum regulae praeceptum ... silentium ... custodiant' are translated as 'æfter regules bebode ... swigean ... hældan'.[62] This wording is very close to that of the *Indicia*, although there are orthographic variations. A glance at Kornexl's tables of *Regularis Concordia* glosses reveals a number of other similarities with the sign list, so the question arises whether the two texts might have had a common origin. Kornexl believes that its paucity of characteristic 'Winchester School' vocabulary rules out a Winchester home for the interlinear version, although its dialect is apparently southern, with a small Anglian admixture.[63] On the basis of similarities with other interlinear glosses attributed to Canterbury, she concludes that Christ Church is the most likely origin for the Old English gloss to the *Regularis Concordia*. Its language is clearly not identical with that of the *Indicia*; for instance, it translates 'in claustro' as 'on claustre', rather than 'on mynstre'. A detailed comparison of the vocabulary of the two texts would be required to establish their relationship more securely, and unfortunately many of the items indicated by signs are not mentioned in the *Regularis Concordia*. Indeed, its attention to everyday concerns largely ignored in other reforming texts is one of the main features that makes the sign list of scholarly interest.

If it is hard to choose between a Winchester and a Canterbury origin for our text, our attention may be drawn to a figure who has connections with both establishments, and indeed with Tiberius A. iii, in which both the *Monasteriales Indicia* and the interlinear Old English *Regularis Concordia* are preserved. This is Ælfric Bata, pupil of Abbot Ælfric, who wrote a number of colloquies for teaching Latin,[64] as well as adapting his

---

61  The text of the *Indicia* is on fols. 97r–101v, between the Old English directions for a confessor and an Old English lapidary.

62  Lucia Kornexl, *Die Regularis Concordia und ihre altenglische Interlinearversion*, Münchener Universitäts-Schriften 17 (Munich, 1993), 115.

63  Kornexl, *Die Regularis Concordia*, pp. ccxxxii–ccxxxvi.

64  See *Anglo-Saxon Conversations: The Colloquies of Ælfric Bata*, ed. Scott Gwara, trans. David Porter (Woodbridge, 1997). Porter's introduction, esp. pp. 2–3, gives what is known of Bata's biography.

master's (which also features, without most of Bata's additions, in Tiberius A. iii). Both Ælfrics were schoolmasters, and it was in the monastic
schoolroom that novices learned the signs they would need after their
profession.[65] Bata is associated with the *Regularis Concordia*, and in fact
with the whole Tiberius compilation, both in the twelfth-century contents
list of our manuscript, and in the entries in the fifteenth-century Christ
Church library catalogue that almost certainly relate to it.[66] The colloquies
of Bata and his master share the *Indicia*'s interest in everyday matters
beneath the notice of higher-minded reforming texts.[67] If the *Indicia* does
belong to Canterbury, and to the second or third generation of the reform,
the Winchester (or Eynsham)-educated schoolmaster Bata could have
brought it with him. Or perhaps he brought the signs, part of the Æthelwoldian inheritance passed on to him by his master Ælfric, but it was a
Canterbury-trained scribe who drew up the list.

That signs eventually became an established part of the conventual
life at Christ Church is not in doubt. At the end of the twelfth century
we have the testimony of Gerald of Wales, shocked by the monks' 'dumb
chattering' ('muta garrulitate'), that he saw 'an excessive superabundance
of signs' ('signorum ... superfluitatem nimiam') at dinner in the cathedral
priory,[68] but this is from a period when signs had fallen into disrepute
among the stricter religious.[69] In the later middle ages, the survival of a
number, albeit not a large number, of sign lists from the fourteenth and
fifteenth centuries shows that signs were by that stage fairly widespread
in English houses.[70] Thus the later history of monastic sign language in
England is fairly well established, at least in outline. The earlier stages

[65] See Bruce, *Silence and Sign Language*, pp. 66–70. Dom Anselme Davril told me that
he was taught the Fleury signs in the same way when he entered the community in the
twentieth century.
[66] See Ker, *Catalogue*, pp. 241 and 248, as well as Kornexl, *Die Regularis Concordia*,
pp. cxxx–cxxxiv.
[67] As noted by Porter, *Anglo-Saxon Conversations*, p. 79.
[68] *De rebus a se gestis* I.5, in *Giraldi Cambrensis Opera*, ed. J. S. Brewer, RS 21 (London,
1861), I. 3–122, at 51.
[69] For discussion, see Bruce, *Silence and Sign Language*, p. 167.
[70] There are two from fourteenth-century Bury St Edmunds (*Signa loquendi*, ed. Jarecki,
no. 6, and David Sherlock and William Zajac, 'Monastic Sign-Language at Bury St
Edmunds in the 14th Century', *Proceedings of the Suffolk Institute of Archaeology and
History* 36 (1988), 251–73); one from Ely cathedral priory, again of the fourteenth
century, but based on the standard list of the Victorines (*Signs for Silence: The Sign
Language of the Monks of Ely in the Middle Ages*, ed. David Sherlock (Ely, 1992));
and one from the nunnery at Syon in the fifteenth century (*History and Antiquities of
Syon Monastery*, ed. G. J. Aungier (London, 1840) pp. 405–9). The Syon list is the
only other one in English.

of its diffusion remain however much less clear. This chapter has begun to penetrate some of the gloom that surrounds them, in particular by illuminating Bishop Æthelwold's important role in the process, but there is much still to do.

# 8

# Wulfsige of Sherborne's Reforming Text

JOYCE HILL

WULFSIGE, bishop of Sherborne, sometimes identified as Wulfsige III because there were two other bishops of Sherborne by this
name in the late ninth and early tenth centuries, hardly springs to mind
when we think of the leaders of the Anglo-Saxon church. Yet Sherborne
is the only see outside the three leading centres of Winchester, Worcester
and Canterbury to have been changed from a clerical to a monastic foundation in the Benedictine reform period, despite the propensity during
the ascendancy of the reform to appoint bishops from the community of
monks. This momentous event, which appears to have been achieved by
Wulfsige's episcopal fiat, occurred in 998. In this respect, what happened
at Sherborne was more akin to the instantaneous change achieved by
Æthelwold in Winchester than the gradualist approach in Canterbury and
Worcester, although there is no indication that Wulfsige adopted Æthelwold's aggressively confrontational methods. He had been consecrated
probably in 993 and there is some evidence, in addition to the lapse of
time, which suggests that he planned for the change. Yet it was a radical
step to take, not matched anywhere else, and it was carried out, apparently successfully, by a man who was at the heart of the reform tradition.
So there is perhaps some justification in including him among the leaders
of the church.

Wulfsige, is, nevertheless, not one of the better-known bishops. This
was partly remedied in 1998 when a conference was held at Sherborne to
celebrate the millennium of the founding of the Benedictine Abbey – that
is to say, the change of the cathedral from a clerical to a monastic community. The outcome was an invaluable collection of essays, published in
2005 under the title *St Wulfsige and Sherborne*,[1] on which I shall draw as
I examine Wulfsige's reforming text: the determinedly reformist Pastoral

---

[1] *St Wulfsige and Sherborne: Essays to Celebrate the Millennium of the Benedictine
Abbey 998–1998*, ed. Katherine Barker, David A. Hinton and Alan Hunt, Bournemouth
University School of Conservation Sciences Occasional Paper 8 (Oxford, 2005). On
monastic cathedrals, see above (Rumble), pp. 21–3.

Letter written by Ælfric on Wulfsige's behalf, and issued in Wulfsige's name for the benefit of the secular clergy.[2] While it is true that this is not about the reformation of the cathedral community, it casts considerable light on Wulfsige's frame of reference and impulse for change, and contributes to an understanding both of his place in reforming circles (to which he demonstrably belonged) and to the influence of the Benedictine reform on the secular church, in aspiration, if not always in practical effect. It is surprising, therefore, that *St Wulfsige and Sherborne* makes little use of this text: Farmer makes no reference to it, even though the subject of his article is the impact on Sherborne of the monastic reform of the tenth century;[3] and although Keynes acknowledges the Letter's value, he fails to examine it, providing instead only a cursory summary of certain issues that it addresses.[4] It seems to me that this was a missed opportunity, given the shortage of direct information about Wulfsige's attitude to reform. There are, after all, no surviving texts that can be attributed to his authorship, with the exception of one, or possibly two, short and somewhat formulaic penitential letters;[5] and the only early *vita* of Wulfsige, written by Goscelin of St Bertin in *c.*1078/1080, tells us little about his activity as a bishop and even less about his 'reformation' of the Sherborne community.[6] A text that Wulfsige commissioned from someone who was an active reformer, and which he then issued in his own name, thus assumes considerable importance as evidence for his concept of the episcopal role and his general reforming interests.

We need first to consider Wulfsige's background. According to Goscelin, he was born in London.[7] It is probable that he was trained under

2  *Die Hirtenbriefe Ælfrics in altenglischer und lateinischer Fassung*, ed. Bernhard Fehr, Bibliothek der angelsächsischen Prosa 9 (Hamburg, 1914), reprinted with a supplement to the introduction by Peter Clemoes (Darmstadt, 1966), Brief I, pp. 1–34. For a translation into modern English, see *Councils & Synods*, ed. Whitelock, no. 40, pp. 191–226.

3  David Farmer, 'The Monastic Reform of the Tenth Century and Sherborne', in *St Wulfsige and Sherborne*, ed. Barker *et al.*, pp. 24–9.

4  Simon Keynes, 'Wulfsige, Monk of Glastonbury, Abbot of Westminster (*c* 990–3), and Bishop of Sherborne (*c* 993–1002)', in *St Wulfsige and Sherborne*, ed. Barker *et al.*, pp. 53–94, at pp. 63, 66–7.

5  *Councils & Synods*, ed. Whitelock, no. 42, pp. 230–1, where one of these letters is printed. She notes the possibility (raised by K. Jost, *Wulfstanstudien*, Schweizer anglistische Arbeiten 23 (Bern, 1950)) 21, that the letter not printed by her was in fact not by Wulfsige. Whitelock disagrees with the basis of Jost's argument. Nonetheless, for a different reason she admits the possibility that Wulfsige was not the author of the letter in question. The two letters are printed as one in *Memorials of Saint Dunstan, Archbishop of Canterbury*, ed. William Stubbs, RS 63 (London, 1874), 408–9.

6  Rosalind Love, 'The Life of St Wulfsige of Sherborne by Goscelin of Saint-Bertin: A New Translation with Introduction, Appendix and Notes', in *St Wulfsige and Sherborne*, ed. Barker *et al.*, pp. 98–123.

7  Love, 'The Life of St Wulfsige of Sherborne by Goscelin', p. 105.

Dunstan at Glastonbury in the early 950s, and subsequently went to West-minster, presumably around the time when it was refounded as a reformed community. There are conflicting traditions as to whether Wulfsige was the monastery's first abbot or whether the monastery was initially led by Dunstan who, at the time of its refounding, was bishop of London. Taking all these traditions into account, and with due attention to abbatial attestations to charters, Keynes has deduced that Dunstan had control of Westminster and that he retained over-all control until his death in May 988, but that at some point in the 960s, then fully occupied as archbishop of Canterbury, he put Wulfsige in charge of the day-to-day business of the Westminster community, a role that Wulfsige held until Dunstan's death.[8] Wulfsige then became the abbot. He went to Sherborne as bishop, probably in 993, and he held the abbacy of Westminster in plurality until he resigned this office, apparently in *c.* 997, the year before the reform of the cathedral community.[9] He died on 8 January 1002.

Whatever the precise circumstances of his earlier career, it is clear that he was influenced by Dunstan and was under his patronage; and it was perhaps in recognition of his former close association with Dunstan that he was given Dunstan's pontifical, probably at the time when he was consecrated bishop.[10] This is Paris, Bibliothèque Nationale lat. 943, written in the second half of the tenth century, almost certainly at Christ Church, Canterbury, but with some Sherborne additions datable to the early eleventh century written on a supplementary quire. One of these is a list of Sherborne bishops; another is a letter of exhortation sent to Wulf-sige by an archbishop whose name is no longer preserved.[11] It could have been Sigeric, archbishop of Canterbury 990–4, if we assume that the letter was sent to Wulfsige on his appointment, or Ælfric, archbishop of Canter-bury 995–1005, if we assume that the letter was sent by an archbishop soon after his own appointment. The latter seems to me to be the more likely circumstance since, in the first sentence after the formal address, the archbishop refers to himself as being appointed by God to the govern-ance of the church. The most natural way to read this is as a reference to a recent development, which suggests that the impulse for the letter was his own appointment rather than Wulfsige's. The sentence goes on to say that this governance is to be carried out 'in tam periculosis et laboriosissimis temporibus',[12] undoubtedly a topical reference to the Viking attacks and

---

[8]  Keynes, 'Wulfsige', pp. 56–9.

[9]  We do not know the exact dates of Wulfsige's appointment as bishop or his surrender of the abbacy of Westminster. The evidence is discussed by Keynes, 'Wulfsige', pp. 61–2.

[10]  Keynes, 'Wulfsige', pp. 62–3; see also figures 5 and 6 on pp. 64–5.

[11]  *Councils and Synods*, ed. Whitelock, no. 41, pp. 226–9.

[12]  'in such dangerous and difficult times'.

the resulting political, economic and military upheavals. Apart from the formal epistolary address, in which Wulfsige is named, there is nothing particularly personal in this letter. It could conceivably have been sent to several bishops with the greeting formula appropriately personalized, as indeed presumably would have been the case if the sender had been Archbishop Ælfric at the time of his appointment. But the context in which it uniquely survives shows clearly that Wulfsige thought it worth preserving. Keynes argues that Wulfsige's decision to reform the community at Sherborne, which he eventually did in 998, was not simply the act of someone from a reformist tradition wishing to make his mark, but was a considered response to the dangerous and difficult times, conceived within a frame of reference that saw the Viking invasions as a manifestation of God's displeasure with the sins of the English.[13] In that frame of reference, the 'upgrading' of the life of the cathedral from the clerical to the monastic, and the exacting of higher standards that this would imply, would be seen as a practical response to threats of attack and destruction that seemed to be gathering apace and from which Dorset would not necessarily be immune.[14]

The archiepiscopal letter does not, in fact, advocate such a radical change of regime, although it was a change that clearly made sense in terms of the tenor of the time and Wulfsige's own background. What the letter does provide, however, is general advice on how a bishop should behave, and how he should ensure that the ealdorman and the *principes* (i.e. reeves and thegns) should conduct their business and discharge their duties in accordance with good Christian custom. The bishop, in other words, is urged to think about the good order of society in the exercise of ecclesiastical and secular authority, with the implication that this is doubly necessary in these troubled times. Good Christian belief and practice are thus presented as bulwarks against contemporary threats.

The reference to the troubled times at the beginning of the letter and the firm advice to the bishop at the end that he should promote Christian conduct in the exercise of secular authority have no known source. The greater part of the letter, however, is taken verbatim from a letter by Alcuin to Eanbald, archbishop of York,[15] although there is nothing in

---

[13]  Keynes, 'Wulfsige', pp. 67–72.

[14]  As Keynes points out ('Wulfsige', p. 71), Wulfsige seems also to have taken practical steps to protect the monastic precinct by enclosing it with hedges and ditches. On the Viking attacks in the region at this time, see Katherine Barker, 'Bishop Wulfsige's Lifetime: Viking Campaigns Recorded in the Anglo-Saxon Chronicle for Southern England', in *St Wulfsige and Sherborne*, ed. Barker *et al.*, pp. 124–32.

[15]  *Councils & Synods*, ed. Whitelock, p. 228, n. 1. For Alcuin's letter, see *Alcuini sive Albini epistolae*, ed. E. Dümmler, MGH, *Epistolae* IV (Berlin, 1895), no. 114; trans.

the passage selected that is circumstantially specific. It spells out, rather, that the bishop should attend to the wellbeing of souls, preach continually, act for the glory of God and not for himself, set a holy example, be proper in the celebration of mass and the anointing of the sick, be continent in fasting, set aside time for reading, and indulge neither in worldly pomp, personal adornments, or excessive drinking. The list of exhortations is long and I have given only a sample of them here, but they are sufficient to make it clear that it was a passage chosen to emphasize the need for high standards in daily life and in the conduct of ecclesiastical responsibilities. As written, this was advice directed at a bishop. But there is nothing here that was not also applicable to the priest for, as Ælfric noted more than once in the Pastoral Letters that he wrote for Bishop Wulfsige and for Archbishop Wulfstan,[16] there is no intrinsic difference between priests and bishops, since both are within the seventh order of the church; the differences are purely functional, in that bishops, in addition to their normal priestly duties, ordain priests, confirm children, bless the chrism, consecrate churches and watch over the collection and distribution of God's dues. The Pastoral Letter that Wulfsige commissioned from Ælfric addresses many of the issues specified in the archbishop's letter to Wulfsige. It seems to me that his interest in setting standards for the clergy, which we see him doing in the Pastoral Letter that Ælfric wrote on his behalf, is the response of someone from a reformist background to the troubles of the time, in just the same way as we may understand his monastic reform of the cathedral community. Furthermore, if the archiepiscopal letter to Wulfsige can be read as indicative of a certain contemporary ecclesiastical mindset, leading to a clearer understanding of why the cathedral community was reformed, its particularities make it yet more pertinent as a prompt for reformist activity in the framework of the secular church.

I now wish to examine the Pastoral Letter itself, and to look at the issues that it addresses and the standards that it sets.[17] It was written in Old English in order all the more effectively to reach out to clergy whose command of Latin, we must imagine, was somewhat limited, although in fact this letter, unlike the first Old English Pastoral Letter that Ælfric wrote for Archbishop Wulfstan a few years later, does not make direct reference

---

Stephen Allott, *Alcuin of York c. A.D. 732 to 804: His Life and Letters* (York, 1974, reprinted 1987), letter 6, pp. 6–10. See also above (Rumble), p. 7.

[16] *Die Hirtenbriefe Ælfrics,* ed. Fehr: p. 11 (Letter for Wulfsige, chs. 43–4); pp. 50–1 (First Latin Letter for Wulfstan, chs. 128–9); and p. 110 (First Old English Letter for Wulfstan, ch.111).

[17] In the following analysis references are given in the body of the article using the chapter numbers in Fehr's edition.

to this difficulty.[18] Be that as it may, it certainly would require much greater linguistic competence to understand an unpredictable, discursive text on a range of topics read aloud in Latin – which is how the text would most likely have been delivered in a clerical synod – than it docs to understand the predictable and repetitive nature of liturgical Latin. So Wulfsige was clearly a pragmatist. By contrast with the Old English Pastoral Letters written for Wulfstan, there is no sign that Ælfric first wrote a version in Latin, and so we must assume that Wulfsige's request was for the vernacular from the outset. The occasion for the reading of the letter to the clergy was evidently a synod shortly before Holy Week, since the instructions given in the letter for the services of Maundy Thursday, Good Friday, Holy Saturday and Easter Day are introduced with the words:

> Ic bidde eow þæt ge gymon eowra sylfra, swa eowere bec eow wissiað, and hu ge don sceolon on þisum towerdum dagum [117].[19]

The letter's opening address [1] sets out Wulfsige's general purpose:

> Ic secge eow preostum, þæt ic sylf nelle beran eowre gymeleaste on eowrum þeowdome; ac ic secge eow soðlice, hu hit geset is be preostum.[20]

There then follows [2–28] a long discussion of the need for 'clænnysse' ('chastity') which, since he is addressing priests, turns out to be a sustained case for priestly celibacy. The authority for this is taken right back to the Council of Nicaea. Within Christian history, this Council, held in 325, was notable for the defeat of Arianism, the heresy which denied the divinity of Christ. And so, in mentioning the Council, the letter refers – unavoidably, one would think – to the defeat and ignominious death of Arius [8–11], which occurred

> For-þan-þe he nolde gelyfan, þæt þæs lifigendan Godes sunu wære ealswa mihtig, swa his mære fæder is [9].[21]

---

[18] The First Old English Letter for Wulfstan opens with the words: 'Us biscopum gedafenað, þæt we þa boclican lare þe ure canon us tæcð and eac seo Cristes boc, eow preostum geopenigan on engliscum gereorde; forþon-þe ge ealle ne cunnon þæt leden under-standan', 'It befits us bishops that we reveal to you priests in the English language the written lore that our canon teaches us, and also the book of Christ [sc. the gospels], because you do not all know how to understand the Latin' (my translation, here and throughout): *Die Hirtenbriefe Ælfrics,* ed. Fehr, p. 68, ch. 2. Fehr's ch. 1, in Latin, is not part of the Pastoral Letter, being the covering note that Ælfric sent to Wulfstan to accompany his two Old English letters.
[19] 'I pray you that you attend to yourselves, as your books direct you, and how you must act in these approaching days'.
[20] 'I tell you priests that I am not willing myself to tolerate your negligence in your service, but I will tell you truly how it is ordained concerning priests'.
[21] 'Because he would not believe that the Son of the living God was just as mighty as his glorious Father is'.

But this is followed by equal attention being given to the Council's decree, which is forcefully described as a unanimous pronouncement, that

> naþer ne bisceop ne mæsse-preost, ne diacon, ne nan riht canonicus, næbbe on his huse nænne wifman, buton hit sy his modor, oððe his swustur, faðu, oððe modrige, and se-þe elles do, þolige his hades [13].[22]

The multiplicity of negatives in the Old English gives the decree extraordinary emphasis, which it is difficult to replicate in translation. Clearly, this was Ælfric's (and by extension Wulfsige's) primary reason for citing the Council of Nicaea in this letter, since reference to the Council is introduced by an assertion of the need to be celibate, as we have seen, and the discussion of celibacy that follows, now with all the authority of the Council behind it, continues to ch. 28. In total, then, the discussion of celibacy, counting from the introduction of the topic to its end at ch. 28, is the most substantial section of the letter dealing with conduct of life, and it is given prominence in being the first. The promotion of clerical celibacy is a feature of the Benedictine reform, and Ælfric in particular was very committed to it, as he was also to sexual continence among the laity.[23] Its importance in this letter can, therefore, be seen as a reflection of his own concerns but, as we shall see below,[24] we have a copy of the letter that was evidently in circulation, so Wulfsige must have subscribed to it himself. This is explicable given his monastic background and his reform credentials. But just as important to an understanding of the position in this letter of the practice of celibacy as a standard for the clergy is the value and power that it had for a bishop concerned with reform in the purposeful sense of seeking to enhance Christian moral authority in the context of the troubled times.

The letter then continues with a discussion of the seven orders of the

---

[22] 'neither bishop nor masspriest, nor deacon, nor any regular canon, is to have in his house any woman, unless it be his mother or his sister, his father's sister or his mother's sister, and he who does otherwise is to forfeit his orders'.

[23] Ælfric vigorously promoted priestly celibacy in his First Latin and First Old English Letters for Wulfstan, although in the latter, where he was conscious of writing for an audience of limited educational sophistication, he decided to modify the complexity of his argument: see Joyce Hill, 'Authorial Adaptation: Ælfric, Wulfstan and the Pastoral Letters', in *Text and Language in Medieval English Prose: A Festschrift for Tadao Kubouchi*, ed. Akio Oizumi, Jacek Fisiak and John Scahill (Frankfurt, 2005), pp. 63–75, at pp. 66–7. See also C. Cubitt, 'Virginity and Misogyny in Tenth- and Eleventh-Century England', *Gender and History* 12 (2000), 1–32, and several publications by R. K. Upchurch, 'For Pastoral Care and Political Gain: Ælfric of Eynsham's Preaching on Marital Celibacy', *Traditio* 59 (2004), 39–78; 'The Legend of Chrysanthus and Daria in Ælfric's *Lives of Saints*', *Studies in Philology* 101 (2004), 250–69; 'Virgin Spouses as Model Christians: The Legend of Julian and Basilissa in Ælfric's *Lives of Saints*', *ASE* 34 (2005), 197–217.

[24] See below, pp. 159–60.

church [29–44], but notably it reverts to the question of celibacy in its discussion of the standard appropriate for deacons, who are required to live the spiritual life 'mid clænnysse' [38], 'in chastity'. As a kind of supplementary note to this discussion, it is explained that the hierarchy of monks and nuns lies outside these seven ecclesiastical orders [45–6].

The following part of the letter [48–60] deals with the due ordering of the priestly life. They are to maintain the services in church, sing the seven canonical hours, as evidently specified in an earlier synod [49]: nocturns, prime, tierce, sext, nones, vespers and compline; they are to pray for the king and the bishop, all who do good to them, and all Christian people; and they are to arm themselves with spiritual weapons in the form of holy books, specified as: a psalter, a book of epistles, a gospel book, a massbook, songbooks (pl.), a passional, a penitential, and a reading book [52].[25] In the copy of the letter which survives in CCCC 190, the statement that such books are essential is given additional emphasis through a comment that is almost certainly non-authorial:[26]

> and he ne mæg butan beon, gif he his had on riht healdan wyle and þam folce æfter rihte wisigan, þe him tolocað' [53].[27]

The underlying transmission of this copy means that the addition is not attributable to Wulfsige,[28] but nonetheless it confirms the importance that was attached to the acquisition by priests of a serviceable library. Furthermore, in harmony with injunctions that we find elsewhere in Ælfric's writings, where he expresses anxiety about the accurate copying of his own work,[29] the priests are told that care must be taken that the books are

---

25  There is another list of books essential for priests in Ælfric's First Latin Pastoral Letter for Wulfstan, see *Die Hirtenbriefe Ælfrics,* ed. Fehr, p. 51, ch. 137. Although this is phrased differently in the Old English version of the same letter (*Die Hirtenbriefe Ælfrics,* ed. Fehr, p. 126, ch. 157), it is clear that Ælfric and his episcopal colleagues had in mind quite a substantial library of around seven to ten items. For an interpretation of the names for the various kinds of book, see Helmut Gneuss, 'Liturgical Books in Anglo-Saxon England and their Old English Terminology', in *Learning and Literature in Anglo-Saxon England: Studies Presented to Peter Clemoes on the Occasion of his Sixty-Fifth Birthday*, ed. Michael Lapidge and Helmut Gneuss (Cambridge, 1985), pp. 91–141.

26  *Die Hirtenbriefe Ælfrics,* ed. Fehr, p. CXXXIV (Clemoes's supplementary introduction).

27  'and he cannot be without them, if he wishes to hold rightly to his order and rightly direct the people who belong to him'.

28  On the development of this manuscript, see Joyce Hill, 'Two Anglo-Saxon Bishops at Work: Wulfstan, Leofric and Cambridge Corpus Christi College MS 190' (forthcoming).

29  *Ælfric's Catholic Homilies. The First Series. Text,* ed. Peter Clemoes, EETS ss 17 (Oxford, 1997), 177; *Ælfric's Catholic Homilies. The Second Series. Text,* ed. Malcolm Godden, EETS ss 5 (Oxford, 1979), 2; *Aelfrics Grammatik und Glossar,* ed. Julius Zupitza (Berlin, 1880), reprinted with a preface by Helmut Gneuss (Berlin, 1966), second reprint with a new introduction by Helmut Gneuss (Hildesheim, 2001), p. 3; *The Old English Version of the Heptateuch and Ælfric's Libellus de Veteri Testamento*

well corrected [54]. Injunctions of this kind are characteristic of the Carolingian reform also, concern with the accuracy of the text being one of
the Carolingians' major preoccupations.[30] We might take it as a reformist
indicator here too, although one has to ask how feasible it was to put
this clearly desirable standard into effect. There are also injunctions here
about the need to have mass-vestments that are suitable for honouring
God and good quality altar cloths, to ensure that the corporal is clean, and
that the chalice and paten are made from clean and imperishable material
(meaning, in effect, material that is impermeable).

This is followed by pronouncements about the importance of preaching
and teaching on Sundays and festivals, when the priest should expound
the meaning of the gospel in English and also the paternoster and creed
[61–7], responsibilities for which Ælfric's homilies would be especially
useful. The clergy are lectured on the importance of book-learning so that
these duties can be properly carried out: 'Þa dumban hundas ne magon
beorcan' [63],[31] lightly paraphrasing Isaiah LVI. 10; and 'Gif se blinda
mann bið þæs oðres blinden lattrow, þonne befeallað hy begen on sumne
blindne seað' [65],[32] echoing Christ's words from Matt. XV. 14.

The focus of attention then shifts to what one might call money matters
and more general conduct [68–82]. Priests must divide the tithes into
three: one part for the repair of the church, one part for the poor and one
part for God's servants who look after the church. Mass may only be
celebrated in a consecrated building, except in cases of great necessity or
if someone is ill; and a child brought for baptism must be baptised immediately so that it does not die a heathen. Priests may not perform services
for money, nor move from one church to another for covetous reasons;
drinking to excess is outlawed, as is engaging in trade, the bearing of
weapons, participation in secular lawsuits, swearing oaths, and deserting
the religious vocation.

Next come directions about penance, about the management of administering the sacrament to the infirm who cannot swallow, or to the sick
who are barely conscious, and about the confessing and anointing of the
sick. [83–92].

---

*et Novo,* I, *Introduction and Text,* ed. Richard Marsden, EETS os 330 (Oxford, 2008), 7
(*Prefatio* to Genesis) and 230 (*Libellus*); *Ælfric's Lives of Saints,* ed. Walter W. Skeat,
EETS os 76, 82, 94, 114 (Oxford, 1881–1900), reprinted in 2 vols. (1966), I. 6.
30 Charlemagne's *Admonitio generalis* refers to the necessity of catholic (i.e. orthodox)
books being carefully emended: *Legum, Sectio II: Capitularia regum Francorum,* I, ed.
A. Boretius, MGH (Hannover, 1883), pp. 52–62, at p. 60, ch. 72. See also Christopher
A. Jones, 'Ælfric's Pastoral Letters and the Episcopal *Capitula* of Radulf of Bourges',
*Notes and Queries* 240 (n.s. 42) (1995), 149–55.
31 'Dumb dogs cannot bark'.
32 'If the blind man is leader of the other blind man, then they both fall into some hidden
pit'.

The letter then refers to the four great synods which, as is noted, established orthodox trinitarian belief and the nature of the incarnate being: Nicaea, Constantinople, Ephesus and Chalcedon.[33] However, as when Nicaea was treated earlier on in the Letter, they are invoked not primarily because of their doctrinal significance, even though that is briefly acknowledged, but rather as the source of the ordinances that govern ecclesiastical life [93–104]. Priests are berated for not properly following their own rule; and in this they are compared unfavourably with monks:

> Hu durre ge ne forseon heora ealra gesetnysse, þonne munecas healdað anes mannes gesetnyssa, þæs halgan Benedictus, and be his dihte lybbað, and gyf hy hwær hit tobræcað, hi hit gebetað eft be heora abbuddes dihte mid ealre eadmodnysse? [101]. Ge habbað eac regol, gyf ge hine rædan woldan, on þam ge magon geseon, hu hit geset is be eow [102]. Ac ge lufiað woruld-spræca and wyllað beon gerefan and forlætað eowre cyrcan and þa gesettnyssa mid ealle [103].[34]

The priestly rule referred to here is not specified. Perhaps, as Whitelock has suggested, it was the Capitulary of Aachen (*c.* 802), known in England under the title the *Iura quae sacerdotes debent tenere* and apparently regarded as the work of Archbishop Ecgberht, an attribution that would have given it considerable authority.[35] To people such as Ælfric and Wulfsige, when compared with the *Regula Sancti Benedicti* and the *Regularis Concordia* it must have seemed rather limited in its prescriptions but, as a framework for priestly conduct within the secular church, it was eminently practical. It addresses what one might call organizational and behavioural matters for priests in a secular context, and for the liturgy specifies the basic requirements by noting the observances required. What it specifies, therefore, is precisely what the Pastoral Letter itself sets out to enforce; and, indeed, it is a direct source for the Letter, particularly chs.

---

[33] Nicaea, in 325, dealt with Arianism, which denied the true divinity of Christ and thus the concept of the Trinity. Constantinople, in 381, dealt with Apollinarianism, which held the view that Christ had a human body but a divine spirit (and was thus incomplete as a man in lacking a human spirit). Ephesus, in 431, dealt with Nestorianism, which argued that there were two separate persons in the incarnate Christ, one divine and one human. Chalcedon, in 451, dealt with Eutychianism or Monophysitism, which held that Christ had one single divine nature.

[34] 'How dare you now despise the ordinances of them all [*sc.* the four church councils just mentioned], when monks keep the ordinances of one man, the holy Benedict, and live by his direction, and if they break it anywhere, they atone for it again by the direction of their abbot with all humility? You also have a rule, if you would read it, in which you can see how it is laid down for you; but you love worldly concerns and wish to be reeves and abandon your churches and ordinances entirely'.

[35] *Councils & Synods*, ed. Whitelock, p. 195. For the text of the Capitulary where the chapters are in the order in which they occur in English manuscripts, see *Legum*, I, ed. G. H. Pertz, MGH (Hannover, 1835), 87–9.

48–84.[36] Another theoretical possibility is the *Enlarged Rule of Chrodegang*, although there are no tenth-century manuscripts from England; the first use may have been by Leofric for the episcopal *familia* at Exeter.[37] This is, in any case, a rule which presupposes some kind of community interaction, which makes it more suitable for a cathedral context than for priests scattered throughout a diocese. It could have been the *Capitula* of Theodulf of Orléans, which was written for the priesthood in Theodulf's diocese and became very popular in England;[38] or it could have been the *De regula canonicorum* attributed to Amalarius of Metz,[39] or something more local, perhaps drawing upon such texts as these, but now no longer extant. In any event, it is clear that both Wulfsige and Ælfric assumed that the clergy would know exactly what was meant, without any further comment. They, as monks, knew full well how much improved standards depended on the full observance of a rule of life, and we see here the same approach being pursued in relation to the secular church – understandably enough, given the background of the author of the letter and its episcopal commissioner. The sentiment, the aspiration, is in line with the archiepiscopal letter already discussed;[40] and the ideal that Wulfsige's Pastoral Letter expresses, captured most neatly in this reference to the importance of a priestly rule, can be seen as an exaction of standards standing in parallel to what he did within the cathedral community, which of course, as a defined episcopal *familia*, presented a different kind of opportunity for reform than did the scatter of priests across the diocese.

At this point, there is a short section on the proper behaviour of ordinary Christians [105–10]: they must go to church frequently, not talk nor

---

[36] *Councils & Synods*, ed. Whitelock, pp. 206–13.

[37] See the note in the Leofric Missal printed by Patrick W. Conner, *Anglo-Saxon Exeter: A Tenth-Century Cultural History* (Woodbridge, 1993), p. 225, item 6. The earliest extant English manuscript of the *Enlarged Rule* is the bilingual version in CCCC 191, written in Exeter and almost certainly to be identified with the *regula canonicorum* in Leofric's Inventory: see Ker, *Catalogue*, pp. 74–5; *The Old English Version of the Enlarged rule of Chrodegang together with the Latin Original. An Old English Version of the Capitula of Theodulf together with the Latin Original. An Interlinear Old English Rendering of the Epitome of Benedict of Aniane*, ed. Arthur S. Napier, EETS os 150 (London, 1916). More generally, see, *The Chrodegang Rules: The Rules for the Common Life of the Secular Clergy from the Eighth and Ninth Centuries. Critical Texts with Translations and Commentary*, ed. Jerome Bertram (Aldershot, 2005).

[38] *Theodulfi Capitula in England. Die altenglischen Übersetzungen, zusammen mit dem lateinischen Text*, ed. Hans Sauer, Texte und Untersuchungen zur englischen Philologie 8 (Munich, 1978).

[39] Noted as a possibility by Whitelock in *Councils & Synods*, ed. Whitelock, p. 216, n. 2, where she also lists the Capitulary of Aachen and the *Enlarged Rule of Chrodegang* as possibilities. For Amalarius, *De regula canonicorum*, see *PL* 105, 812–956, although the authorship is in fact debatable: see *The Chrodegang Rules*, ed. Bertram, pp. 93–4.

[40] See above, pp. 148–51.

hold conversations in church, and not drink, nor fool around while they are there. This, though reasonable enough in what it says, is at odds with the letter's otherwise determinedly priestly focus, and there are grounds for believing that it was a later addition by Ælfric, drawing upon his homily *De oratione Moysi*, extant in the best surviving *Lives of Saints* manuscript, although not necessarily part of Ælfric's original conception of that work.[41]

We return to the behaviour of priests for the rest of the letter. In chs. 111–16 they are enjoined not to rejoice in anyone's death, nor to attend on the corpse unless invited. Even then, there should be no participation in heathen songs or loud laughter, or drinking beside the dead body 'þe-læs-þe ge syndon efenlæce þæs hæðenscypes, þe hy þær begað' [113].[42] Priests are also directed not to be proud, not to adorn themselves with rings, and to dress in moderation, neither too meanly nor too showily. Lay and monastic dress must alike be avoided.

At ch. 117 the letter moves to treating in considerable detail how the services of Maundy Thursday, Good Friday, Holy Saturday and Easter Day – both Mass and Offices – are to be conducted, continuing to ch. 149. The standards here are those we are familiar with in the monastic context although, in the absence of a community, the liturgy is rather less elaborate in its ceremonial. Since, evidently, there were priests who were accustomed to keep the consecrated Easter host for use at a later date, advice is included about how the host is to be kept, for how long and in what conditions, in order to avoid its turning mouldy or being eaten by mice. Priests are reminded that any consecrated host is just as holy as that consecrated on Easter Day, and there follow some theological observations about why this is so. The section concludes with basic advice about the mixing of water and wine, the need for cleanliness and general care, and the inappropriateness of Mass being celebrated by someone who is blind, since he cannot see whether what he offers to God is clean or dirty.

This original letter ends at this point [149], although there was presumably a concluding sentence or two, now lost. But there is a surviving manuscript which has an added section on feasts and fasts [150–61]. In order to interpret this, it is necessary to take into account all of the extant manuscripts.

---

[41] *Die Hirtenbriefe Ælfrics,* ed. Fehr, p. CXXXIV (Clemoes's supplementary introduction). The passage from *De oratione Moyse* is lines 68–86: *Ælfric's Lives of Saints,* ed. Skeat, I. 288. On the manuscript tradition of the *Lives of Saints,* see Joyce Hill, 'The Dissemination of Ælfric's *Lives of Saints*: A Preliminary Survey', in *Holy Men and Holy Women: Old English Prose Saints' Lives and Their Contexts,* ed. Paul E. Szarmach (Albany, 1996), pp. 235–59, at pp. 235–42.

[42] 'lest you are imitators of the heathenism which they practise there'.

There are three copies of the Ælfric's Pastoral Letter for Wulfsige.[43] One is on spare leaves at the end of Cambridge University Library, Gg.3.28, s.x/xi, the earliest surviving copy of Ælfric's two series of Catholic Homilies and a manuscript which is 'either a product of Ælfric's own scriptorium or a remarkably faithful copy of such a manuscript'.[44] The occurrence of the letter here suggests that it was an Ælfrician file copy. Unfortunately it is incomplete because of the loss of the manuscript's final leaves. However, because it breaks off at ch. 108, part way through the passage that seems to be an insertion from Ælfric's *De oratione Moysi*, we can perhaps assume that this alteration was made by Ælfric. There is another copy in Bod, Junius 121, s. xi (3rd quarter).[45] This is a manuscript within the Wulfstan commonplace book tradition, but Wulfsige's Pastoral Letter is not in other manuscripts of this tradition, so that we cannot be sure if Wulfstan ever had it. However, it would be just the kind of text that Wulfstan was interested in, and there is a close relationship between the Wulfsige Letter and the Pastoral Letters that Ælfric subsequently wrote for Wulfstan,[46] so it is conceivable that the Junius text derives from a copy sent by Ælfric to Wulfstan, perhaps in the course of their correspondence about these matters. This copy includes the *De oratione Moysi* extract (which would be consistent with the exemplar being furnished by Ælfric), but not the concluding feasts and fasts addendum. Finally, there is the copy in CCCC 190, where it is among the additions by Bishop Leofric, who died in 1072.[47] By contrast with Cambridge University Library, Gg.3.28 and Junius 121, this text does not have the Latin covering letter from Ælfric to Wulfsige, which one might expect to be preserved in Ælfric's file copy and which might thus form part of any copy supplied by him to someone else for reference, but which is hardly likely to have been retained by Wulfsige in the version that he used for public consumption. It follows, therefore, that a text derived from the version issued by Wulfsige would also not have the covering letter. This copy of the letter also lacks the *De oratione Moysi* passage, which further supports the view that it is traceable to Wulfsige rather than Ælfric, if we assume that the

---

[43] What follows summarizes my more detailed study of the manuscripts in 'Monastic Reform and the Secular Church: Ælfric's Pastoral Letters in Context', in *England in the Eleventh Century: Proceedings of the Harlaxton Symposium*, ed. Carola Hicks (Stamford, 1992), pp. 103–17.

[44] *Ælfric's Catholic Homilies. The Second Series*, ed. Godden, p. xliii. For a description, see Ker, *Catalogue*, pp. 13–21, no. 15.

[45] For a description, see Ker, *Catalogue*, pp. 412–18, no. 338.

[46] *Die Hirtenbriefe Ælfrics*, ed. Fehr, pp. 35–221. Fehr also prints (at pp. 222–7) a private letter written by Ælfric to Wulfstan, evidently in response to some questions posed by the latter.

[47] For a partial description, see Ker, *Catalogue*, pp. 70–3, no. 45. See also Hill, 'Two Anglo-Saxon Bishops at Work'.

*De oratione Moysi* passage was added by Ælfric after he had sent the Letter to Wulfsige, or that he deleted it from the text he finally sent to Wulfsige, on the grounds that it was inappropriate. However, uniquely of the three surviving copies it does have the addendum on feasts and fasts, which Whitelock believes was added by Wulfsige.[48] Since the folios on which the Pastoral Letter survives were added at Exeter during Leofric's episcopacy to a mid-eleventh-century manuscript, it seems as if we have here a witness to a circulating copy, traceable to the version issued by Wulfsige, which has found its way to the neighbouring diocese,[49] and into a manuscript context not unlike that of Junius 121: a context that is concerned with regulatory matters and the good ordering of the church from an episcopal point of view. On the evidence of the CCCC 190 copy, then, it is reasonable to say that the contents of the letter bear the *imprimatur* of Wulfsige, just as much as they undoubtedly reflect the concerns of Ælfric as the actual author.

Why, finally, did Wulfsige call upon Ælfric? Ælfric was in a reformed monastery not many miles from the cathedral, in Wulfsige's own diocese, and already had the patronage of powerful supporters of the reform, both ecclesiastical and lay; his lay patrons, moreover, were the leading figures of the region where the Sherborne diocese was situated.[50] Although we do not know precisely when Wulfsige commissioned the Pastoral Letter, knowledge of Ælfric's ability in promoting reform standards through his vernacular Catholic Homilies had begun to spread, as witness Ælfric's correspondence with Sigeric, archbishop of Canterbury.[51] Additionally, Ælfric had the right credentials through his Winchester connection (the neighbouring diocese), and was probably known locally as someone who was engaged in Benedictine reform writing, mainly in the vernacular, at Cerne Abbas, where he went simply as monk and masspriest, and was thus without the distractions of major office. We might put Wulfsige's commission down to convenience, contacts, and recognition of appropriate experience on Ælfric's part; and perhaps Ælfric in return would have found it, in its attention to the secular church, a suitable complement to the work that he was already doing. Not only was he completing

---

[48] *Councils & Synods*, ed. Whitelock, pp. 193–5.
[49] The circumstances under which this might have occurred are discussed in Hill, 'Two Anglo-Saxon Bishops at Work'.
[50] Catherine Cubitt, 'Ælfric's Lay Patrons', in *A Companion to Ælfric*, ed. Hugh Magennis and Mary Swan (Leiden, 2009), pp. 165–92.
[51] Joyce Hill, 'Ælfric: His Life and Works', in *A Companion to Ælfric*, ed. Magennis and Swan, pp. 35–65. Ælfric's letters to Sigeric are discussed at pp. 42–3. The article as a whole explores in more detail the evidence, briefly referred to here, for the various contexts in which Ælfric worked and the impetus given to his literary activity by the circumstances of his career.

and then revising the Catholic Homilies (which are ideal examples of the priestly preaching that the letter advocates), but he was also working at this time on various other texts, including *De falsis diis*,[52] *De oratione Moysi*, which he then used to supplement his own file-copy of the Pastoral Letter for Wulfsige, [53] *De xii abusivis*,[54] *Esther*, [55] and *Judith*,[56] and all of these, in their different ways, could be seen to be inspired by contemporary conditions.[57] Yet, by the time Ælfric sent the Pastoral Letter to Wulfsige, whenever precisely that was, there was more to it than expediency and the convenience of good contacts. There seems also to have been a personal relationship, which allowed Ælfric to be exceptionally forthright in the Latin letter that he wrote to accompany the Old English text. It is worth quoting in full:

> Ælfricus humilis frater uenerabili episcopo Wulfsino salutem in domino. Obtemperauimus iussioni tuæ libenti animo. Sed non ausi fuimus aliquid scribere de episcopali gradu, quia uestrum est scire quomodo uos oporteat optimis moribus exemplum omnibus fieri et continuis ammonitionibus subditos exhortari ad salutem quę est in Christo Ihcsu. Dico tamen quod scpius deberetis uestris clericis alloqui et illorum neglegentiam arguere, quia pęne statuta canonum et sanctę aecclesiae religio uel doctrina eorum peruersitate deleta sunt. Ideoque libera animam tuam et dic eis quę tenenda sunt, sacerdotibus et ministris Christi, ne tu pereas pariter, si mutus habearis canis. Nos uero scriptitamus hanc epistolam, quę anglice sequitur, quasi

---

[52] *Homilies of Ælfric: A Supplementary Collection*, 2 vols., ed. John C. Pope, EETS os 259–60 (London, 1967–8), II. 667–724.

[53] See above, p. 159.

[54] *Early English Homilies from the Twelfth Century MS. Vesp. D. XIV*, ed. Rubie D-N. Warner, EETS os 152 (London 1917), pp. 11–16.

[55] *Angelsächsischen Homilien und Heiligenleben*, ed. Bruno Assmann, Bibliothek der angelsächsischen Prosa 3 (Kassel, 1889), reprinted with a Supplementary Introduction by Peter Clemoes (Darmstadt, 1964), pp. 92–101.

[56] *Angelsächsischen Homilien und Heiligenleben*, ed. Assmann, pp. 102–16.

[57] For recent discussion of Ælfric's concern with contemporary issues, see, for example, Mary Clayton, 'Of Mice and Men: Ælfric's Second Homily for the Feast of a Confessor', *Leeds Studies in English*, n.s. 24 (1993), 1–26; *eadem*, 'Ælfric's *Esther*: A *Speculum Reginae*?', in *Text and Gloss: Studies in Insular Learning and Literature Presented to Joseph Donovan Pheifer*, ed. H. C. O'Briain, A. M. D'Arcy and J. Scattergood (Dublin, 1999), 89–101; *eadem*, 'Ælfric's *Judith*: Manipulative or Manipulated?', *ASE* 23 (1994), 215–27; *eadem*, 'Ælfric and Æthelred', in *Essays on Anglo-Saxon and Related Themes in Memory of Lynne Grundy*, ed. Jane Roberts and Janet Nelson, King's College London Medieval Studies 17 (Exeter, 2000), 65–88; Malcolm Godden, 'Apocalypse and Invasion in Late Anglo-Saxon England', in *From Anglo-Saxon to Early Middle English: Studies Presented to E. G. Stanley*, ed. Malcolm Godden, Douglas Gray, and Terry Hoad (Oxford, 1994), pp. 130–62; Stacy S. Klein, 'Beauty and the Banquet: Queenship and Social Reform in Ælfric's *Esther*', *Journal of English and Germanic Philology* 103 (2004), 77–105; and Simon Keynes, 'An Abbot, an Archbishop and the Viking Raids of 1006–7 and 1009–12', *ASE* 36 (2007), 151–220.

ex tuo ore dictata sit et locutus esses ad clericos tibi subditos, hoc modo
incipiens: [...]⁵⁸

The change to the plural in the sentence beginning 'Dico tamen' is a
comment by Ælfric on the responsibility of all bishops. The rest of the
covering letter is in the singular, addressed to Wulfsige directly.

As already noted, Ælfric's reputation for orthodox writing in the
vernacular, supportive of the Benedictine reform, had already begun
to spread by the time Wulfsige became bishop,⁵⁹ and we should not, in
any case, underestimate the extent to which the relatively small circle of
learned, reform-minded activists were known to each other by name, if
not in person. Even so, we should probably allow for some lapse of time
after 993 before Ælfric felt able to address Wulfsige in the way that he
does in this letter, and write a Pastoral Letter for public dissemination in
the bishop's voice, particularly if we set the tone of this covering letter
against that of his letters to Sigeric and Wulfstan. These, though characterized by an underlying sense of confident authority, are formally defer-
ential. Yet the covering letter to Wulfsige is vigorous, personal, and sharp.
Sisam believed that this was an indication that Ælfric wrote it very soon
after Wulfsige's consecration, driven, perhaps, by a still fresh sense of
the contrast between what he had known at Winchester under Æthelwold
and what he was now experiencing in the area around Cerne, and driven
too by a fear that Wulfsige might take a gradualist approach to reform,
coming as he did from the Dunstanian rather than the Æthelwoldian
camp.⁶⁰ But while it was probably the case that Ælfric was inspired to
develop his vernacular corpus because of the relative intellectual poverty
that he saw outside Winchester, the shock that the move to Cerne (in
c. 987) must have administered was hardly recent, and he had already
responded positively and systematically to the problems of the broader

---

⁵⁸ *Die Hirtenbriefe Ælfrics,* ed. Fehr, p. 1. 'Ælfric a humble brother, to the venerable
   bishop Wulfsin, greeting in the Lord. We have obeyed your command with an open
   mind, but we have not dared to write anything concerning the episcopal office, because
   it is for you to know how it befits you to be an example to all through the best practices
   and to exhort those set under you through continual admonitions to the salvation which
   is in Jesus Christ. I say, nevertheless, that you ought to speak to your clerics more often
   and point out their negligence, because canon law and the religion and doctrine of the
   holy church have nearly been destroyed by their perversity. Therefore, free your mind
   and tell them what things must be held by priests and ministers of Christ lest you perish
   likewise, if you are reckoned a dumb dog. Indeed, we have written this letter, which
   follows in English, as if it were dictated from your mouth and you had spoken to the
   clerics under your charge, beginning in this way: [...]'. On the variation in the form
   of Wulfsige's name, see Rebecca Rushforth, 'Wulfsige's Name: The Writing and the
   Spelling', in *St Wulfsige and Sherborne,* ed. Barker *et al.,* pp. 15–19.
⁵⁹ See above, p. 160.
⁶⁰ Kenneth Sisam, *Studies in the History of Old English Literature* (Oxford, 1953),
   p. 169.

church.[61] It is in fact difficult, given what we know of Ælfric and the tone of his other letters, to see the covering letter to Wulfsige as being written in any context other than that of an established and secure personal relationship which had already included discussion of the problems alluded to here and in the Pastoral Letter itself. We can only assume that Ælfric's willingness to give voice to his sense of frustration and urgency relied upon its being understood by the recipient because they were men who understood each other's point of view.

The upgrading of the cathedral *familia* was something that was formalized five years after Wulfsige's consecration; but his resignation of the abbacy of Westminster in the previous year suggests that he recognized that some focused attention would be needed to carry it through. Even so, there was a certain 'tidiness' about this reform, concerned as it was only with the cathedral community. Raising the standards of the secular clergy across the diocese will have been more difficult, probably more uneven, and more long drawn out, in a sense an altogether more ambitious task. But there is clear evidence that Wulfsige had this as one of the goals of his episcopacy, and the reforming text that he commissioned from Ælfric as a way of carrying it forward is consistent with the aims that we have come to recognize as his motivation for making Sherborne a monastic cathedral. Wulfsige's reforming text gives us a glimpse of two ecclesiastics nurtured in the monastic tradition striving to raise the standards of the secular church, perhaps spurred on in the immediate context by a recognition that this was how they could contribute to moral resistance 'in tam periculosis et laboriosissimis temporibus'.[62]

---

[61]  For the circumstances of Ælfric's career at Cerne Abbas, see Hill, 'Ælfric: His Life and Works', pp. 52–60.

[62]  See above, p. 149.

# 9

## From Winchester to Canterbury: Ælfheah and Stigand – Bishops, Archbishops and Victims

THE final chapter of this book on leaders of the Anglo-Saxon church reconsiders the lives and contrasting reputations of two late Anglo-Saxon bishops of Winchester, both of whom were subsequently promoted to be archbishops of Canterbury.[1] One (Ælfheah) was a monk who was later canonized as a martyr, the other (Stigand) was a secular priest who was vilified even before his death as a pluralist and a usurper. Each played an active part, as advisers to the current king, in important national events. Both of them eventually died as the result of invasions of England from the Continent. Both are mentioned in contemporary accounts and documents, but their reputations were however mainly fossilized after the Norman Conquest when chroniclers assessed their lives in accordance with monastic and papal ideals of behaviour.

### Ælfheah of Winchester and Canterbury

Ælfheah was born *c*. 953 and appears to have had the byname Godwine, probably a patronym.[2] He seems first to have lived as part of the clerical minster at Deerhurst, Gloucestershire, before moving south to Somerset

---

[1]  The only other Anglo-Saxon bishop of Winchester who was translated to Canterbury was Ælfsige I, in 958. This was not an auspicious precedent, however, as he died in 959 on his way to Rome to collect his *pallium*. See Nicholas Brooks, *The Early History of the Church of Canterbury: Christ Church from 597 to 1066* (Leicester, 1984), pp. 237–8 and 375 n. 98; also Wassenhoven, above, p. 102.

[2]  David Hugh Farmer, *The Oxford Dictionary of Saints*, 4th edn (Oxford, 1997), pp.17–18, *sub* Alphege (1); *HBC,* pp. 214 (Canterbury), 223 (Winchester); *HRH*, pp. 28–9, 241; Henrietta Leyser, 'Ælfheah (*d.* 1012)', *ODNB*, article 181; PASE, *sub* Ælfheah 44 (Male) ; see also Brooks, *Early History*, p. 279. For the byname, see *ASC* 984 A: *The Parker Chronicle and Laws (Corpus Christi College Cambridge, MS. 173)*, ed. Robin Flower and Hugh Smith, EETS os 208 (London, 1941 for 1937, repr. 1973), 29b: 'se ðe oðran naman þæs geciged godpine' 'he who was called by the second name Godwine'.

and there associating himself with the monastic reform. According to William of Malmesbury he was at some point monk and prior of Glastonbury Abbey.[3] However, according to Osbern's late-eleventh-century *Vita Sancti Aelfegi*, upon leaving Deerhurst he is said to have dwelt as a hermit at Bath, before joining (or refounding) the reformed monastery there.[4] He became abbot by 982, probably *c.* 977, in succession to Æscwig with whom he may already have shared some authority since 968.[5]

As a monk of Bath, if not as joint abbot, he would have been among the 'micel muneca ðreat', the 'great throng of monks', involved with Edgar's coronation there in 973.[6] In October 984, on the recommendation of Archbishop Dunstan (who is said to have been inspired by a vision of St Andrew),[7] he was appointed the successor to Æthelwold as bishop of Winchester.[8] There he completed and extended Æthelwold's building works at the Old Minster: these included the addition of a ring-crypt at the eastern end and a five-staged tower with a golden weathercock.[9]

---

3   *The Early History of Glastonbury: An Edition, Translation and Study of William of Malmesbury's* De antiquitate Glastonie ecclesie, ed. and trans. John Scott (Woodbridge, 1981), ch. 67, p. 137.

4   Osbern, *Vita S. Aelfegi Cantuariensis archiepiscopi et martiris*, in *Anglia Sacra sive collectio historiarum antiquitus scriptarum de archiepiscopis & episcopis Angliæ*, ed. Henry Wharton, 2 vols. (London, 1691), II. 122–42, at 123–4. Cf. comments by Patrick Wormald, 'How Do We Know So Much About Anglo-Saxon Deerhurst?', Deerhurst Lecture 1991 (Deerhurst, 1993), pp. 7–9.

5   *HRH*, pp. 27–8, 241; Simon Keynes, *An Atlas of Attestations in Anglo-Saxon Charters, c. 670–1066* (Cambridge, 1995), tables LV, LXI.

6   *ASC* 973 A: *Parker Chronicle*, ed. Flower and Smith, 28b. On the coronation of 973, see Simon Keynes, 'Edgar, *rex admirabilis*', in *Edgar, King of the English 959–975: New Interpretations*, ed. Donald Scragg (Woodbridge, 2008), pp. 3–58, at pp. 48–51. On the poem recording it, see Mercedes Salvador-Bello, 'The Edgar Panegyrics in the *Anglo-Saxon Chronicle*', *ibid.*, pp. 252–72.

7   According to Adelard, *Vita Sancti Dunstani*, lectio viii, in *Memorials of Saint Dunstan, Archbishop of Canterbury Edited from Various Manuscripts*, ed. William Stubbs, RS 63 (London, 1874), 61–2. This *vita*, written between 1004 and 1011, was dedicated to Ælfheah, *ibid.*, p. 53; see also Antonia Gransden, *Historical Writing in England c. 550 – c. 1307* (London, 1974), p. 78. Dunstan's obedience to St Andrew is also referred to by Eadmer in his *Vita S. Dunstani*, see *Eadmer of Canterbury, Lives and Miracles of Saints Oda, Dunstan, and Oswald*, ed. and trans. Andrew J. Turner and Bernard J, Muir (Oxford, 2006), pp. 96–7, 102–3, 148–9 (chs. 28, 31 and 61). See also William of Malmesbury, *The Deeds of the Bishops of England* (Gesta Pontificum Anglorum), trans. David Preest (Woodbridge, 2002), pp. 21–2, 112 (chs. 19 and 76); and William's *Vita Dunstani*, II. 24. 5–6 in *William of Malmesbury, Saints' Lives: Lives of SS. Wulfstan, Dunstan, Patrick, Benignus and Indract*, ed. and trans. M. Winterbottom and R. M. Thomson (Oxford, 2002), pp. 279–80.

8   He was consecrated on 19 October and instituted on 28 October (SS Simon and Jude), see *ASC* 984 A: *Parker Chronicle*, ed. Flower and Smith, 29b.

9   'Special Dedicatory Letter to Ælfheah', in Wulfstan of Winchester, *Narratio metrica de S. Swithuno*, ed. and trans. Michael Lapidge, in *The Cult of St Swithun*, Winchester Studies 4, *The Anglo-Saxon Minsters of Winchester*, part ii (Oxford, 2003), 372–97, especially 380–1 and 386–9.

The refurbished church was dedicated in 993 or 994.[10] On 10 September 996, he translated Æthelwold's body to a new tomb within the choir.[11] Ælfheah also took steps to safeguard the church's endowment: in 984 × 1001 he obtained a confirmation from King Æthelred II of the Old Minster's right to the beneficial hidation of its estate of Chilcomb which surrounded the city;[12] and in 996 he persuaded King Æthelred to restore a tenement in Winchester which had been bequeathed to the Old Minster by the noblewoman Ælfswith but had been subsequently alienated.[13] In 997, in recognition of Ælfheah's 'sedulous humility', King Æthelred restored to the Old Minster the important Wiltshire hundred of Downton (including 45 hides of detached upland at *Eblesburna*, the place now called Bishopstone), which he admitted to having unjustly seized in his youth.[14] Although it has been suggested that Ælfheah himself had been party to an alienation in 986 to a layman of 5 hides of this property (at *Ebbleshurne*),[15] this is probably to do him an injustice as the bounds of the 5 hides described in the relevant royal diploma which he witnessed seem to identify it as Stratford Tony (also on the River Ebble), which was not later part of Downton Hundred which it presumably would have been if Æthelred's restoration of 997 were effective. Besides using his influence with the king to obtain new confirmations or restorations of land, Ælfheah may himself have been responsible for commissioning the Old Minster Refoundation Charter in the form of a commemorative codex containing copies of documents previously issued by King Edgar at the instigation of Bishop Æthelwold.[16]

On at least two occasions Ælfheah played a key role in national politics in relation to Viking attacks. One of these, as is well known and as will be discussed below,[17] was in 1011–12 but it should be noted that on an earlier occasion in 994 he had been involved in a symbolic act which strengthened the peace treaty negotiated (with payment of tribute) between the English and a Viking army whose leaders included Olaf Tryggvason.[18]

---

[10] Lapidge, *The Cult of St Swithun*, p. 390 n.

[11] *Wulfstan of Winchester: Life of Æthelwold*, ed. and trans. Michael Lapidge and Michael Winterbottom, (Oxford, 1991, repr. 1996), ch. 43, pp. 66–7; and *ibid.*, pp. xlii, xcix–ci.

[12] S 946; Rumble, *Property and Piety*, no. XXX.

[13] S 889; Rumble, *Property and Piety*, no. XXVI. The same document also recorded the grant of half a fish-weir at Brentford, Middlesex.

[14] S 891; KCD 698; apparently authentic according to Simon Keynes, *The Diplomas of King Æthelred 'The Unready' 978–1016: A Study in their Use as Historical Evidence*, Cambridge Studies in Medieval Life and Thought 3rd ser., 13 (Cambridge, 1980), 255.

[15] Keynes, *Diplomas*, pp. 39 (n. 69), 180, 182. S 861; KCD 655.

[16] Rumble, *Property and Piety*, no. V. For discussion of this putative codex (containing S 814–19, 821–7), see *ibid.*, pp. 99–104.

[17] See below, pp. 169–70.

[18] *ASC* 994 C–F; *The Anglo-Saxon Chronicle according to the Several Original Authorities*, ed. and trans. Benjamin Thorpe, 2 vols., RS 23 (London, 1861, repr. 1964),

After hostages had been given to the Vikings, Ælfheah, with Ealdorman Æthelweard of Hampshire, escorted Olaf from Southampton to the royal estate of Andover and then, as diocesan bishop, officiated at Olaf's confirmation as a Christian, with King Æthelred acting as godfather.

> Then the king sent Bishop Ælfheah and Ealdorman Æthelweard for King Olaf, and hostages were given to the ships meanwhile. And they then brought Olaf to the king at Andover with much ceremony, and King Ethelred stood sponsor to him at confirmation ['se cyning Æþelred his onfeng æt bisceopes handa'],[19] and bestowed gifts on him royally. And then Olaf promised – as also he performed – that he would never come back to England in hostility.[20]

It is worth considering whether the successful outcome of events of 994 may possibly have made Ælfheah fatally over-confident in his later dealings with a different group of Vikings in 1012.

Ælfheah was appointed archbishop of Canterbury in 1006, at the age of about 53.[21] As successor first of Æthelwold at Winchester and then of Dunstan at Canterbury, Ælfheah was heir to two variant traditions of the monastic reform in England (one coming from Abingdon/Winchester and the other found at Glastonbury/Canterbury) and he took care actively to promote the cults of the leaders of both.[22] At Winchester, as mentioned above,[23] he continued and expanded the building work begun by Æthelwold and also translated the latter's relics. At Canterbury, he commissioned Adelard of Ghent to write a life of his patron Dunstan.[24]

---

I. 242–3. The reference to Ælfheah at the end of *ASC* 991 A is an early-twelfth-century Canterbury interpolation, see *Parker Chronicle*, ed. Flower and Smith, 29b; *The Anglo-Saxon Chronicle MS A*. ed. Janet Bately, The AS Chronicle: A Collaborative Edition, ed. David Dumville and Simon Keynes 3 (Cambridge, 1986), xli, Scribe 9. For text, translation and discussion of a general peace-treaty apparently made earlier in 994 and now known as II Æthelred, see Simon Keynes, 'The Historical Context of the Battle of Maldon', in *The Battle of Maldon AD 991*, ed. Donald Scragg (Oxford, 1991), pp. 81–113, at pp. 103–7.

[19] *The Anglo-Saxon Chronicle MS C*, ed. Katherine O'Brien O'Keeffe, The AS Chronicle: A Collaborative Edition, ed. Dumville and Keynes 5 (Cambridge, 2001), 87.

[20] Translation from Whitelock, *EHD*, pp. 235–6.

[21] *ASC* 1006 C–F; *The Anglo-Saxon Chronicle*, ed. and trans. Thorpe, I. 254–5. *ASC* 1006 A is an interpolation of s. xi/xii, see *Parker Chronicle*, ed. Flower and Smith, 30a; *ASC MS A*, ed. Bately, p. xxxix, hand 7a. For arguments in favour of an ordination date of 16 November 1006, see Keynes, *Diplomas*, p. 262.

[22] Cf. *Bishop Æthelwold: His Career and Influence*, ed. Barbara Yorke (Woodbridge, 1988, repr. 1997), pp. 9–10; and D. J. Dales, 'The Spirit of the *Regularis Concordia* and the Hand of St Dunstan', in *St Dunstan: His Life, Times and Cult*, ed. Nigel Ramsay, Margaret Sparks, and Tim Tatton-Brown (Woodbridge, 1992), pp. 45–56, especially pp. 49, 55.

[23] See above, pp. 166–7.

[24] See above, p. 166, n. 7.

As both an experienced royal counsellor and a national spiritual leader, Archbishop Ælfheah was present at Enham, Hampshire, at Pentecost 1008, with his archiepiscopal colleague Wulfstan of York, when an attempt was made to emulate Continental peace assemblies as a way of countering, through prayer and spiritual reforms, the threat to the kingdom from the Vikings. There a new law-code, V and VI Æthelred, whose three final written forms (two vernacular and one Latin) were composed by Archbishop Wulfstan, seems to have been discussed and approved.[25] This, according to Margaret Deanesly, amounted 'to a complete restatement of English law about the church'. [26] In V Æthelred, twenty-five out thirty-five chapters dealt with the church and in VI Æthelred, the longer version, thirty out of fifty-two.[27]

In September 1011, however, disaster struck Ælfheah when he and others, including Godwine the bishop of Rochester, Ælfweard the king's reeve and an Abbess Leofrun, were captured by a marauding Viking force which had been allowed to enter the cathedral city of Canterbury through the treachery of one Ælfmær whose life Ælfheah is said to have previously saved.[28] The Vikings stayed in Canterbury for 'as long as they pleased' and when they departed they took Archbishop Ælfheah with them:

> He was then a captive ['ræpling'][29] who had been head of the English people and of Christendom.[30]

25 See M. K. Lawson, 'Archbishop Wulfstan and the Homiletic Element in the Laws of Æthelred II and Cnut', *English Historical Review* 107 (1992), 565–86; reprinted in *The Reign of Cnut: King of England, Denmark and Norway,* ed. Alexander R. Rumble (London and Cranbury, NJ, 1994), pp. 141–64; and Simon Keynes, 'An Abbot, An Archbishop, and the Viking Raids of 1006–7 and 1009–12', *ASE* 36 (2007), 151–220, at 177–9.

26 Margaret Deanesly, *Sidelights on the Anglo-Saxon Church* (London, 1962), p. 60.

27 Deanesly, *Sidelights*, p. 61.

28 These Vikings were part of the army led by Earl Thorkell the Tall which had landed in 1009; on him, see Simon Keynes, 'Cnut's Earls', in *The Reign of Cnut*, ed. Rumble, pp. 43–88, at pp. 54–7. For the attack on Canterbury, see *ASC* 1011 C–F: *The Anglo-Saxon Chronicle*, ed. and trans. Thorpe, pp. 266–7. MSS E and F have Leofwine in error for Leofrun. John of Worcester identified her as abbess of St Mildryth's, Thanet, and Ælfmær as an archdeacon, see *JW, s.a.* 1012; II. 468–9. *ASC* is careful to distinguish this Ælfmær from the identically named abbot of St Augustine's, Canterbury, who managed to escape. PASE calls him Ælfmær 9.

29 *ASC MS C*, ed. O'Brien O'Keeffe, p. 96. The OE noun *ræpling*, literally 'one bound' is related to the verb *rǣpan* 'to bind (with a rope [*rāp*])' which had been used earlier in the same annal in the passage 'hi … heregodon ure earme folc, ⁊ hi rypton ⁊ slogon' (O'Brien O'Keeffe, p. 95), 'they harried our wretched people and they bound and slew them' [my translation]; see *An Anglo-Saxon Dictionary based on the Manuscript Collections of the late Joseph Bosworth*, ed. T. Northcote Toller (Oxford, 1898, repr. 1975), p. 784.

30 Whitelock, *EHD*, p. 244.

Although a huge tribute of £48,000 was paid at London to these Vikings just after Easter 1012,[31] according to John of Worcester a further ransom of £3000 was demanded for Ælfheah.[32] This he appears to have refused to allow to be paid, an action which seems to have cost him his life. While being kept at the Vikings' camp on the River Thames at Greenwich, he was killed on 19 April during an assembly or public meeting (*husting*). While this may possibly be a reference to the holding of a formal trial with passing of sentence, his being pelted with ox-bones by those present accords well enough with literary references to bone-throwing in later Scandinavian written sources to suggest that he was made the object of ritual entertainment at a drunken feast.[33]

> [...] the army became greatly incensed against the bishop because he would not promise them any money, but forbade that anything should be paid for him. They were also very drunk, for wine from the south had been brought there. They seized the bishop, and brought him to their assembly ['to hiora hustinge'][34] on the eve of the Sunday of the octave of Easter, which was 19 April, and shamefully put him to death there: they pelted him with bones and with ox-heads, and one of them struck him on the head with the back of an axe, that he sank down with the blow [...].[35]

His captors, perhaps regretting what had occurred when they had been drunk on 'wine from the south', presumably meaning wine brought from Normandy, next day allowed his body to be taken to London. There it was received with honour by Bishop Eadnoth of Dorchester-on-Thames and by Bishop Ælfhun and the citizens of London and was buried on the following day in St Paul's Cathedral.[36] Ælfheah was canonized very soon after.[37] The annals in the Anglo-Saxon Chronicle for 1011–12 (written

---

[31]  Easter Sunday was on 13 April.

[32]  *JW, s.a.* 1012; II. 470–1.

[33]  Ian McDougall, 'Serious Entertainments: An Examination of a Peculiar Type of Viking Atrocity', *ASE* 22 (1993), 201–25.

[34]  *ASC MS C*, ed. O'Brien O'Keeffe, p. 96.

[35]  Whitelock, *EHD*, p. 245. John of Worcester (*JW, s.a.* 1012; II. 470–1) gives the name of the man who struck the final blow as Thrum and claims that he had been confirmed by Ælfheah the day before. Keynes ('Cnut's Earls', p. 64) suggests identity with Thrymr, a thegn who occurs as witness to Cnut's diplomas in the early 1020s.

[36]  A change to the word-order was made in MS E (s. xii[1]), or its exemplar, in order to imply that the body was carried to London by the two bishops and the citizens themselves but there is no other evidence for this: *The Anglo-Saxon Chronicle MS E*, ed. Susan Irvine, The AS Chronicle: A Collaborative Edition 7 (Cambridge, 2004), 69. Bishop Eadnoth was himself later killed in the battle against Cnut at *Assandun* on 18 October 1016: *Liber Eliensis*, II.71: ed. E. O. Blake, Camden Soc. 3rd ser., 92 (London, 1962), p. 141; *Liber Eliensis: A History of the Isle of Ely from the Seventh Century to the Twelfth, Compiled by a Monk of Ely in the Twelfth Century*, trans. Janet Fairweather (Woodbridge, 2005), p. 169.

[37]  Benedictions for both Ælfheah's festival (19 April) and translation (8 June) were included in the supplementary leaves (fols. 85–111) added at Christ Church Canterbury

before the year 1023, when his relics were returned to Canterbury) already referred to him as a holy martyr:

> They kept the archbishop with them till the time that they martyred him ['oð þæne timan þe hi hine gemartiredon']. [1011]

> [...] and his holy blood fell on the ground, and so he sent his holy soul to God's kingdom. [1012]

> And God now reveals there [at St Paul's] the powers of the holy martyr ['þær nu God sutelað þæs halgan martires mihta'].[1012] [38]

Some extra details were added to the story by the contemporary though geographically distant chronicler Thietmar, bishop of Merseburg in East Saxony (c. 975–1018), who wrote that he had heard (from an eyewitness whom he named as Sewald) of the killing by an army led by Earl Thorkell of 'the noble prelate of the city of Canterbury, called Dunstan' [named thus in error for Ælfheah]. Thietmar asserted that the prelate had at first promised to give a ransom but had not been able to raise it and that Earl Thorkell had tried unsuccessfuly to prevent the killing.[39] This latter assertion contrasts with William of Malmesbury's version of events in the twelfth century, which stated that Thorkell had himself instigated the killing.[40] It may be, however, that Ælfheah overplayed his hand, having miscalculated that he could negotiate a better deal because of his experience of the successful treaty made with Olaf Tryggvason in 994.

Ælfheah's bodily relics (apart from a finger which was later said to have been given by King Cnut to Westminster Abbey)[41] were later trans-

---

in the middle of the 11th century to the benedictional now Paris, BN, lat. 987, see David N. Dumville, *Liturgy and the Ecclesiastical History of Late Anglo-Saxon England: Four Studies* (Woodbridge, 1992, pp. 84–5 and 92–3, n. 167. The festival but not the translation was included in the kalendar in the Arundel Psalter (BL, Arundel 155, fol. 3v); *English Kalendars before A.D. 1100*, ed. Francis Wormald, HBS 72 (1934, repr. 1988), 173; this fact has been used to date the manuscript, see Richard W. Pfaff, 'Eadui Basan: Scriptor Princeps?', in *England in the Eleventh Century: Proceedings of the 1990 Harlaxton Symposium*, ed. Carola Hicks, Harlaxton Medieval Studies 2 (Stamford, 1992), 267–83, at 273.

[38] Translation from Whitelock, *EHD*, pp. 244–5; quoted text from *ASC MS C*, ed. O'Brien O'Keeffe, pp. 96–7.

[39] Whitelock, *EHD*, no. 27, chs. 42–3, pp. 349–50, For the relevant passage quoted from the edition by R. Holtzmann (Berlin, 1935), see McDougall, 'Serious Entertainments', pp. 206–7.

[40] 'Turkillus [...] qui incentor necis beati Elfegi fuerat','Thurkil [...] who had provoked the murder of St Ælfheah': *William of Malmesbury, Gesta regum Anglorum, The History of the English Kings*, I, ed. and trans. R. A. B. Mynors, completed by R. M. Thomson and M. Winterbottom (Oxford, 1998), ch. 181.3 (pp. 320–1).

[41] M. K. Lawson, *Cnut: The Danes in England in the Early Eleventh Century* (London and New York, 1993), p. 155 and n. 177, referring to a 15th-century chronicle (see *The History of Westminster Abbey by John Flete*, ed. J. A. Robinson (Cambridge, 1909), p. 70). Ælfheah's bloodied monastic cowl was given by Bishop Ælfweard of London to

lated to Canterbury to be placed to the north of the high altar, near those of Dunstan.[42] This translation from London to Canterbury in 1023 appears to have been a political act by Cnut, once the Vikings had finally won the kingdom, designed to bring together the king's Danish and English subjects after years of warfare.[43] It also served to isolate potential trouble-makers among former followers of Earl Thorkell who had been party to the killing of Ælfheah.[44]

Later, the post-Conquest Archbishop Lanfranc (1070–89), an Italian, questioned the categorization of Ælfheah's murder as a martyrdom, saying that Ælfheah had died in a dispute over a ransom rather than for his faith.[45] However, after Ælfheah had been successfully defended by the learned Abbot Anselm of Bec who confirmed him as a martyr because 'he died for truth and justice, which was to die for Christ',[46] Lanfranc commissioned from the Canterbury monk Osbern not only a hymn commemorating Ælfheah but also a prose *vita*.[47] In the latter, Osbern compared Ælfheah to St Stephen the protomartyr who had met his death by stoning (*c.* 35 A. D.).[48] Osbern's account of the 1023 *translatio* may also have been composed at the behest of Lanfranc.[49] These texts succeeded in confirming Ælfheah's right to his position as one of the most

Ramsey Abbey when he retired thither in 1044, see *Chronicon abbatiae Rameseiensis a. saec. x. usque ad an. circiter 1200 in quatuor partibus*, ed. W. Dunn Macray, RS 83 (London, 1886), 158.

[42] *ASC* 1023 D: *The Anglo-Saxon Chronicle MS D*, ed. G. B. Cubbin, The AS Chronicle: A Collaborative Edition 6 (Cambridge, 1996), 64; Whitelock, *EHD*, pp. 253–4. See also Brooks, *Early History*, pp. 41–3 and p. 38, fig. 2.

[43] For a late-eleventh-century account of this translation, see '*Translatio Sancti Ælfegi Cantuariensis archiepiscopus et martiris* (*BHL* 2519): Osbern's Account of the Translation of St Ælfheah's Relics from London to Canterbury, 8–11 June 1023', ed. Alexander R. Rumble, trans. Rosemary Morris and Alexander R. Rumble, in *The Reign of Cnut*, ed. Rumble, pp. 283–315.

[44] Cnut seems to have reached an accommodation with his former rival Thorkell by 1023 when he acted as Cnut's regent in Denmark: *ASC* 1023 C; *ASC MS C*, ed. O'Brien O'Keeffe, p. 104; Keynes, 'Cnut's Earls', pp. 54–7.

[45] H. E. J. Cowdrey, *Lanfranc: Scholar, Monk, and Archbishop* (Oxford, 2003), pp. 175–6, 180–1.

[46] Cowdrey, *Lanfranc*, p. 180. See further, *The Life of St Anselm, Archbishop of Canterbury, by Eadmer*, ed. and trans. R. W. Southern (London, 1962), pp. 50–4.

[47] Cowdrey, *Lanfranc*, p. 181. The hymn has not survived: R. W. Southern, *Saint Anselm and his Biographer: A Study of Monastic Life and Thought, 1059–c. 1130* (Cambridge, 1963), p. 250. For the *vita*, see above, p. 166, n. 4. On Osbern, see Antonia Gransden, *Historical Writing in England c. 550–c. 1307* (London, 1974), pp. 127–9; and Southern, *Saint Anselm and his Biographer*, pp. 248–52. An early-twelfth-century mass for St Ælfheah is in a manuscript probably from Rochester, see Daniel J. Sheerin, 'Masses for Sts. Dunstan and Elphege from the Queen of Sweden's Collection at the Vatican', *Revue Bénédictine* 85 (1975), 199–207.

[48] McDougall, 'Serious Entertainments', pp. 205–6. For Stephen, see Acts VI–VII; and Farmer, *Oxford Dictionary of Saints*, p. 453.

[49] See above, n. 43; and *The Reign of Cnut*, ed. Rumble, pp. 284–6.

important saints whose relics were preserved at Canterbury. In 1105 his body was discovered to be incorrupt,[50] and a new shrine was constructed on the left of the high altar in the cathedral as rebuilt by Anselm.[51] One of his successors, Thomas Becket, referred to him as Canterbury's first martyr and commended himself to God and St Ælfheah at the time of his own martyrdom in 1170.[52]

Ælfheah's appeal to his venerators seems to have derived from his apparent personal bravery in refusing to let himself be ransomed, his action contrasting with the general conciliatory attitude of the secular leaders of the English at this time, many of whom thought it better to buy off the Vikings with tribute rather than to fight them.[53] Despite his lasting cult at Canterbury, however, there are only a few recorded church dedications to Ælfheah (Alphege, Elphege), mainly in Kent, but also one in the City of London and one in Winchester.[54]

### Stigand of Winchester and Canterbury

Stigand, the second subject of this chapter, came from the generation that succeeded Ælfheah. He was a priest of the royal household of Cnut and his successors whose service was rewarded by the grant of various rich livings. [55] Probably his first reward was the nationally significant church which had been founded by Cnut in 1020 to commemorate all those on both sides who had died in the battle of *Assandun* (1016), although it is not proven that Stigand was its first incumbent.[56] To be already a priest (aged

---

[50] Farmer, *Oxford Dictionary of Saints*, p. 18; R. W. Southern, *Saint Anselm: A Portrait in a Landscape* (Cambridge, 1990), p. 323.

[51] Cowdrey, *Lanfranc*, p. 182; Southern, *Saint Anselm: A Portrait*, pp. 325–7.

[52] Farmer, *Oxford Dictionary of Saints*, p.18.

[53] See the many payments of tribute recorded at this period in *ASC*. For the distinction between tribute and 'Danegeld', see Ann Williams, *Æthelred the Unready:The Ill-Counselled King* (London and New York, 2000), pp. 151–3, Appendix,'A Note on "Danegeld"'.

[54] In Kent at Canterbury, Seasalter and Greenwich, see Tim Tatton-Brown, 'The City and Diocese of Canterbury in St Dunstan's Time', in *St Dunstan*, ed. Ramsay *et al.*, pp. 75–87, at pp. 81 and 85 n. 42. Tatton-Brown's list omits the one in Winchester, for an account of which see Derek Keene, *Survey of Medieval Winchester*, Winchester Studies 2 (Oxford, 1985), 113, 118, 134, 886–7; this was first recorded in 1284 but was apparently disused by 1428.

[55] *HBC*, pp. 214 (Canterbury), 217 (Elmham), 223 (Winchester); *John Le Neve, Fasti Ecclesiae Anglicanae 1066–1300*, II, *Monastic Cathedrals (Northern and Southern Provinces)*, compiled by Diana E. Greenway (London, 1971), pp. 3 (Canterbury) and 85 (Winchester); PASE, *sub* Stigand 1 ; H. E. J. Cowdrey, 'Stigand (*d.* 1072)' *ODNB*, article 26523; Frank Barlow, *The English Church 1000–1066: A History of the Later Anglo-Saxon Church* (2nd edn, London and New York,1979), especially pp. 77–81, 209–11, 302–10; Brooks, *Early History*, pp. 304–10.

[56] *ASC* 1020 F: the statement 'gi\e/f hit his anum preoste þas nama was Stigand' is part

at least thirty) in 1020 he would have had to be born by 990 and would thus have been at least eighty-two on his death in 1072, a very advanced age upon which the surviving sources do not comment. Designated as a priest he witnessed surviving royal diplomas from about 1033.[57] Near the beginning of the reign of Edward the Confessor, on 3 April 1043, he was appointed bishop of Elmham although he was soon deprived of the position because of the fall from favour of his patron, Queen Emma.[58] However, it was restored to him early in 1044 and he held it until 1047.[59] He was then translated to Winchester (after 29 August) which he retained in plurality on his appointment to Canterbury (after 14 September 1052) until he was deprived of both in 1070.[60] Not much is known of him in his role as bishop of Winchester before or after his elevation to Canterbury beyond his acting with the community at the Old Minster to lease three estates to different individuals.[61] While archbishop, he may have unfairly treated a number of abbeys. He is said to have broken the terms of an exchange of lands made with Abbot Spearhafoc of Abingdon.[62] According to the compiler of the *Liber Eliensis*, he appropriated to himself profits from the vacant abbacies of [New Minster] Winchester, Glastonbury, St Augustine's and Ely, although he is also credited with the gift of valuable vestments and religious artefacts to the latter.[63] He may also have had powers over St Albans in 1066.[64]

of a marginal addition (datable s.xi/xii), on fol. 66v of the manuscript, made by the first scribe of F and associated with an erasure of text. See *The Anglo-Saxon Chronicle MS F*, ed. Peter S. Baker, The Anglo-Saxon Chronicle: A Collaborative Edition 8 (Cambridge, 2000), pp. lxi, 111. For the siting of the battle at Ashdon, Essex, see Cyril Hart, 'The Site of Assandun', *The Danelaw* (London and Rio Grande, 1992), pp. 553–65, especially 562–5; and Warwick Rodwell, 'The Battle of *Assandun* and its Memorial Church: A Reappraisal', in *The Battle of Maldon: Fiction and Fact*, ed. Janet Cooper (London and Rio Grande, 1993), pp. 127–58.

57  S 967, 969, 975, 979, 982 (?spurious), and 993: see Simon Keynes, 'Regenbald the Chancellor (*sic*)', *Anglo-Norman Studies* 10 (1988), 185–222, especially fig. 1 (p. 193). PASE lists these subscriptions under Stigand 2 (together with the *ASC* 1020 F reference to *Assandun*).

58  *ASC* 1043 C; *ASC MS C*, ed. O'Brien O'Keeffe, p. 108; trans. Douglas and Greenaway *EHD*, p. 105. See also Barlow, *Edward the Confessor*, p. 77.

59  *HBC*, p. 217.

60  *HBC*, pp. 223, 214.

61  S 1402–3 and 1476; Robertson, *ASCharters*, nos. 106–7, 114. He is also recorded in S 1588/BCS 479 as having an estate near Wanborough, Wiltshire.

62  See *Charters of Abingdon Abbey*, ed. S. E. Kelly, AS Charters 7–8 (Oxford, 2000–1), clxiv; *Chronicon monasterii de Abingdon*, ed. Joseph Stevenson, RS 2 (London, 1858), I.462–3. Cf. GDB, fol. 169r; *DB Gloucestershire* 56: 2.

63  *Liber Eliensis*, II.98: ed. Blake, p. 168; trans. Fairweather, p. 200. Cf. Simon Keynes, 'Ely Abbey 672–1109', in *A History of Ely Cathedral*, ed. P. Meadows and N. Ramsay (Woodbridge, 2003), pp. 3–58, at pp. 42–3.

64  See *Charters of St Albans*, ed. Julia Crick, AS Charters 12 (Oxford, 2007), 28–30.

It is thought that Stigand's family came from Norfolk.[65] In 1066, apart from his own considerable landholding in the county,[66] his brother Æthelmær held the church of SS Simon and Jude in Norwich 'de patrimonio', that is by ancestral right, while their sister (unnamed) held 32 acres in the same borough.[67] The choice of personal names made by Stigand's parents for the two brothers reflected the Anglo-Scandinavian nature of eastern England in the later tenth century. His own name derived from ON *Stigandr*, a byname meaning 'he who goes with long strides' or 'the swift footed one',[68] but his brother was called by the OE name Æthelmær.[69] It is interesting that his own son was called Robert, a Continental Germanic name (from OG *Hrodebert*) favoured by the Normans.[70] Although, apart from references to our man, the name *Stigandr* is not common in documents from Anglo-Saxon England, it was held by at least six people in Normandy before 1066, reflecting Scandinavian influences there, and by the Norman bishop of Selsey/Chichester 1070 87. A few individuals with the name are recorded in the twelfth century in East Anglia, where Archbishop Stigand held much land, but it is not certain after whom they were named.[71]

While bishop of Elmham, Stigand helped his brother to obtain a lease on two estates belonging to the abbey of Bury St Edmunds.[72] In 1047 he arranged for Æthelmær to succeed him to the see of Elmham.[73] It is just possible that, immediately after having himself become bishop of Winchester, Stigand again helped his brother's affairs, if he were the same Æthelmær to whom, together with his son Sæman, one hide of land at Sparsholt, Hampshire, about three miles to the north-west of the city, was leased by the bishop and the community at the Old Minster; however, as

---

[65]  Barlow, *English Church*, pp. 77–8
[66]  See below, p. 176.
[67]  LDB, fol. 117b (*DB Norfolk* 1: 61). Stigand himself held the churches of St Martin and St Michael in Norwich, but they are not said to be patrimonial: LDB, fol. 116b (*DB Norfolk* 1: 61).
[68]  John Insley, *Scandinavian Personal Names in Norfolk: A Survey Based on Medieval Records and Place-Names*, Acta Academiae Regiae Gustavi Adolphi 62 (Uppsala, 1994), 345–7; Olof von Feilitzen, *The Pre-Conquest Personal Names of Domesday Book*, Nomina Germanica 3 (Uppsala, 1937), 374–5.
[69]  Olof von Feilitzen, *Pre-Conquest Personal Names*, pp. 184–5. For Æthelmær, see below, n. 73.
[70]  For Robert's holding in Stainsfield, Lincs., see GDB, fol. 375c (*DB Lincolnshire* CS 30). For the personal name, see Thorvald Forssner, *Continental-Germanic Personal Names in England in Old and Middle English Times* (Uppsala, 1916), pp. 216–17, s.n. *Ro(d)bert*.
[71]  Insley, *Scandinavian Personal Names*, pp. 346–7.
[72]  S 1468; Robertson, *ASCharters,*, no. 97 (1043×1044).
[73]  *HBC*, p. 217 ; Barlow, *English Church*, p. 217. The assertion that Æthelmær did not succeed to Elmham until 1052 (Frank Barlow, *Edward the Confessor* (London, 1970), p. 87) is refuted by Brooks, *Early History*, p. 389 (n. 152).

Æthelmær is not designated a bishop in the lease, this transaction would probably have to be dated within a very narrow time-frame in 1047.[74] Stigand would need to have been translated to Winchester before his brother was consecrated to Elmham.

Stigand's own leasing from Bath Abbey in 1061×1065 of the estate of Tidenham, in Gloucestershire on the Welsh border, may have led to the drawing up of the custumal which survives with the lease.[75] This is of both social and economic interest to modern Anglo-Saxonists as it describes riding-service owed by the *geneats*, labour services owed by *geburs* and also fishing-rights on the rivers Severn and Wye.

Stigand was the epitome of a very rich, secular ecclesiastic. Besides his ecclesiastical appointments, he is shown by the Domesday records to have been in possession of many manors and lordships, particularly in East Anglia. It has been calculated that the value of these personal holdings, in ten counties, was more than £750.[76] In Norfolk he held more land than the king and about the same as him in Suffolk and Dorset. More than a thousand thegns and freemen in East Anglia had him as their lord, as did a further 100 elsewhere.[77]

In the manner of a modern civil servant, Stigand seems until just before his death to have been able to accommodate himself to the requirements of the current ruler: he served equally Cnut, Harald Harefoot, Harthacnut, Edward the Confessor,[78] Harold II[79] and William I.

---

[74] S 1402; Robertson, *ASCharters*, no. 106. The inclusion as witness of Abbot Ælfwine of the New Minster only narrows the date to 1047×1057; see *HRH*, pp. 81, 258. The lessor is probably to be identified with *Æilmer* the former tenant of 1 hide in Chilcomb Hundred in 1086 (GDB, fol. 41a : *DB Hampshire* 3:1). He is not designated there as a bishop, but as Æthelmær had been deposed in 1070 and had been besides the bishop of a different and distant diocese, his status may have been forgotten, suppressed or excluded by those drawing up the church of Winchester's Domesday return. There is no mention of Sæman here or elsewhere in Domesday Hampshire.

[75] S 1426, 1555; Robertson, *ASCharters*, nos. 109, 117. Tidenham was taken from Stigand and granted to Earl William of Hereford (d. 1071). It was part of the *Terra Regis* in 1086: GDB, fol. 164r; *DB Gloucestershire* 1: 56.

[76] Mary Frances Smith, 'Archbishop Stigand and the Eye of the Needle', *Anglo-Norman Studies* 16 (1993, published 1994), 199–219, especially 204–11. See also Barlow, *English Church*, p. 79, n. 2.

[77] Smith, 'Archbishop Stigand', p. 205.

[78] Apart from the time of his temporary loss of the see of Elmham in 1043–4 due to his connection with Queen Emma, see above, p. 174.

[79] Archbishop Stigand is depicted on the Bayeux Tapestry, standing with arms outstretched in acclamation, in front and on the left of the enthroned King Harold; see Fig. 6.5. Despite the later assertion by William of Poitiers, it is unlikely, however, that Harold had been crowned by the uncanonical Stigand rather than by Archbishop Ealdred of York, see Sir Frank Stenton, 'The Historical Background', in *The Bayeux Tapestry: A Comprehensive Survey*, ed. Sir Frank Stenton, 2nd edn (London, 1965), pp. 9–24, at 17–18, and *ibid.*, plate 34; also Brooks, *Early History*, p. 307. For the opposite view, see Barlow, *English Church,* p. 60, n. 4; and cf. Owen-Crocker, above, pp. 123–4. For

During the Confessor's reign he kept on good terms with Earl Godwine and his family, from a similar Anglo-Scandinavian background, and was able to act as a mediator between them and the king on more than one occasion.[80] In 1052, on their triumphal return from exile, he was chosen as archbishop to replace their enemy, Robert of Jumièges, who had fled from his see at Canterbury.[81] Stigand was the first non-monk to hold the see since the ill-fated Archbishop Ælfsige (958).[82] In allowing himself to be appointed in Robert's place, and for then making use of the latter's *pallium* until he got his own, Stigand stored up eventual disaster for himself in later years with the papacy.[83] Although after his deposition in 1070 he was said, in two episcopal professions to his successor Archbishop Lanfranc, to have been excommunicated by five successive popes (Leo IX, Victor II, Stephen IX, Nicholas II and Alexander II),[84] it was also recorded that in 1062 he was allowed to join the papal legates and Ealdred, the archbishop of York, in the process of choosing Wulfstan (II) as bishop of Worcester.[85] The latter was, however, then consecrated by Ealdred and not by Stigand. Nevertheless Stigand did consecrate individuals as abbots at this time (Æthelsige of St Augustine's in 1061, Baldwin of Bury in 1065, and Thurstan of Ely in 1066), though this caused problems for them later.[86]

Any role that Stigand had in the negotiations over the succession to Edward the Confessor has been obscured by later sources, but he seems to have supported Harold in 1066[87] and Edgar the ætheling immediately after the battle of Hastings. When, before Edgar's own surrender at

---

the deliberate ambiguity of the Tapestry here, see Barbara English, 'Le couronnement d'Harold dans la Tapisserie de Bayeux', in *La Tapisserie de Bayeux: l'art de broder l'Histoire*, ed. Pierre Bouet, Brian Levy, François Neveux (Caen, 2004), pp. 347–81, at pp. 377–80.

[80]  Frank Barlow, *The Godwins: The Rise and Fall of a Noble Dynasty* (Harlow, 2002), pp. 42, 46; and *The Life of King Edward Who Rests at Westminster Attributed to a Monk of Saint-Bertin*, ed. and trans. Frank Barlow, 2nd edn (Oxford, 1992), ch. i. 3 (pp. 34–5).

[81]  *HBC*, p. 214; Brooks, *Early History*, p. 304.

[82]  Brooks, *Early History*, p. 306. Cf. Barlow, *English Church*, p. 209. See above, p. 165, n. 1.

[83]  Brooks, *Early History*, pp. 306–7. For his own *pallium*, see below, p. 178.

[84]  The professions of Wulfstan of Worcester and Remigius of Dorchester, see *Canterbury Professions*, ed. Michael Richter, Canterbury and York Society 140 (1973), nos. 31–2. Cowdrey, in *ODNB*, however, is of the opinion that 'For any such sustained papal campaign there is neither evidence nor probability'; see also H. E. J. Cowdrey, *Lanfranc: Scholar, Monk, and Archbishop* (Oxford, 2003), p. 82. The statement of excommunication is also doubted by Barlow, *English Church*, pp. 306–7.

[85]  *The Vita Wulfstani of William of Malmesbury*, ed. Reginald R. Darlington, Camden Society 40 (1928), 18. For a full discussion of Wulfstan's promotion to the bishopric, see Emma Mason, *Wulfstan of Worcester c.1008–1095* (Oxford, 1990), pp. 76–87.

[86]  Brooks, *Early History*, p. 307.

[87]  As evidenced by the Bayeux Tapestry: see above, p. 176, n.79.

Berkhamstead, Stigand submitted to Duke William at Wallingford, he was at first allowed to keep his appointments, though it seems that he was not subsequently allowed to crown the new king.[88] In 1067 he accompanied William I on his return to Normandy, probably so that William could keep him under his control.[89]

When it was clear, after some secondary resistance had been quelled, that the Norman invasion had succeeded, King William seems to have decided to stop supporting Stigand. When Archbishop Ealdred of York died on 11 September 1069 the ensuing vacancy meant that a new incumbent would eventually need to be consecrated.[90] Knowing that such a consecration made by Stigand would not be accepted by the pope, William did not challenge his deposition by the papal legates the cardinal-priests John and Peter, with Ermenfrid, bishop of Sion, at the Council of Winchester *c*.11 April 1070.[91] Stigand was accused of having unlawfully taken the place of his Norman predecessor Archbishop Robert of Jumièges and to have subsequently made use of his *pallium*.[92] Even though he had been confirmed in his position and was said to have been given his own *pallium* by Benedict X, pope between 5 April 1058 and 24 January 1059,[93] this

---

[88]   *The* Gesta Guillelmi *of William of Poitiers*, ed. and trans. R. H. C. Davis and Marjorie Chibnall (Oxford, 1998), bk. II, chs. 28, 30 (pp. 146–7, 150–1). This work was probably written 1071×1077, see *ibid.*, pp. xx–xxi.

[89]   *ASC* 1066 D: ed. Cubbin, p. 81; trans. Douglas and Greenaway, *EHD*, pp. 149–50. *The* Gesta Guillelmi *of William of Poitiers*, ed. and trans. Davis and Chibnall, bk. II, ch. 38 (pp. 166–9).

[90]   *HBC*, p. 224.

[91]   '7 or 11 April 1070. Legatine Council at Winchester', *Councils & Synods with Other Documents Relating to the English Church*, I, *A.D. 871–1204*, part ii, 1066–1204, ed. D. Whitelock, M. Brett and C. N. L. Brooke (Oxford, 1981), no. 86; *JW*, III.10–13. For discussion of the deposition, see Barlow, *English Church*, pp. 302–8 and Appendix I; and Cowdrey, *Lanfranc*, pp. 79–84.

[92]   For the significance of the *pallium*, see above, p. 6, n. 26 (Levison and Lamb).

[93]   *JW*, II.584–5; also *Councils & Synods*, I, ii. 569. For Benedict X, see J. N. D. Kelly, *The Oxford Dictionary of Popes* (Oxford, 1986, repr. 1988), pp. 150–1. Note that at Canterbury in the early 12th cent. it was believed that Stigand had been sent a *pallium* by Pope Victor II (13 April 1055 – 28 July 1057; Kelly, *Dictionary*, pp. 148–9), via Godric, dean of Christ Church. This is stated in the list of *pallia* that appears, written in the same hand (s.xi/xii), both in CCCC 173A, 54v and in BL, Cotton Tiberius A.vi, 35r; see *ASC MS A*, ed. Bately, pp. xliii, 94 (hand 15); *The Anglo-Saxon Chronicle MS B*, ed. Simon Taylor, The AS Chronicle: A Collaborative Edition, ed. David Dumville and Simon Keynes 4 (Cambridge, 1983), xxi–xxii, 58; Ker, *Catalogue*, nos. 39 and 188. In the CCCC manuscript the statement concerning Stigand's *pallium* is at the foot of the first column and below the horizontal ruling but is by the same hand as the other entries (although rather cramped); see *Parker Chronicle*, ed. Flower and Smith, 54b. It may, however, have been added as an afterthought, subsequent to those of Archbishops Lanfranc and Anselm written at the top of the next column. Cowdrey (*Lanfranc*, p. 82, n. 37) is of the opinion that 'This statement cannot be dismissed out of hand'. If true, the involvement of Godric would be an interesting link between Stigand and Ælfheah, as in his youth Godric is said to have been one of the two Christ

was the act of an anti-pope in the eyes of the Normans and of the current pope Alexander II. Stigand was also accused of pluralism (holding the sees of Winchester and Canterbury together).[94] Although undeniable, this charge of pluralism was not however pursued with much rigour, as it was not so unusual a practice at that time.[95] Thus, the sees of Worcester and York had frequently been held together (for example, by such notable ecclesiastics as St Oswold from 971 to 992 and Wulfstan the homilist from 1002 to 1016), and had only since 1062 (on the appointment of Wulfstan II to Worcester) been permanently separated.[96] Nearer home, Archbishop Ælfric of Canterbury (d. 1005) had retained the see of Ramsbury for ten years after his promotion in 995.[97] We might note also the later tenure of the abbacy of Glastonbury, the bishopric of Winchester and the decanate of St Martin le Grand, London, in the mid twelfth century by Henry of Blois, King Stephen's brother and a man who was for a time himself papal legate.[98] It may be suggested then that Stigand was unlucky to live so long that he saw in his lifetime not only the end of the Anglo-Saxon state but also the challenging of uncanonical, but hitherto tolerated, practices by a wave of papal reforms.[99] For this he suffered the loss of everything and was vilified by the Norman and later monastic chroniclers.[100] He died a prisoner in the king's castle at Winchester on 21

Church monks who opened Ælfheah's first tomb in St Paul's, London, prior to the translation of the relics to Canterbury on the orders of King Cnut. See *'Translatio Sancti Ælfegi archiepiscopi et martiris'*, ed. and trans. Alexander R. Rumble and Rosemary Morris, in *The Reign of Cnut*, ed. Rumble, pp. 283–315, at pp. 304–5, where Godric is said to have been once a disciple (*discipulus*) of Ælfheah and to have been Osbern's chief source for the events described in the *Translatio*.

94   *JW*, III. 10–13; also *Councils & Synods*, I, ii. 569.
95   Barlow (*English Church*, p. 304, n. 1) refers to Popes Leo IX and Victor II as pluralists. Note also that even the reformer Nicholas II (1058–61) retained the see of Florence while pope, see Kelly, *Dictionary*, p. 151.
96   *HBC*, p. 224. On Wulfstan's appointment, see Mason, *Wulfstan of Worcester*, pp. 76–87.
97   *HBC*, pp. 214, 220.
98   On Henry, see David Knowles,'Henry of Winchester', *Saints and Scholars: Twenty-five Medieval Portraits* (Cambridge, 1963), pp. 51–8; and Lena Voss, *Heinrich von Blois, Bischof von Winchester (1129–71)*, Historische Studien 210 (Berlin, 1932), where Henry's decanate of St Martin's is discussed on pp. 100–7.
99   Cf. Barlow, *English Church*, pp. 301–8.
100  The *Gesta Guillelmi of William of Poitiers*, ed. and trans. Davis and Chibnall, II.1 (pp. 100–1); *The Ecclesiastical History of Orderic Vitalis*, ed. and trans. Marjorie Chibnall, 6 vols (Oxford, 1968–80), II. 236–9; Eadmer, *Historia novorum in Anglia*, ed. Martin Rule, RS 81 (1884), 9. On Stigand's declining posthumous reputation, see Smith, 'Archbishop Stigand and the Eye of the Needle', pp. 214, 217. William of Malmesbury had been somewhat less vicious in his treatment of Stigand: *Willelmi Malmesbiriensis monachi, De gestis pontificum Anglorum libri quinque*, ed. N. E. S. A. Hamilton, RS 52 (London, 1870), 35–7; William of Malmesbury, *The Deeds of the Bishops*, trans. Preest, ch. 23 (pp. 25–6). Malmesbury's work was used as a source for the Winchester annals, *s.a.* 1069, see *Annales monasterii de Wintonia (A.D.*

or 22 February 1072.[101] It seems however, that by 1164 details of his exact
misdemeanours had been forgotten by some. In that year, Thomas Becket
was taunted by Henry II's barons with Stigand's end only as an example
of what happened to clerics who went against their king. They reminded
him that William I 'threw Archbishop Stigand of Canterbury in a dark pit
and condemned him to perpetual imprisonment'.[102]

## The Reputations of Ælfheah and Stigand

Later, as is still often the case, Ælfheah and Stigand were held up respectively as 'good' and 'bad' leaders of the late Anglo-Saxon church. The
lives of both have generally been manipulated, however, by subsequent
writers for their own purposes.[103] More equitably, the actions of each
should be seen within a contemporary context rather than with hindsight.
In a sense both were victims of changing circumstances; each suffered
as a result of invasions of England by foreigners with different cultural
beliefs and political agendas.

Stigand has been less fortunate in his later reputation than Ælfheah. It
should be remembered, though, that he was not bound by a monastic rule
and was a member of the hitherto fairly independent English church at a
time of alien reforms coming via Normandy. Ælfheah, as both a monk-
bishop and a national hero, has been treated more favourably by contemporary and later commentators. Nevertheless, even his probity may be
capable of being questioned in one relatively small way. Was he perhaps
responsible for the removal of certain quite significant objects from his
earlier living at Winchester when he moved to Canterbury? Were these
free gifts or enforced ones?

    *519–1277), in Annales monastici*, II, ed. Henry Richards Luard, RS 36 (London,
    1865), 28. See also, Mary Frances Giandrea, *Episcopal Culture in Late Anglo-Saxon
    England*, Anglo-Saxon Studies 7 (Woodbridge, 2007), 20–3.

[101] His bodily remains were however placed in the cathedral, according to the inscription
    on one of the mortuary chests still today on top of the screens in the presbytery.
    Stigand's obit at Winchester and Ely was on 21 February, but at St Augustine's,
    Canterbury, on 22 February: *John Le Neve, Fasti Ecclesiae Anglicanae*, II, *Monastic
    Cathedrals*, compiled Greenway, 3.

[102] *English Lawsuits from William I to Richard I*, ed. R. C. van Caenegem, 2 vols., Selden
    Society 107 (London, 1991), II, *Henry II and Richard I (nos 347–645)*, no. 421 (8–13
    October 1164, Council at Northampton), at p. 423.

[103] In 1572, Matthew Parker, drawing on sixteen sources, devoted a chapter of his *De
    antiquitate Britannicæ ecclesiæ* to Stigand, but as an example of the expression of
    papal power over the English church after 1066; see Timothy Graham, 'Matthew
    Parker's Manuscripts: An Elizabethan Library and its Use', in *The Cambridge History
    of Libraries in Britain and Ireland*, I, *To 1640*, ed. Elisabeth Leedham-Green and
    Teresa Webber (Cambridge, 2006), 322–41, at 336.

Thus the manuscript which included version 'A' of the Anglo-Saxon Chronicle (CCCC 173, fols. 1–56), which had been at Winchester since *c*. 900, certainly moved to Canterbury in the eleventh century. Since the episcopal lists in it were compiled and added to it 985×988, when Ælfheah was bishop of Winchester, it is probable that he removed the manuscript in 1006 to be with him as a source of reference in his new position at Canterbury.[104] Unfortunately for modern scholars interested in the eleventh-century text of the Chronicle, once it reached Canterbury the booklet of the manuscript containing the annals was not kept up to date and seems to have been largely ignored until after 1066.[105] However, this booklet was both added to and used as a source *c*. 1100 by the scribe and compiler of the F manuscript of the Chronicle, working at Christ Church.[106]

Other manuscripts may also have been moved at this time as a consequence of Ælfheah's promotion. As the Arundel Psalter reflects a change at Canterbury at this time from the Glastonbury kalendar to a version which included several saints venerated at one or other of the Old and New Minsters at Winchester, it is probable that a manuscript containing this different version went from Winchester to Canterbury as an exemplar, although perhaps only on temporary loan.[107] The Arundel Psalter also contains the earliest known use in a Canterbury manuscript of 'Winchester style' decorative frames.[108] Another manuscript, now in Paris, a benedictional possibly written at Winchester *c*. 970 by Godemann, the scribe of the slightly later Benedictional of St Æthelwold, was apparently at Christ

---

104  For the date of these episcopal lists, see Simon Keynes in *HBC*, p. 210 (MS C). For the date of the hand (s.x ex.), see Ker, *Catalogue,* no. 39, art. 5. For the suggestion that it was 'regarded as "the bishops' copy"' of *ASC,* [as opposed to being the property of the Old Minster community], see M. B. Parkes, 'The Palaeography of the Parker Manuscript of the Chronicle, Laws and Sedulius and Historiography at Winchester in the Late Ninth and Tenth Centuries', *Scribes, Scripts and Readers: Studies in the Communication, Presentation and Dissemination of Medieval Texts* (London and Rio Grande, 1991), pp. 143–9, at pp. 167–8.

105  Paradoxically, however, this may have ensured its survival in the sack of Canterbury in 1011.

106  See *Parker Chronicle,* ed. Flower and Smith, 30a–31b. After the entry for 1001, the annals are barren therein except for post-Conquest insertions, several of them written by the first scribe of BL, Cotton Domitian viii: see Ker, *Catalogue,* no. 148 (s.xi/xii); and *ASC MS F,* ed. Baker, pp. xx–xxii.

107  The kalendar is now BL, Arundel 155, fols. 2–7v. See above, p. 170, n. 37; and Pfaff,'Eadui Basan', pp. 274–6. Cf. Brooks, *Early History,* pp. 264–5.

108  Richard Gameson, 'Manuscript Art at Christ Church, Canterbury in the Generation after St Dunstan', *St Dunstan,* ed. Ramsay *et al.,* pp. 187–220, at pp. 209–11 and plates XV, XVI; Elżbieta Temple, *Anglo-Saxon Manuscripts 900–1066,* A Survey of Manuscripts Illuminated in the British Isles, ed. J. J. G. Alexander, 2 (London, 1976), no. 66.

Church by the 1020s.[109] Liturgical additions made to it then are thought to reflect the interest of Ælfheah in the cult of St Æthelwold.[110]

Most significantly, however, in relation to the history of the Benedictine reform at Winchester, it seems that the head of St Swithun, a hugely important relic, was taken thence to Canterbury in the time of Ælfheah's archiepiscopacy and given a place on the high altar there.[111] It is, however, now at Evreux, where it may have been since the late fourteenth century.[112]

Whether Æthelwold would have approved of this removal of the (literally) chief part of the Old Minster's principal treasure is an interesting question to contemplate. Perhaps Ælfheah, having apparently lived as part of three or four different monastic institutions (Bath, Winchester, Canterbury and perhaps Glastonbury), saw himself as the spiritual leader of a more inclusive church, rather than of one tied to narrow local allegiances? With such a view, significant items might be moved between institutions to be used or placed where they were considered to be of most value in promoting a common agenda.[113] This would accord more with a Benedictine view of communal property than did the competitive nature of localized cult-centres, vying with each other for alms and patronage, of the sort that had been developed at various monasteries in the later tenth century.

In summary then, Ælfheah may be seen as a forward-looking and proactive leader of the Anglo-Saxon church whose life was violently cut short, while Stigand, although apparently willing to fulfil his duties as archbishop during the reigns of a succession of very different kings of England, was someone who was unable to match new standards of clerical behaviour imposed by the forces of papal reform, to his eventual cost. Ælfheah's designation as a martyr has not been questioned since the late eleventh century, but perhaps Stigand may be seen too as a hapless victim, if only of changing political circumstances.

---

[109] Paris, BN, lat, 987. Gameson, 'Manuscript Art', pp. 209–11; Temple, *Anglo-Saxon Manuscripts*, no. 25; see also above, p. 170, n. 37.

[110] A supplementary tripartite benediction in the name of Æthelwold: see *Wulfstan of Winchester: The Life of Æthelwold*, ed. and trans. Lapidge and Winterbottom, pp. cxxxviii–cxxxix.

[111] Michael Lapidge, *The Cult of St Swithun*, pp. 38, 40, 60; Brooks, *Early History*, p. 41.

[112] John Crook, 'The Rediscovery of St Swithun's Head at Évreux', in Lapidge, *The Cult of St Swithun*, pp. 61–5 and pl. XVI.

[113] Archbishop Ælfheah's bloodied stole is said to have been taken to Ramsey Abbey in 1044 by Bishop Ælfweard of London (see above, p. 171, n. 41), while both the arm of St Swithun and the hair of St Æthelwold were at Peterborough in the 12th century, see Pauline Stafford, *The East Midlands in the Early Middle Ages* (Leicester, 1985), p. 175.

# Index

The ancient counties of England are used, as delimited by the English Place-Name Society.